DANGEROUS
DIPLOMACY

DANGEROUS DIPLOMACY

HOW THE STATE DEPARTMENT THREATENS AMERICA'S SECURITY

JOEL MOWBRAY

Since 1947
REGNERY
PUBLISHING, INC.
An Eagle Publishing Company • Washington, DC

Library of Congress Cataloging-in-Publication Data

Mowbray, Joel.
Dangerous diplomacy : how the State Department threatens America's security / Joel Mowbray.
p. cm.
ISBN 0-89526-110-3 (alk. paper)
1. United States. Dept. of State. 2.   United States—Foreign relations.
I. Title.
JZ1480.A4.M69 2003
327.73—dc22

2003018048

Published in the United States by
Regnery Publishing, Inc.
An Eagle Publishing Company
One Massachusetts Avenue, NW
Washington, DC 20001

Visit us at www.regnery.com

Distributed to the trade by
National Book Network
4720-A Boston Way
Lanham, MD 20706

Printed on acid-free paper

Manufactured in the United States of America

10 9 8 7 6 5 4 3 2 1

Books are available in quantity for promotional or premium use. Write to Director of Special Sales, Regnery Publishing, Inc., One Massachusetts Avenue, NW, Washington, DC 20001, for information on discounts and terms or call (202) 216-0600.

To my parents,
for teaching me to question authority

Contents

1

Detained: My Own Road to Damascus

★ *"I HAVE SOME PEOPLE HERE I'D LIKE YOU TO MEET."*

The middle-aged blond woman from the State Department press office was standing in the hallway—five feet from the press briefing room—surrounded by four armed guards. She indicated that she wanted me to meet them. The conversation had started out friendly enough moments earlier, just as I was walking out of a daily press briefing. She greeted me with a smile: "Hi Joel, how are you?"

But friendliness and smiles did not last long.

Since I was relatively new in the building—this was maybe the fifth press briefing I had attended—I figured she just wanted the guards to get to know me. I shook each guard's hand and introduced myself as if I were at a cocktail party. But when I attempted to excuse myself, she calmly informed me, "That's not possible."

I offered to come back later that afternoon, but the press officer replied just as coolly, "Someone is coming here to speak with you." *Something* was not right.

"Am I being detained?" I asked.

"Someone is coming here to speak with you," she repeated robotically.

I didn't know what was happening, but I knew that whoever was coming to greet me was not a welcoming committee.

I grabbed my cell phone. There was no reception, so I started walking down the hallway. The guards immediately followed in step. To prevent any misunderstandings, I explained that I was just trying to get a signal. The blond woman tried to escort me into a back room to use a State Department land line, but I had seen enough movies to know that that would not be a good move. Until I knew what was going on, I wanted to remain out in the open, where others could see what was happening to me.

After a long minute, my cell phone had a signal. I called everyone I could think of: *National Review* (my employer), multiple attorneys, and several other people. I still didn't know what was going on, and no one would tell me. Some ten to fifteen minutes later, a plainclothes Diplomatic Security officer approached me. With the four guards flanked behind him—and four more blocking the front entrance/exit—he started questioning me. He didn't indicate what he was looking for. A few moments later, I asked him, "Am I being detained?"

He replied simply, "No."

I took a step toward the exit, and the agent stepped in front of me and said, "*Now* you're being detained."

The plainclothes officer grabbed my notebook. He flipped through it, found nothing, then handed it back to me. Next he searched me to see if I had any paper on me. He sent several of the guards back into the press briefing room—the press briefing had ended minutes earlier—but they did not find anything either. I eventually realized what they were looking for: a classified State Department memo that I had questioned the press spokesman about at the briefing, a memo about which the spokesman was caught trying to lie. I knew this because the officer wanted to know who had given me the cable. In other words, he wanted to know who my source was. I was stunned—and silent. They did not find the cable on me, nor did they find it in the briefing room. And they certainly did not learn from me the identity of any of my sources.

The whole affair ended a few minutes later—about half an hour had passed altogether—not because of any legal finding, but because the *National Review* public relations office had warned them the detainment would backfire. It did. Before I returned home that day, I was besieged with calls from reporters, many of whom had been at the press briefing and witnessed my detainment. I was fine, and I got more than fifteen minutes of fame as a result. But the fact that anyone at State even contemplated detaining a journalist is frightening—and revealing. Even more revealing about State is what happened moments earlier in the press briefing.

Earlier that week—the briefing was on a Friday—the *Washington Post* and *National Review Online* (in a story by me) had reported on the contents of a classified memo (also known as a "cable") in which the U.S. ambassador to Saudi Arabia, Robert Jordan, had requested that the program known as Visa Express—a program that had let in three of the September 11 terrorists in the three months it was in operation before September 11, 2001—be shut down. But state was trying to deny the story. Top officials at State were "trying to pretend the news reports about the cable were inaccurate, because they were still trying to save Visa Express, which they were hoping to expand to other countries," a State Department official told me.[1] Knowing that State was attempting to mischaracterize the contents of the ambassador's cable, I decided to ask press spokesman Richard

Boucher a pointed question. Few are better than Boucher at evading questions or answering with non-answers, making my task a difficult one indeed.

Knowing that the entire purpose of the cable from Ambassador Jordan was to request the elimination of Visa Express, I pressed Boucher with the following: "The ambassador asked, in the cable this week, to terminate the program formerly known as 'Visa Express'... is that correct?"

Boucher's response? "Well, no."[2] But the subject line of the cable says it all: "Request for Guidance on Termination of Visa Express." Boucher lied — live on national television. The degree of temerity is what shocked me; the lie itself did not.

For the previous month, I had battled with State over the Visa Express program — and had contended with a series of lies in the process. The first story on the program ran at *National Review Online* (an abbreviated version of a *National Review* magazine piece) on June 14, 2002. The story caught traction quickly. It was easy to see why. Nine months after September 11, all residents in the country that produced fifteen of the nineteen terrorists were still submitting their visa application forms to private Saudi travel agents — and almost no Saudi nationals were being interviewed before receiving visas. Whereas the rest of the country was trying to adjust to the new, post–September 11 reality, State was pretending that the world had not changed — at least with respect to Saudi Arabia.

After almost a week of attempting to ignore the growing controversy, State dropped the name "Visa Express" on the same day *National Review* (with the longer story) hit newsstands, making it the program formerly known as Visa Express. At the same time, State revamped the description of the program on the website for the U.S. Embassy in Riyadh. It previously had read like a full-page advertisement, enticing people to take advantage of the "convenience" of a program that was "designed to help qualified applicants obtain U.S.

visas quickly and easily."[3] But days after the original Visa Express story was published, the embassy's website was overhauled, with marketing hype replaced by the language of bureaucracy.

A sample sentence from the updated description: "When the applicant has completed and signed the application forms and has compiled the requirement [sic] documentation, these travel agencies bring the application to the Embassy in Riyadh or Consulate General in Jeddah with the required application fee and any applicable visa issuance fee."[4]

State's "reforms" to the program formerly known as Visa Express consisted of dropping the name and changing the description on the U.S. Embassy's website. That was it. There were no reforms, no changes to a program that had let in three of the September 11 terrorists and continued to be a gaping loophole in United States border security.

When State finally did respond—fully one week after the Visa Express story first broke—its defense was telling. Ed Vazquez, the spokesman for Consular Affairs, the bureau within State in charge of visas, defended the program formerly known as Visa Express on Fox News. It was the first public defense any State official had made.

Vazquez jeered: "Mr. Mowbray reminds me of a comment made by Mary McCarthy about Lillian Hellman, that every word that she writes is a lie, including 'the' and 'and.'"[5]

He then proceeded to tell a whopper of his own: "Twelve of the hijackers were interviewed."[6] Maybe he didn't know the truth, but the General Accounting Office did. When the GAO, the investigative arm of Congress, conducted an investigation of visa policies in 2002, it discovered that, "consular officers granted visas to 13 of these 15 Saudi and Emirati hijackers without an interview."[7]

One of the other half-truths told by Vazquez during that interview was State's primary defense of the program: "No travel agent is deputized to do a U.S. visa any place in the world, least of all in Saudi

Arabia." He further explained, "Travel agents collect applications in remote locations and pass it on to the embassy or consulate. That's all they do."

But "collecting" applications was not all they did. Travel agents, who had a financial incentive in having people qualify for visas so they could then purchase travel packages, were expected to help applicants complete the forms. Travel agents were also in charge of pre-interviewing, and, according to one Consular Affairs official familiar with the program, they also entered the information from the applications into a computer program.[8] The applications were eventually passed on to the consulate or embassy; a consular officer was in fact the person who actually issued a visa, but consular officers spent an average of two to three minutes reviewing each application. And in the case of almost all Saudi nationals, visas were being issued without any interviews at all.

Within another week, State resorted to still more ad hominem attacks, issuing a three-page memo to Congress and the media called "*National Review* Article on Visa Express: Myths & Facts." But the document was little more than a written version of Vazquez's earlier defense, though it did not contend that "every word" I had written was a lie. It was the distribution of this particular document, in fact, that convinced me to attend State's daily press briefings. If State was going to assail me personally, I was not going to let those attacks go unchallenged.

Most Americans who learned of Visa Express probably wanted to believe that their government would be incapable of sacrificing their security so recklessly. I know I didn't believe it when I first heard it. Only a few months before the Visa Express story broke, I knew very little about the State Department. I knew nothing about how visas were issued or the relevant laws. As cynical as one can become when following politics, I originally refused to accept as true what a State Department official told me. It was only after I had obtained absolute proof—in the form of official documents—that I was able to believe that my government was refusing to protect Americans from a known terrorist threat well after September 11.

In a *National Review Online* story in April 2002 on the possibility of suicide bombings happening here in America, I cited border security as the central weakness in our prevention efforts—but I did not even mention State or its handling of visas. A source then approached me with details of the Visa Express program, which was still operating more than six months after September 11. I thought this person was crazy, but I followed up on the off chance that there was something there. As it turned out, there was a *lot* there.

A source provided me with cables exposing shocking "policies," such as people without criminal records being considered automatically eligible for a visa if they could afford a fancy vacation. "If the travel agency is reasonably satisfied that the traveler has the means to buy a tour 'package,' there will be little further evaluation of the applicant's qualifications."[9] That's from the "Best Practices" handbook, which constitutes policy governing consular officers on visa issuance—and it was not changed in the aftermath of the worst terrorist attack in our history.

In the course of my investigation, I thought the whole Visa Express debacle was solely the result of problems at the Consular Affairs (CA) bureau. The fact that it was a CA spokesman who had attacked me initially only reinforced that belief. When the "Myths & Facts" sheet was distributed by State's main press office, my attitude shifted somewhat, though I still believed the problems I was investigating were largely confined to that one bureau.

But all that changed on July 12, 2002, the day I was detained. Being told that I was not free to leave the building and then being surrounded by four armed guards was scary. But being asked by the plainclothes Diplomatic Security officer for the identity of my source was scandalous.

I eventually realized the Visa Express problem represented something far deeper and more pervasive than what I had uncovered at Consular Affairs—it represented a systemic problem throughout the State Department, stemming from a corrosive culture that puts the interests of other nations ahead of America's.

State's motives are not inherently sinister, but being driven by its twin obsessions with "stability" and maintaining "smooth relations,"makes coddling dictators almost an end in itself for the State Department. Making visas easy to obtain, for example, made the Saudi royal family happy. Not challenging in any meaningful way the obscene abuses of despots ensures that the regimes will not be undermined and "relations" will not be soured. In the Middle East in particular, State's dual emphasis on "stability" and "smooth relations" has often created chummy relations with the ruling elites— with an implicit understanding that the United States will not push for reforms that might threaten the control these dictators wield over their people.

As we will see, the VIP treatment the U.S. State Department gives the Saudis epitomizes everything that is wrong with the State Department.

2

Unbreakable:
The State-Saudi Alliance

★ *"TEXAS, WE HAVE A PROBLEM."*

The date was April 24, 2002. Standing on the runway at Elling-ton Air Force Base in Houston, Texas, the cadre of FBI agents, Secret Service, and Customs agents had just been informed by law enforcement officials that there was a "snag" with Crown Prince Abdullah's oversized entourage which was arriving with the prince for a visit to George W. Bush's Western White House in Crawford, Texas. The flight manifest of the eight-plane delegation accompanying the Saudi would-be king had a problem. Three, to be exact: one person on the list was wanted by U.S. law enforcement authorities and two others were on a terrorist watch list.

This had the potential to be what folks in Washington like to refer to as an "international incident." But the State Department was not about to let an "international incident" happen. Which is why this story has never been written—until now.

Upon hearing that there was someone who was wanted and two suspected terrorists in Abdullah's entourage, the FBI was ready to "storm the plane and pull those guys off," explains an informed source.[1] But given the "international" component, State was informed of the FBI's intentions before any action could be taken. When word reached the Near Eastern Affairs (NEA) bureau, NEA's reaction was classic State Department: "What are we going to do about those poor people trapped on the plane?" To which at least one law enforcement official on the ground responded, "Shoot them"—not exactly the answer State was looking for.

State, Secret Service, and the FBI then began what bureaucrats refer to as an "interagency process." In other words, they started fighting. The FBI believed that felons were to be arrested, even the Saudi variety. State had other ideas. Secret Service didn't really have any, other than to make sure that the three Saudis in question didn't get anywhere near the president or the vice president. State went to the mat in part because it was responsible for giving visas to the three in the first place. Since it was a government delegation—where all applications are generally handled at one time—the names were probably not run through the normal watch lists before the visas were issued.

Details about what happened to the three men in the end are not entirely clear, and no one at State was willing to provide any facts about the incident. What is clear, though, is that the three didn't get anywhere near Crawford, but were also spared the "embarrassment" of arrest. And the House of Saud was spared an "international incident." That normally staid bureaucrats engaged in incredible acrobatics to bail out three guys who never should have been in the United States in the first place says a great deal about State's "special relationship" with the Saudis.

THE OIL FACTOR

The State-Saudi alliance really does boil down to one thing: oil. At least that's what former secretary of state George Schultz seems to think: "They're an important country. They have lots of oil. You do pay a lot of attention to that."[2] Foggy Bottom (the nickname for the State Department—due to the location of the department in the Foggy Bottom neighborhood of Washington, D.C.) agrees, and has been conditioned to do so by the 1970s oil shocks. When the infamous oil crisis of 1973 was ballooning, America was confident that its tight relationship with the Saudis would ensure an uninterrupted flow of cheap oil. This confidence was shattered—and world oil prices more than tripled when the Saudis pursued their own economic interests. Saudi power inside Washington skyrocketed, with bureaucrats realizing that the House of Saud could not be taken for granted.

When the next oil crisis struck in 1979, prices shot up by more than 150 percent—but that was mostly driven by other countries: a substantial drop in Iraqi production and the sudden halt in Iranian production. Consumer panic, hoarding by nervous companies and individuals, and price-gouging also contributed. Saudi Arabia did little to deepen the crisis—Saudi-controlled OPEC implemented two comparably modest price increases in 1979—and actually was seen by many as an invaluable ally. The balance of power managed to shift even further in the Saudi direction in following years—and State became ever more willing to accede to Saudi demands.

THE HUMILIATION OF HUME HORAN

One man who was at the center of one of the most significant milestones in U.S.-Saudi relations—not a particularly good one for the United States—was Hume Horan. In a test of wills, the Saudis made an outrageous demand, and State not only caved, it went one step further.

Before becoming ambassador to Saudi Arabia in 1988, Horan was already intimately familiar with the country, having served as deputy chief of mission in Riyadh, the embassy's number-two position, from 1972–1977. Fluent in Arabic, Horan had a keen insight into Saudi culture that his mostly non-Arabic-speaking predecessors had lacked. So when he received instructions to express "surprise and disapproval" over a secret 1985 Saudi purchase of Chinese missiles that could have reached Turkey and Israel, he knew that King Fahd would not take the tongue-lashing kindly. But, after reassurances from Washington, Horan did as he was told.

When he got back from the unpleasant exchange with the king, he noticed a written message had arrived for him rescinding the previous directive. Unbeknownst to Horan, Prince Bandar (his Saudi counterpart) had convinced officials in Washington that the missiles would be positioned in such a way as to make clear that they weren't threats to Turkey or Israel.[3] Bandar's successful lobbying set in motion Horan's ouster. As Horan said, "My goose was cooked."[4]

In a meeting with former undersecretary of state Philip Habib, who had been sent to smooth over tensions, King Fahd personally demanded—with Horan standing behind Habib—that Horan be replaced. State quickly complied. But perhaps in an effort to "teach a lesson" or simply to show the Saudis how tough it could be on its own people, State forced Horan to humiliate himself. The fluent Arabic speaker had to go back before King Fahd to ask the king's "permission" for State to reappoint Horan's predecessor, Walter Cutler, who was not an Arabic speaker. It was clear that the move was designed as a "kowtow," which is the word Horan uses to describe the experience. It worked. And it showed the Saudis who had the upper hand. As Horan notes, "It put the United States in a weak and servile position."[5]

ROOTS OF THE RELATIONSHIP

The bond between Washington and Riyadh may have deepened because of the oil crises, but its roots began decades earlier. FDR initiated the oil-for-protection relationship in 1945. Eisenhower enshrined this arrangement as a strategic goal with his Eisenhower Doctrine in 1957, where he declared the protection of the Arab world—with particular focus on Saudi Arabia—to be a national security priority.

While official policy was coziness with the House of Saud and Foggy Bottom was dominated by Arabists, there was some degree of tension, with many officials uncomfortable with the radical Wahhabi clerics who dominate everyday life in Saudi Arabia. In 1962, President Kennedy became increasingly concerned that the civil war in Yemen—in which Egypt backed the pan-Arab revolutionaries and Saudi Arabia backed the royalists—posed a tremendous threat to the stability of the region.[6] According to Hermann Eilts, a former ambassador to both Saudi Arabia and Egypt, Kennedy pushed the House of Saud to engage "in internal economic and political reform and end all aid to the Yemeni royalists."[7] Such pressure, though, turned out to be short-lived. Eilts, in a review of a book by a fellow Arabist, former ambassador to Saudi Arabia Parker Hart, noted that promotion of reform—something Eilts himself found unpleasant and unhelpful—was abandoned entirely just a few years after it started.

Not until the Johnson administration did then–secretary of state Dean Rusk wisely discontinue all such exhortations for reform, which by then had become almost rote and counterproductive. The Saudi leadership, Rusk believed, was best qualified to judge its own best interests.[8]

But in the intervening years, the State Department's refusal to press for reform in Saudi Arabia turned into humiliating obsequiousness. Wahhabi Islam—the militant strain endorsed by the ruling family—is the only permitted religion in the kingdom. Christians are not allowed to worship on Saudi soil—and Jews are not even allowed in the country. Even Shi'ites, the majority population in the oil-rich Eastern Province, are not free to practice their denomination of Islam. Not only does State not push to change this flagrant violation of religious liberty, it behaves like the House of Saud when asked to do so. In 1997, the U.S. consulate in Jeddah banned the offering of Catholic Mass on the premises—Protestant services had already been relegated to the British consulate—because of the Saudi government's "displeasure."[9]

FEEDING AT THE SAUDI TROUGH

Perhaps former assistant secretary (the lead position of a bureau) for Near Eastern Affairs (NEA) Ned Walker said it best when he told the *Washington Post*, "Let's face it, we got a lot of money out of Saudi Arabia."[10] Walker meant "we" as in the U.S. government, but he easily could have used it to refer to former Foggy Bottom officials who benefit financially after retirement. Some do it directly—and in public view, because of stringent reporting requirements—while most, including Walker, choose a less noticeable trough.

The gravy train dates back more than twenty-five years. In that time, it has created a circle of sympathizers and both direct and indirect lobbyists. But the most important—and most indirect—byproduct of lining the pockets of former State officials is that the Saudi royal family finds itself with passionate supporters inside Foggy Bottom. Which is precisely the intended effect. Prince Bandar bin Sultan, the Saudi ambassador the United States, was quoted in the *Washington Post* as having said, "If the reputation then builds that the Saudis take care of friends when they leave office, you'd be surprised how much better friends you have who are just coming into office."[11] This is not to say that State officials make decisions with visions of dollars dancing in their heads, but at the very least, they probably take a more benign view of the royal family that "takes care of" their friends and former colleagues.

Among the first former Foggy Bottom officials to work directly for the House of Saud was former assistant secretary for Congressional Affairs Frederick Dutton, starting in 1975. According to a 1995 public filing (mandated for all paid foreign agents), Dutton earns some $200,000 per year.[12] Providing mostly legal services, Dutton also flacks for the House of Saud and even lobbies on the royal family's behalf from time to time. One of his successors as head of Congressional Affairs, Linwood Holton, also went to work for the Saudis, starting in 1977.[13] Rounding out the current team of retired State officials now directly employed by the Saudis is Peter Thomas Madigan, deputy assistant secretary for Legislative Affairs in the first Bush administration.[14]

Most of the Saudi money, though, goes indirectly to former State officials, most commonly by means of think tanks. This approach pays dividends in many ways: Foggy Bottom retirees get to have their cake—without the public realizing they're eating it—and the Saudis get to have "indirect" lobbyists, who promote the Saudi agenda under the cover of the think tank label. Three organizations in particular are the primary beneficiaries of Saudi petrodollars, and all are populated with former State officials: the Meridian International Center, the Middle East Policy Council, and the Middle East Institute.

After a long and "distinguished" career in the Foreign Service, Walter Cutler took the reins at the Meridian International Center. He had served as ambassador to Zaire and Tunisia, and twice in Saudi Arabia, and he stayed close to the Saudis after leaving State. Cutler told the *Washington Post* that the Saudis had been "very supportive of the center."[15] Meridian is not alone. The Middle East Policy Council, which also receives significant Saudi funding,[16] counts among its ranks former ambassadors—career Foreign Service members all—Charles Freeman, Frank Carlucci, and Hermann Eilts. The Middle East Institute, officially on the Saudi payroll, receives some $200,000 of its annual $1.5 million budget from the Saudi government, and an unknown amount from Saudi individuals—often a meaningless distinction since most of the "individuals" with money to donate are members of the royal family, which constitutes the government. MEI's chairman is Wyche Fowler, who was ambassador to Saudi Arabia from 1996–2001, and its president is Ned Walker, who has served as both deputy chief of Mission in Riyadh and ambassador to Saudi Arabia. Also at MEI: David Mack, former ambassador to the United Arab Emirates and deputy assistant secretary for NEA; Richard Parker, former ambassador to Algeria, Lebanon, and Morocco; William Eagleton, former ambassador to Syria; Joseph C. Wilson, career FSO and former deputy chief of Mission in Baghdad; David Ransom, former ambassador to Bahrain and former deputy chief of Mission in Yemen, UAE, and Syria; and Michael Sterner, former ambassador to UAE and deputy assistant secretary of NEA.

For Meridian and MEI, at least, the House of Saud is not the only government entity lining up to fund them; Foggy Bottom is as well. Meridian does significant amounts of work with State, particularly in coordinating the International Visitors Program, which determines the individuals and groups invited—and not invited—to Washington for a chance to curry favor with State officials in person. MEI last year was slated to handle a conference of Iraqi dissidents—which was going to exclude the umbrella organization of pro-democracy groups, the Iraqi National Congress (INC)—in London. (The conference was cancelled after public outcry over MEI's role.) The grant for holding the conference was a staggering $5 million—more than three times MEI's annual budget.[17]

The money, the favors, and State's affinity for Saudi elites over the decades have all helped contribute to the "special relationship" between State and the House of Saud. Notes Hudson Institute senior fellow Laurent Murawiec, "This is a relationship that has been cemented by forty years of money, power, and political favors that goes much deeper than most people realize."[18]

VISA EXPRESS

State has by no means been acting as a rogue department in dealing with Saudi Arabia, somehow coddling a nation that various White Houses considered hostile. But the lengths to which State goes to pamper the Saudis is something largely carried out of its own volition. There is no better example of this than Visa Express, the program that required all Saudis (including non-citizens) to turn in their visa applications at private Saudi travel agencies, which then sent them in bundles to the embassy in Riyadh or the consulate in Jeddah. Visa Express was entirely of State's own making; it was conceived of and planned for while Clinton was president, and was officially launched when Bush was in the White House. And in the three months it was operational before September 11, Visa Express let in three of the September 11 terrorists. But State did not shut it down. It took ten months—and tremendous public pressure— before that happened.

From the moment in early 1993 that Mary Ryan became head of Consular Affairs (CA), the division that oversees visa issuance, consulates, and embassies, traditional requirements for visa applicants started getting pared down (discussed in detail in Chapter 8). Partial versions of Visa Express—though not by that name—were implemented in various countries in the mid- to late-1990s. But nowhere in the world had State launched a program whereby all residents, citizens and non-citizens alike, would be expected to submit visa applications to local, private travel agencies. It was a bold—and untested—plan. Yet State chose to try out this ambitious project in a nation that was a known hotbed of al Qaeda extremists. To be fair, most Americans were not thinking about national security in late 2000 and early 2001, but State should have been. That's its job. Khobar Towers, the U.S. military dormitory, had been attacked by Hezbollah terrorists in 1996, killing nineteen U.S. soldiers, and wounding 372.[19] And State had ample information that al Qaeda was fully operational inside Saudi Arabia. Yet State went ahead in that environment with plans to launch its first nationwide Visa Express program.

Although State vociferously defended Visa Express when it came under intense scrutiny—claiming that it was almost irrelevant that travel agencies had been deputized to collect visa applications (and more, as it turned out)—the truth is that Visa Express was an incredible threat to U.S. border security. State's official line was that travel agencies did no more than, say, FedEx would in collecting and passing on applications. This was simply not true.

According to internal State documents, travel agencies were expected to conduct pre-interviews and ensure compliance. In other words, people with financial incentive to obtain visas for others were helping them fill out the forms. At first blush, this might not sound significant. But the average visa application is approved or refused in two to three minutes,[20] meaning that there are key indicators a consular officer looks for in making his decisions. With a two-page form—one page of which has questions like "Are you a member of a terrorist organization? (Answering 'yes' will not necessarily trigger a refusal)"—a travel agent who handles dozens or hundreds of applications daily could easily figure out the red flags that are to be avoided. Armed with that information, it would be relatively easy to help an applicant beat the system. Visa Express also arranged it so that the overwhelming majority of Saudi applicants never came into contact with a U.S. citizen until stepping off the airplane onto American soil.

Apparently oblivious to the glaring security loopholes created by Visa Express, State proudly implemented the program in June 2001. In an e-mail that, in hindsight, is shocking for its gleeful tone, the deputy chief of mission in Riyadh, Thomas P. Furey, wrote to Mary Ryan about Visa Express being a "win-win-win-win"—with nary a mention of security concerns. In the e-mail, Furey notes that the program started with Saudi nationals—whom he amazingly refers to as "clearly approvable"—and then says that Visa Express had been expanded to include non-Saudi citizens one day earlier, on June 25, 2001. Visa Express also resulted in the overwhelming majority of Saudi applicants never coming into contact with visa applicants. "The number of people on the street and coming through the gates should only be fifteen percent of what it was last summer," Furey wrote.

The four wins Furey boasts about? From his e-mail:

> The RSO [regional security officer, an American responsible for coordinating embassy security with local police] is happy, the guard force [Saudi residents who provide embassy and consulate security] is happy, the public loves the service (no more long lines and they can go to the travel agencies in the evening and not take time off from work), we love it (no more crowd control stress and reduced work for the FSNs [Foreign Service Nationals, Saudi residents]) and now this afternoon Chuck Brayshaw and I were at the Foreign Ministry and discovered the most amazing thing—the Saudi Government loves it!

It would be easier to defend State's creation of Visa Express if it had abandoned it on September 12, 2001—or at least had done so after it realized that fifteen of the hijackers were Saudis, including three who got in through the program. But in the month after September 11, out of 102 applicants whose forms were processed at the Jeddah consulate, only two were interviewed, and none was refused.

When word leaked to the *Washington Post* that fifteen of the nineteen terrorists were Saudis, the embassy in Riyadh assured the Saudis that the U.S. had "not changed its procedures or policies in determining visa eligibility as a result of the terrorist attacks of Sept. 11, 2001."[21] And after my investigative story on Visa Express came out in mid-June, State's initial change was cosmetic—literally. It dropped the name "Visa Express," but changed nothing about the program itself. Only after a month of a full-court press defending the suddenly nameless program did State shutter it. And even then, it was not because it had realized the error of its ways, but because it needed to offer some proof to Congress—set to vote near the end of July to strip State of the visa authority altogether—that it was indeed fit to handle such a vital function of U.S. border security. (The gambit worked—Congress sided with State.)

After the program was sacked, officials at State "openly worried that Saudi relations would worsen with the stricter requirements," according to an official there.[22] If only they had expressed such "worry" about the wisdom of fast-tracking visas in a nation teeming with Islamic extremists.

Saudi Arabia, after all, is the home of Wahhabi Islam, and Wahhabi true believers' favorite catch phrase is "Death to America"—well, maybe the second favorite, after "Death to Israel." But look again at Furey's e-mail. He was clearly—frighteningly—blind to this reality. He referred to Saudi nationals as "clearly approvable." What he saw was a nation filled with people he believed belonged in the United States. Furey, in his e-mail, summed up his idealized vision of Saudi Arabia quite succinctly: "This place really is a wonderland."

EXPRESS NEGLIGENCE

State's obliviousness to reality—and security—had an even more incredible result: one of the ten travel agency companies contracted as a Visa Express vendor is a subsidiary of a suspected financier of terrorism. Fursan Travel & Tourism is owned by the Al-Rajhi Banking & Investment Corporation (RBIC), which is one of the alleged financiers of al Qaeda listed in the "Golden Chain" documents seized in Bosnia in March 2002 (detailing the early supporters of al Qaeda back in the late 1980s, after the Soviets left Afghanistan). RBIC was also the primary bank for a number of charities raided in the United States after September 11 for suspected ties to terrorist organizations. RBIC maintained accounts for the International Islamic Relief Organization, the Saudi Red Crescent Society, the Muslim World League, and the World Assembly of Muslim Youth. RBIC also was used to wire money to the Global Relief Foundation in Belgium, which the United States has designated as a terrorist organization.

Records recovered by Spanish authorities show that several members of an al Qaeda affiliate there held accounts at RBIC, and the terror cell's chief financier told a business partner to use RBIC for their transactions in a fax recovered by Spanish police.[23] And they were not the only al Qaeda terrorists who did business there. Abdulaziz Alomari, who helped Mohammed Atta crash American Airlines Flight 11 into the north tower of the World Trade Center and was one of the three terrorists who received a visa through Visa Express, held an account at RBIC as well.[24] Because his visa application form—which was obtained by this author—does not indicate which travel agency he used, it is not known whether Alomari submitted his application to the agency owned by RBIC.

The founder and namesake of RBIC, Suleiman Abdul Aziz al-Rajhi, also started the SAAR Foundation, whose clone successor, Safa Trust (SAAR liquidated, but most of the same people and operations carried over to Safa[25]) was at the center of the FBI's investigation into the extensive financial network of mostly Saudi-financed terrorist activities in the United States. Operation Greenquest, as it was called, resulted in the raiding of twenty-three different Muslim

organizations' offices, including Safa Trust and several charities that
had bank accounts with RBIC. Although the raids occurred after
September 11, the FBI had been investigating the elaborate financial arrangements—which regularly included SAAR—for years
before the September 11 attacks.

Yet the State Department was so careless in choosing its Visa
Express vendors that one owned by a suspected financier of terrorism became deputized to handle the collection and initial processing of U.S. visas.

IGNORING TERROR FUNDING

The State Department is well aware of the Saudi royal family's open
support for the families of suicide bombers who kill innocent Israelis.
The Saudi Committee for Support of the Intifada al Quds—al Quds
(the "Holy City") is the Arabic name for Jerusalem—spearheaded a
$109.6 million Saudi fundraising telethon in spring 2002 for Pales-
tinian "martyrs." The money raised was earmarked, contrary to what
the Saudis originally claimed, to support the families of suicide
bombers. The State Department's response to such fundraising
never went beyond Secretary of State Colin Powell's statement on
Fox News Sunday that such funding was a "problem."[26]

Documents seized by Israel during its West Bank incursion earlier in 2002 showed that the Saudi Committee—headed by Saudi
interior minister Prince Nayif bin Abd al-Aziz and financially supported by the royal family—knowingly gave money to terrorists and
the families of suicide bombers responsible for attacks that killed
more than ninety Israelis and wounded over six hundred.[27] And that's
just in the first of ten payment rounds analyzed by the Israelis. No
one at State denied the authenticity of the documents, yet most—
particularly those at NEA—did not really care, according to an
administration official.[28] The group the committee gave money
through—with explicit instructions on who the recipients were—was

the Tulkarm Charity Committee (TCC), which distributes social welfare benefits to Palestinians in order to garner political support for Hamas, an avowed terrorist organization. The headquarters of TCC (which was raided by the Israeli Defense Forces) had materials encouraging the murder of Jews, and even a celebratory poster of the suicide bomber who murdered twenty-nine and injured 140 in the Netanya Passover massacre.[29]

In funding the families of suicide bombers, the Saudi Committee—with the tacit approval of the Saudi government—was rewarding terrorists and their families, fueling more terrorism, and consequently undermining America's objective of an Israeli-Palestinian peace agreement. State should have issued a stern rebuke to the Saudis—publicly or privately. But instead, the Saudis got a free pass.

SEE NO EVIL, REPORT NO EVIL

When driving from Jeddah to Mecca, one encounters two road signs. The first tells Muslims that Mecca is straight ahead. The other tells non-Muslims to proceed no further and take the last available exit. Welcome to Saudi Arabia, where some Muslims can practice their religion freely, and no one else can. Shi'ite Muslims, the majority population of the oil-rich Eastern Province, are not only *not* free to practice their version of Islam, but they can be imprisoned and tortured for doing so.[30] History helps explain some of this disdain and contempt for non-Wahhabists. Mohammed Ibn Saud, ancestor to the current king, struck a pact with Mohammed ibn Abd al-Wahhab some 250 years ago, whereby Wahhab's fundamentalist clerics and followers would support the Saud family, in exchange for the royal family's generous financial support of Wahhabism, Wahhab's militant version of Sunni Islam. Modern-day Wahhabists hate nothing more—aside from Christians, Jews, and other infidels—than Muslims practicing non-Wahhabist Islam.

In a June 28, 2000, letter to then–secretary of state Madeleine Albright, the U.S. Commission on International Religious Freedom, which was established by Congress in 1998 to advise Foggy Bottom, wrote:

> In Saudi Arabia, the government brazenly denies religious freedom and vigorously enforces its prohibition against all forms of public religious expression other than that of Wahabi Muslims. Numerous Christians and Shi'a Muslims continue to be detained, imprisoned and deported. As the Department's 1999 Annual Report bluntly summarized: "Freedom of religion does not exist."

Even worshipping or praying in the dark of night can be a dangerous activity in Saudi Arabia, for Saudi police regularly storm into homes if they have reason to believe Christians are attempting to worship. If "caught," the punishment can be severe. In 1998, a Christian Ethiopian got one thousand lashes—carried out over several months—after merely being *accused* of distributing religious materials.

The worst punishments are reserved, though, for those who leave Islam. The punishment for people who commit apostasy—the "crime" of converting from Islam to another religion—is beheading. The House of Saud, however, promotes conversions of a different kind—bringing people *into* Islam, particularly those who work in embassies. Paid on a sliding scale, those who cajole others into converting to Islam are rewarded with bounties of up to $20,000. The highest payment is for converting an American diplomat; lower payments of a few hundred dollars are given for converting a foreign national from one of the non-Western embassies.

Based on overwhelming evidence of religious persecution and overall denial of any form of religious liberty, the Commission on

International Religious Freedom recommended—for the fourth year in a row—that State designate Saudi Arabia as one of the handful of nations considered a "country of particular concern (CPC)." According to the commission, Saudi Arabia qualified under every criterion—and was actually seen as the worst offender in the world.[31]

But for the fourth year in a row, State didn't comply. The CPC designation is despised by listed countries, because it automatically triggers sanctions, though those sanctions can be easily waived for reasons of U.S. national interest. Under the International Religious Freedom Act of 1998, which both created the Commission and mandated that State provide annual reports on international religious freedom, State has no leeway on whether or not to report a country that meets certain standards of religious persecution or denial of religious liberty.

There is a simple explanation for the Saudi exclusion: higher-ups at State put their collective foot down. According to an administration official familiar with the internal squabbling surrounding the Saudi-CPC question, "It was Armitage's decision. He made the call."[32] That was Richard Armitage, Foggy Bottom's number two official, Powell's right-hand man, and a trusted friend of the Saudis. In the Powell State Department, Armitage is the filter through which all major policy changes must go. And Armitage made it quite clear, according to another official, that Saudi Arabia was not to be given the CPC designation.[33] A different administration official, however, says that although politics played a part, Armitage's role in the process was a bit more nuanced, meaning those writing the report were made to "know" early on how things operate and what wouldn't be tolerated. "Let's put it this way: the decision [on Saudi Arabia] was made a long time before it was actually 'made,'"[34] explains the official. Either way, the House of Saud received another free pass.

SAUDI SLAVERY IN AMERICA

"Saida," a young Filipino woman, was brought into a hospital emergency room one night in 1998, unconscious and covered in blood. But the Saudi man who had carried her there was not a Good Samaritan; he was the man who had raped her. When the Saudi couple who employed her as a domestic worker found out about the attack, they rushed to the hospital. Not to help Saida, but to force her out of there before she could implicate their friend. They brought her back into their custody, where she came into contact again and again with her rapist.[35] This happened not in Saudi Arabia, but in Northern Virginia, just outside Washington, D.C. Saida did escape and was able to seek refuge—but no thanks to the State Department. State has known for years about the widespread problem of Saudis bringing domestics with them to America, abusing—and some would say enslaving—them, yet State does nothing to stop it.

Many of the domestic servants employed by Saudi families come from poor areas in nations where the women have responded to agency-placed ads. Many of the women are promised $800 a month only to be informed almost immediately after landing in the kingdom that they will instead receive just $200, if that much. But what often happens next is far worse. The horror stories typically involve women locked inside the home, worked up to twenty hours a day, passed off to friends and neighbors like mere property, and enduring repeated verbal and physical abuse. They are paid so little, if at all, that they typically cannot afford expensive travel back home when their contracts expire. So when offered the chance to work for the Saudi employer—or a friend or relative of the employer—in the United States, the women often jump at the chance, believing that conditions will be far better in America. Sadly, that assumption is generally wrong.

Once in America, the domestics often face the same fate as in the kingdom. This is no secret to the State Department. According to an official at Diplomatic Security (DS), the law enforcement arm of State, DS has received "many" calls from local police stations about abuse of domestics by Saudi diplomats.[36] And human rights activists have been struggling to make State aware of the issue, but to little effect. "We don't want to anger those who are politically connected, such as the Saudis, so the State Department chooses not to provide oversight. It's appalling," complains human-rights attorney Jean Bruggeman.[37]

It's not that State is powerless to do anything about the problem. Many simple measures could be taken, the easiest of which would be to inform women—in their native language—of their rights when they receive their visas to come to the United States. Consular officers could tell them it is illegal for their passports to be confiscated or for an employer to change the contract terms to pay less than minimum wage. The women could be told that abuse can be reported, and doing so does not result in deportation—something they are often told by Saudi employers. It would not be a panacea, but it would be a start. But State doesn't want to hand out even a single sheet of paper warning and informing the women. One State official (who is extremely loyal to Foggy Bottom) snapped, "It's not like those women are our responsibility." Given that the United States is giving them visas—and the abuse is happening in America—*yes*, it is State's responsibility. Which is bad news for the abused women.

Keith Roderick, president of the Coalition for the Defense of Human Rights, who personally helped a woman escape a Saudi home, notes, "When you meet these women and hear their horror stories, it breaks your heart. But after you think about it, it gets you angry, really angry—because State should be doing something about this, and then they turn a cold shoulder to women who want nothing more than to live free."[38]

SMALL FAVORS

In 1982, Prince Turki was in trouble for fighting with the police in Miami. Unfortunately for him, he didn't have diplomatic immunity because he wasn't serving in any governmental capacity in the United States. But fortunately for him, he had something better than diplomatic immunity: a former State Department official ready—and able—to "bend" the rules for the prince. It shouldn't be difficult to predict how the story ends.

On February 26, 1982, Dade County police—reacting on a tip from an informant that Turki had an abused domestic worker trapped there—raided the prince's home.[39] A fight ensued—no domestic worker was found—and police claimed they were kicked and spat upon. An audio recording of the incident captured a royal screaming, "I'll break your nose." It was not Turki making the physical threat, though. It was his wife. Police wanted to charge Turki with assault. State, as usual, had other ideas. Foggy Bottom dispatched former ambassador to Saudi Arabia John C. West to Miami to fix matters. He did.

West, who had a $10,000-per-month contract at the time with a private Saudi firm,[40] came to Prince Turki's defense. With Foggy Bottom's help, he arranged for the prince to receive retroactive diplomatic immunity—even though Turki served no role in or on behalf of the Saudi government whatsoever.[41]

To show that there were no hard feelings for having to "twist" the law in the midst of a highly public situation, West threw a gala bash in Turki's honor that May.[42] At the festivities at the swank Mount Vernon room in the Madison Hotel in Washington, D.C., many high-ranking officials from State were among those sipping cocktails, slurping oysters, and nibbling on prime rib sandwiches. Prince Turki addressed the assembled crowd in praise of U.S.-Saudi relations. After all, they had done wonders for him. To show his gratitude to West personally, he gave an undisclosed sum to the West Foundation (named after the former ambassador and run by his brother); the West Foundation had earlier received a generous $500,000 contribution from another wealthy Saudi benefactor.[43]

Witnessing with disgust how the whole series of events unfolded, Sergeant John Collins, who participated in the raid, told the *New York Times*, "Something has to be done to protect Americans in this country from their own State Department."

PROTECTING BANDAR

Prince Bandar is often considered the most politically savvy of all the foreign ambassadors living in Washington. That may or may not be true—but he certainly is the best-protected. According to a Diplomatic Security (DS) official, Prince Bandar has a security detail that includes full-time participation of six highly trained and skilled DS officers. (DS officers are federal government employees charged with securing American diplomatic missions.)[44] The DS officers and a contingent of private security officers guard him at his northern Virginia residence and travel with him to places like Florida or his ski resort in Aspen, Colorado.

A State Department official, speaking on condition of anonymity, claimed that State was reimbursed by the Saudi government for the use of the DS officers, though he refused to provide any specifics or evidence to that effect.[45] Even if the salaries are reimbursed, though, six skilled DS agents are diverted from meaningful work, such as investigating visa fraud, in order to protect *one person*.

To show his appreciation for their presence, Bandar provides the DS agents with catered meals every day, and with fresh-brewed coffee and gourmet pastries to start out the mornings. The agents enjoy these delicacies from the comfort of an extra house on the premises reserved for the security staff. When the DS agents join Bandar in Aspen—where they have their own ski chalet—he typically buys them full ski outfits and other gifts.

But each agent who works for Bandar is cycled off-rotation very quickly: on average about thirty days after arriving. There doesn't seem to be any real reason for this, other than that Bandar might hope that the more agents he serves catered meals and buys fancy gifts for, the more friends he is likely to have. But with the number of "friends" he—and the rest of the Saudi royal family—already have at Foggy Bottom, one wonders why he would need more.

3

Cold Shoulder: State's Smallest Victims

★ *"THIS IS NOT A HOTEL."*

Monica Stowers had just rescued her son and daughter from her Saudi ex-husband—their father and captor. When she arrived at the U.S. embassy in Riyadh in November 1990, the consul general, Karla Reed, told her, "This is not a hotel." Monica was desperate: her children had been trapped in the abusive custody of their father, Nizar Rasheed Radwan, since 1985.

Radwan had actually allowed his ex-wife to get a visa—in Saudi Arabia, women cannot enter or exit without the "permission" of a husband or father—to see their son, Rasheed, who was having his appendix removed. Because she knew she might never have an opportunity to rescue her children again, Monica went with her still-sore son to her daughter Amjad's school. Even though Monica's face was covered with an *abaya* (veils women in the kingdom must wear), Amjad knew it was her mother because of the shoes she wore.

The seven-year-old ran into her mother's loving embrace, and the reunited family went to the one place where Monica thought she would be protected: the U.S. embassy in Riyadh.

With an American flag prominently displayed nearby, Reed and her number-two official, Frederick Pauleski, combined forces to destroy whatever idealism Monica and her children had harbored about the United States. After telling the scared and helpless family—Monica risked arrest and the kids faced further abuse—they had to leave, Reed snapped, "You cannot claim asylum here. The Saudis can come in and take you." Pauleski helped Reed make the threat a reality. Claiming that Radwan was a "reasonable guy," Pauleski called Monica's ex-husband and told him where she and her children were.

Despite Monica's begging and pleading, Reed, a career diplomat, ordered two Marine guards to force the family out of the embassy. Standing next to the Marines, Pauleski grabbed Rasheed's arm, making the twelve-year-old boy cry out, "Ouch!" Embarrassed, Pauleski took a step back. Monica held out her family's three passports "like a shield," telling her children, "You will remember what your government did to you when you went to them for help."[1]

As the Marines moved closer to the family, one of them apologized to Monica, saying, "I'm sorry, ma'am. I'm just doing my job."[2] The other Marine scooped up little Amjad—she was cowering next to her mother—and dropped her outside the door of the embassy. Monica had no choice but to follow. Supporting her son—who was still weak from the recent surgery—Monica says, "It was the longest walk I ever took."[3] Monica was being thrown out on the street by the very same government her father had admirably served in World War II. His "thanks" was that he never got to see his granddaughter before he passed away in 1992.

With no money and no place else to go, Monica had the embassy van take her family to the mother of her ex-husband. By the next morning, Amjad was locked up inside Radwan's house. Monica took her son and went into hiding.

But then things got worse. The following June, Monica was arrested. When State notified her mother in Texas, she asked them, "Why don't you help her?"[4] State indicated they had no plans to do so, because Monica had "overstayed" her visa—true in fact, but more than understandable given that she was trying to rescue her abducted daughter. Reed actually stopped to visit her at the woman's prison, but only because she was on her way to see a drug dealer in the men's prison. Reed did nothing to help Monica get released. But a Saudi princess whom Monica had tutored bailed her out after three days in jail.

In 1996, Rasheed paid someone $20,000 to escape over the border into Bahrain. He eventually made it to New York, where he visited Harlem—and then was overcome with emotion when he was able to touch the World Trade Center. That year proved to be not as good for his sister, however, who was married off at age twelve to an older Saudi man. Eventually, Amjad fled from her "husband" and went into hiding with her mother. But since they couldn't obtain exit visas to leave the country—a husband or father must provide consent for females to receive visas—the women lived secretly in an abandoned school.

But then Amjad encountered some good fortune. Her grandmother, Ethel Stowers, testified before Congress about her situation in June 2002. The following month, the *Wall Street Journal* ran an editorial excoriating State for its treatment of Amjad—and President Bush one month later personally raised the issue with Prince Bandar, the Saudi ambassador to the United States. That August, Congressman Dan Burton—armed with a list of fifteen cases of Americans held against their will inside the kingdom—led a bipartisan delegation to get Amjad and other Americans out of Saudi Arabia and into freedom.

When the congressional delegation arrived in Saudi Arabia, they were in for a shock: nineteen-year-old Amjad (whose first "husband" from seven years before had divorced her) had been married off to an already-married Saudi father of five who was in his forties.[5] (The middle-aged Saudi was acting in accordance with Islamic law, which allows a man to have up to four wives.) Overweight and overwhelmed by teenage emotions, Amjad was vulnerable—and her Saudi father preyed on her insecurities, telling her that she was fat and could never make it in America. Then—right before the long-scheduled delegation arrived—Amjad underwent major surgery, having her stomach stapled. Burton was able to meet with Amjad in a Riyadh Starbucks, where the emotionally scarred girl was trembling with fear.[6] Because of pressure exerted by the Burton delegation, Amjad was given an exit visa to leave the kingdom—but she was so confused that she didn't know what to do. She said she wanted to leave Saudi Arabia, but not just then.[7]

Amjad eventually did try to leave Saudi Arabia. But when she attempted to cross over into Bahrain in February 2003, Saudi officials blocked her because she didn't have written permission from her husband. This, despite the fact that Burton had been promised— just a few months earlier—by Foreign Minister Prince Saud al-Faisal, "Any American woman in Saudi Arabia who wants to leave will be free to do so."[8] When Monica Stowers e-mailed Maura Harty, the head of Consular Affairs (which handles abduction cases), Harty's response mentioned nothing about Saudi malfeasance or bad faith. She only asked Monica if the U.S. embassy had had advance notice of Amjad's plans. In subsequent e-mails, Harty blandly assured Monica, "We want to work with you to get that exit permit." Frustrated that Harty repeatedly refused to acknowledge that the Saudis had violated their own recent promise, Stowers shot back, "What is so complicated about it? Freedom is easy." If only.

MISSION CONFLICT

Because international child abductions involve foreign nations, State becomes the primary intermediary, if for no other reason than because it is the only governmental body with people and resources on the ground adequate to handle the cases. But whereas a law enforcement agency might gear up for action right away, State does the only thing it knows how to do: it "raises the issue" with foreign governments. That's it. State might "raise" the hopes of parents, but it does little else. And foreign governments know how to read between the lines—delay, stall, and obfuscate—and American children will most likely stay trapped with the abducting parent.

As of 2002, there were some 16,000 American children trapped overseas—only 170 of whom were returned in the previous year[9]—and most of whom did so with little or no help from State. The most celebrated of these abduction cases involve American mothers and Saudi fathers. The typical tale is that an American woman marries a foreign man, usually a Saudi national she met at college, and then, after they divorce, the father uses an unsupervised visit to take the children to Saudi Arabia, often with the help of the Saudi embassy. The mothers are distraught, but Foggy Bottom isn't. Perhaps trying to be "high-minded" and "objective," State officials often handle the child abductions in a clinical and detached manner. And because Foggy Bottom is driven by a constant desire to get a deal—any deal—State sets its sights on "reasonable" goals such as monitored phone calls and supervised visits in the foreign country, *not* on getting an abducted American child back home.

State views child abduction cases as part of the overall relationship with a foreign nation, giving them no higher human priority than, say, a business issue. So when foreign governments—the House of Saud is masterful at this—create a legal maze to make it "legally" impossible to recover a child, State sees the rules as new obstacles that must be respected, not necessarily removed.

Notes the American Enterprise Institute's Danielle Pletka, "It's not that the State Department doesn't care about abducted children; it's that they care much more about maintaining 'smooth relations.'"[10] Getting forceful with State's foreign counterparts, after all, might "upset" them—and might "damage" otherwise "friendly" relations. This is why State is a mere spectator when girls and women in Saudi

Arabia are not allowed exit visas without the consent of a husband or father—and girls as young as twelve risk being sold off into "marriage."

Just ask Margaret McClain, another woman whose story was told to Congress.*

FIGHTING FOR HEIDI

On July 11, 1992, Margaret McClain fell in love with her new daughter, Heidi. Heidi came late in her mother's life—Margaret was in her forties—but the new mother couldn't have been happier. She was widowed in 1988, but had found love again a little over a year later, marrying Heidi's father, Abdulbaset Alomari, in December 1989. A student at Arkansas State University in Jonesboro, Alomari was twenty years her junior. The wedded bliss, however, soon dissipated, with Alomari becoming an increasingly radical Islamist—he became an assistant imam in 1991 at a Wahhabist mosque—and physically abusing his wife.

After Heidi was born, matters got worse. Alomari's violence had become routine, and Margaret worried that she would not be able to shield Heidi from his rage. In 1993, Margaret received an order of protection—and local police had to escort Alomari from the premises. The following year, the two were divorced—though Alomari had found time in the interim to marry his cousin. Despite evidence of physical abuse or Alomari's incestuous bigamy, the judge granted him unsupervised visitation—even though McClain warned the judge that her ex-husband might abduct Heidi to Saudi Arabia, which he did in August 1997 with the apparent help of the Saudi embassy.

Sharp and determined, Margaret got local police and the FBI involved the moment she learned her ex-husband had taken Heidi out of Arkansas, which he was prohibited by the court from doing. State and federal warrants were issued for his arrest, and Alomari was listed

* Stories cited in this chapter are sourced from congressional testimony provided to Congress, congressional hearings, and court records and transcripts.

on Interpol. But since he had managed to enter safely into Saudi Arabia, the only U.S. government agency with the jurisdiction to handle the case was the State Department. Knowing that her ex-husband had connections to Aramco, the U.S.-Saudi oil conglomerate, Margaret told State to look there for her husband. State did nothing.

Margaret knew that time was crucial. Heidi had allegedly been sexually molested by her father at age three, and though a psychiatrist had believed the girl, the police didn't have enough evidence to prosecute. Margaret had then seen Alomari's fury firsthand. As she was backing her car out of the driveway one day — about one week before the court issued the protection order — Alomari pulled in from the street, blocking her. He rushed to her car, pounding on the driver's side window, demanding to know where she was going. Margaret got out of the car, locked it, and asked him to calm down. When he kept yelling — it was around 9 a.m. — she started walking next door to call the police, and maybe get some help from a physically imposing neighbor. But Alomari walked around to the other side of the car and started kicking the window that was mere inches from his daughter's head. Margaret raced back and was able to calm him down. With Heidi now alone with her father in Saudi Arabia, Margaret feared the worst.

After more than six months with no indication of where her husband was — or if her daughter was even alive — Margaret received several threatening e-mails from Alomari. Without any help from the FBI or State — neither wanted to act quickly — Margaret had a friend of her grown son trace the e-mails to a server at Aramco, exactly where she had told State to look for Heidi's abductor. But even with this information, State still did nothing. Not deterred, Margaret e-mailed every Aramco employee with an "English-sounding" name, pleading for any information about Alomari. Several months later, in summer 1998, she received an anonymous e-mail from an Aramco employee who had just arrived in Texas, telling her Alomari's phone number and city of residence—even the location of Heidi's day care. With that information in hand, State did...nothing. After a few more months, State finally arranged phone contact. In all, it took State more than two years to set up a "welfare visit," where a consular officer was finally able to see Heidi in person—though it would take an extra three years (five total since the abduction) before Margaret could do the same.

When she was finally able to see her daughter in Saudi Arabia in July 2002—that was the first time her ex-husband agreed to give her "permission" to enter the kingdom—her planned five-day visit was reduced to three hours. The night before she arrived, Alomari informed the consulate in Dhahran that there was a "family emergency" that required him to take Heidi with him to Riyadh. The consular officer in Dhahran, Margaret says, was actually "very upset with him," and the official arranged to have two local Saudi residents travel with Margaret to Riyadh so she wouldn't be walking alone into a potentially nasty situation. After traveling halfway around the world, Margaret saw her ten-year-old daughter for three hours—at a McDonald's. She was overwhelmed at seeing Heidi, but afterward, she feared what fate might befall her daughter in the next few years—particularly because of something Alomari had once told her.

Shortly before their separation in 1993, Alomari had told Margaret that it was religiously acceptable for him to have married a woman nearly twenty years his senior, because the prophet Mohammed had done so. He then told her that when he was older, he could take a wife as young as nine, because that was the age of Mohammed's last wife.[11] By the time she saw her daughter in 2002, Heidi was already one year past that age.

State has never demanded the return of Heidi; it has only "raised the issue" with the Saudis. Not wanting to cause "unnecessary" turmoil in the U.S.-Saudi relationship, it is not aggressively fighting to rescue Heidi from the abusive custody of the man who kidnapped her. As the House Government Reform Committee noted in documents related to hearings it held in October 2002, "The State Department's current efforts in the McClain case are focused on facilitating future visits by Margaret to Saudi Arabia, rather than on the return of Heidi."[12]

NOT JUST MOTHERS LEFT BEHIND

Quiet and unassuming, Michael Rives knows firsthand how Monica Stowers and Margaret McClain feel. His two children are trapped in Saudi Arabia, unable to see their gentle and loving father. Aside from the abductor being the mother, Michael's case is different in one key respect: he is the legal custodial parent under not just U.S. law, but Saudi law as well. Even though the case doesn't even give the abducting mother the fig leaf cover of Saudi "law," State does not demand the return of Michael's children, Sami and Lilly. Michael wants his children back before they forget their father.[13] The State Department apparently doesn't care if they are never returned at all.

While working in Saudi Arabia, Michael met and married a Syrian woman named Roua al-Adel in 1996. Al-Adel, who lived in the kingdom because her Syrian father had been a powerful government official there, "thought of herself as being very Western," he explains, "which is why we got married." She gave birth to Lilly on October 8, 1997. A year later, they moved to Texas. But al-Adel found adjusting to life in America much more difficult than she had anticipated, so she made regular visits to the kingdom. On one such trip, Sami was born, on July 22, 1999. (Although Lilly and Sami were born in the kingdom, Saudi and U.S. law both consider the children U.S. citizens because their father is American.) In July 2001, al-Adel took four-year-old Lilly and two-year-old Sami with her to Saudi Arabia—with Michael's permission. It was supposed to be a two-month vacation. But after she was supposed to have returned, al-Adel sent word to Michael that she was keeping the children in Saudi Arabia and that he would "never" be able to see them again.[14]

Even though the law was not on her side, al-Adel had something else working in her favor. Her father, the minister of education and commerce in Syria in the early 1970s, also served as a longtime advisor to the Saudi minister of labor. And her brothers were also politically well connected. To make sure she would have the full protection of the Saudi government, al-Adel's father convinced the Saudis to make his daughter a Saudi citizen.

After spending $33,000, Michael won a divorce and full custody of Sami and Lilly. But then began the back-and-forth with the Saudi government, and when Michael pushed State to take a tough line, he complained, "It was almost as if State was waiting for any Saudi excuse so they could tell me that they couldn't help me."[15]

After Republican Congressman Dan Burton of Indiana intervened on Michael's behalf in his August 2002 trip to the kingdom, State "treated me much better, and became more aggressive," Michael notes. But nearly two years after Lilly and Sami were taken, he still does not have his kids back. He has received a few photos — the first of which he got only after they had been gone a year — so at least he can see how they look. And Michael has been able to talk on the phone "a few times" with Lilly and Sami. But they speak very little English, since al-Adel is teaching them only Arabic. So how does he communicate with them? "I listen to their voices, and they listen to mine," he says, his voice cracking with emotion.[16]

NOT JUST SAUDI ARABIA

"I remember the last time I heard his voice. It still breaks me up inside just thinking about it," says Larry Synclair in a subdued voice.[17] The last time he talked to his son, Larry Jr., was May 10, 2001, which came almost a year after he saw him that final time before he was taken by his mother. Larry has encountered the same willful disregard from State about his plight, and has received the same degree of "help" that Margaret McClain and Michael Rives have had in trying to get their children back. But Larry's case is different, in that his son is in Russia, not Saudi Arabia. It hasn't proven a key difference, though, in terms of getting more effective assistance from Foggy Bottom.

In Russian cases, as Larry Synclair has discovered, there is the same hesitancy by officials at State to pressure the foreign government to return an abducted American child. With Russia—as with Saudi Arabia—State acts as if its hands are tied because Russia is not a signatory to The Hague Convention, which covers the civil aspects of international child abductions. Even presented with substantial evidence suggesting that the mother is abusing Larry Jr., State has done precious little to rescue him.

Larry Synclair first met Svetlana Gavrilova, a Russian national, when he toured what was then the Soviet Union in October 1990 with a group of National Public Radio reporters and producers. When he returned just over a year later—a month before the official fall of the Soviet Union—Larry started dating Gavrilova. Almost three years later, in 1994, they married in Russia—and Larry Jr. was born one year after that, on May 14, 1995. But by 1997, Larry could sense that his happy marriage was crumbling. Gavrilova started exhibiting extreme mood swings, and she would go away for entire weekends for "yoga" sessions. Larry figured out the following spring that, in fact, his wife had joined a cult and was hooked on drugs—and the "yoga" weekends were actually marathon orgies (dubbed "Cosmic Lovefests" in Internet advertisements) where the participants partook of hallucinogenic drugs. Over the next few months—after they separated in early May 1998—Gavrilova kidnapped Larry Jr. *twice.*

But because she wanted money more than she wanted to keep Larry from seeing his son, Gavrilova allowed him very limited weekend visitation rights in October 1998 in exchange for monthly "child support" payments. When he was with his son, he noticed a marked change from just months earlier. After making a simple mistake or creating any kind of a mess, Larry Jr. would cower in fear—as if waiting for harsh punishment. The three-year-old had also started wetting his bed. And when Larry heard something break in the kitchen one weekend, he found his son curled up in a corner, crying.

Larry went to the U.S. embassy in Moscow for help—twice, once after each kidnapping. Nothing was done after either visit. Pleas to have the U.S. government protect one of its citizens from persistent and chronic abuse went unheeded. Larry soon faced a crisis, and he was forced to act because his government would not. A few days after Christmas, Gavrilova threatened that she would kidnap her son again if Larry didn't pay her more. Ten days later, Larry and his son boarded a train out of Russia, flew from Belarus to Britain, and landed in California on January 11, 1999.

But the freedom Larry Jr. achieved upon touching U.S. soil proved fleeting. Larry initiated divorce proceedings in February and received temporary sole custody, but Gavrilova actually came to the United States to fight for custody. In September 1999, the court allowed Gavrilova to take Larry Jr., to Russia, awarding her temporary custody. The decision was heart-stopping not just because the authorities failed to investigate Larry's allegations of child abuse—which were supported by the sworn statement of a former nanny in Russia—but because Gavrilova *admitted* in her declaration to the court that she had abducted her son. Within days of returning to Russia, Gavrilova broke off all contact with her ex-husband.

In February 2000, without any assistance from State, Larry's attorney arranged a meeting with Gavrilova and Larry Jr., through local Russian authorities. Larry, holding several wrapped gifts, waited outside the Universitet Metro subway station with an official from the local court and his lawyer hovering nearby. He saw his son approaching from across the street, walking hand-in-hand with his mother and her boyfriend, one on either side of the boy. Seeing that staged entrance, Larry knew something was not right. When Larry was standing five or six feet from his son—who was wearing only mud-covered jogging pants and a yellow plastic raincoat over his clothes in the bitter Russian winter—he set the gifts on the car parked next to him.

Larry Jr., pulled away from his mother and her boyfriend and thrust toward his dad. Larry crouched down, embracing the son he hadn't seen in five months—and his son clutched his little hands around the back of his dad's neck. The child's heart was racing, and Larry could feel his body starting to quiver. Not wanting to "spook" Gavrilova—who could end the meeting at any moment—Larry stayed low to the ground, clinging to his son. His ex-wife started screaming, demanding Larry's passport—something she wanted merely as a power play since Larry was not going to be alone with his son. Larry—still in the same position, holding his son—handed her a proposed custody agreement, which would have granted him custody for six months each year.

Gavrilova was indignant, and threw the agreement, page by page, into the mud next to her son's feet. Ten minutes after the meeting began, Gavrilova grabbed her son—but the four-year-old would not let go of his dad, who was still crouching low to the ground. As much as he wanted to hold his son forever, he let go, reassuring Larry Jr., that everything would be fine. Crying, the boy was whisked away by his mother—never opening the gifts from his dad. It was the last time Larry has seen his son.

Fearing the worst, Larry pushed State to do something—anything. On June 14, 2000, State performed a "welfare check," where the Foreign Service officer (FSO), who was not a child psychiatrist, made a determination that Larry Jr., looked "healthy and happy."[18]

The embassy finally arranged a phone call between father and son nearly a year later, on May 10, 2001. Because Gavrilova was teaching Larry Jr., only Russian, Larry needed a translator to speak with his son. State recommended to Larry that he accede to his ex-wife's demands that she pre-approve all "questions" he had for his son. He did. When he asked his son a question, he could hear Gavrilova whispering in the background. She instructed her son to only answer with "da" and "nyet." Like the ill-fated meeting the year before, the phone call lasted just ten minutes. Two "welfare visits"—where the FSO did Gavrilova's bidding by declaring the boy "happy and healthy" the first time and "healthy and safe" after the second visit in December 2000—and one brief phone call. That's all State has done for Larry in over three years. Even with the only final custody order that has ever been issued—in the U.S. or Russia—awarding Larry sole legal custody in December 2002, State has taken no further action.

Things have gotten a little better, though. Before Congressman Burton turned up the heat on State with hearings and the delegation trip to Saudi Arabia in August 2002, officials at Foggy Bottom insisted to Larry that his case was nothing more than a "child custody" issue. But after the congressional pressure was applied, State conceded that Larry Jr., had, in fact, been abducted. Larry, of course, already knew this—but it was still significant to hear his own government admit the obvious.

When asked what he'll do if—when—he sees his son again, Larry says, "I don't like to think about that." He pauses for a moment, his voice falling almost to a whisper. Choking back tears, he finally answers, "When I see him again, I know I'm going to want nothing more than to hold him in my arms. But it depends on his initial reaction; I don't know whether he'll see me as his father or look at me like I'm a stranger."

TREATY'S FALSE HOPE

Toiling away at his government-issued desk day after day, Tom Johnson is an attorney with an encyclopedic grasp of the law. His measured tone and meticulous attention to detail hint at his life as a Marine some two decades earlier. When he's not working or taking time to be a devoted father to his three little girls, Tom spends almost every waking moment fighting to get back his daughter Amanda, who was never sent back from what was supposed to be a temporary stay with her mother overseas in 1995. Tom has poured countless hours into his quest—and has nearly depleted himself financially, spending more than $250,000. But Tom has had to go to these lengths to get his daughter back not from a desert prison like Saudi Arabia or a semi-lawless state like Russia, but from democratic Sweden. And the biggest enemy in his struggle has been his employer: the U.S. Department of State.

Particularly maddening in cases involving Sweden—and countries such as Austria and Germany—is that the "law" should provide an easy compass for State to follow in recovering abducted American children from these countries. The law in question is a treaty known as The Hague Convention, which is intended to strip abducting parents of the strongest incentive they have: getting a second chance in court—or just a first one—in their own homeland. Originated in 1980, The Hague Convention has fifty-one signatories—not Saudi Arabia or Russia—and it declares that child abduction cases must be handled in the place of the child's "habitual residence." The only exception allowed is when doing so would pose a "grave risk." Even though, at first blush, the treaty seems rather straightforward, Hague Convention nations such as Sweden and Austria play games with "habitual residence" and "grave risk." And State lets these cheaters prosper.

Pursuant to a Virginia custody order, seven-year-old Amanda was in Sweden with her mother. But when she failed to return in time for her third grade classes in the United States in 1995, Tom knew something was wrong. His ex-wife then filed for sole custody in her local district court in Sweden—even though the Virginia court had issued an order that granted her shared custody. Her gambit failed—but only initially. Tom won in the lower Swedish courts—at considerable financial expense to himself—but the seventeen-month ordeal ended with Sweden's high court ruling against him. Seemingly rewarding the mother for stalling, the court ruled that Amanda's "habitual residence" had changed to Sweden because at that point Amanda had been there for more than two years—even though the Virginia custody order had explicitly noted that her "habitual residence" was Virginia.[19] Despite the flagrant violation of the clear spirit and intent—if not the letter itself—of The Hague Convention by Sweden, State has never demanded Amanda's return.

For a while, State went about as far as it ever goes in abduction cases: it cited Sweden as a Hague Convention violator. From 1999 to 2002, Amanda's case was featured prominently in State's annual reports to Congress on child abduction cases involving signatories of The Hague Convention. But State did nothing else to exert pressure on Sweden to actually comply with the treaty. No threats of punishment or sanctions. No threats not to honor Hague rulings in the United States or to refuse to send children back to Sweden. While Tom was pleased that State went as far as it did—something of a minor miracle for the institution—he believed more was necessary. So he testified before Congress multiple times and appeared on television programs, including *Nightline*. Amanda's plight was written up in places as varied as *Reader's Digest* and the *Wall Street Journal*. Tom even wrote scholarly papers, including one for New York University's prestigious law journal, on why State was not doing everything it was allowed to under The Hague to seek the return of American children. In other words, he became a thorn in the State Department's side.

This was too much for the folks at Foggy Bottom. In the 2003 report to Congress on Hague compliance, all references to Amanda were excised, and Sweden was given a clean bill of health.[20] Maura Harty—the same head of Consular Affairs (CA) that Monica Stowers found so unhelpful—specifically "cleansed" Sweden in the report to exact revenge on Tom Johnson, according to a senior CA official.[21] "Harty and her deputies don't know how to deal with troublesome parents, so they want to make it clear that parents who speak out will be punished," notes the official. This "whitewash"—as one State Department official termed it—erased references not just to Amanda, but also to thirteen other American children in situations not unlike Amanda's. So not only do Swedish parents have their legal expenses paid for by their generous socialist government, but American parents have to pay their own way *and* fight *both* governments.

At times, Tom seems resigned, telling *Nightline* in May 2000, "The reality is that, short of sending in a Marine battalion landing team, she's not coming back." Yet he soldiers on, in large part because there are other children like Amanda. The odds against him are long. A senior official at State estimated that roughly ten percent of Hague cases overseas involving an American parent result in the child being returned to the United States. According to the Center on Missing and Exploited Children, more than ninety percent of Hague cases heard in the United States result in the child being sent overseas—often with State's help. Foggy Bottom has on a number of occasions filed what's known as an *amicus curiae* (friend of the court) brief, recommending that the court should side with the foreign parent. On an individual basis, there is nothing insidious about this. But State has almost never—if ever—filed a petition on behalf of an American parent.

HAPPY ENDINGS—WITH NO HELP FROM STATE

With a State Department unwilling or unable to help mothers or fathers get their children back from tyrannies like Saudi Arabia or democratic nations like Sweden, some parents turn elsewhere for help. One such parent is "Sara"—she wishes to remain anonymous for fear of retribution—who hired a specialty firm to rescue her ten-year-old son, "Kevin," and thirteen-year old daughter, "Kathleen," from Syria. Sara had no other option, because State refused to help her.

Kevin and Kathleen were on an unsupervised visit with their father, a Syrian national living in the U.S., one weekend in 1993, when the father loaded his three- and six-year-old children onto a flight bound for Syria. Since she had full custody of the children and the father had broken the law in kidnapping them—state and federal warrants were issued for his arrest, and he was listed on Interpol—Sara initially believed that State would help her recover Kevin and Kathleen. But after five years, State had not even arranged for her to see her children in Syria. The most "help" she received were a few phone calls over the years. She finally realized that if she were to rescue Kevin and Kathleen, she would have to do so without help from Foggy Bottom.

After Sara started searching for a private firm that would help rescue her children—it's a thriving industry, but one filled with con men and hustlers—Kathleen, then thirteen years old, told her mother that she was about to be sold off into marriage. Sara's need to get her children out of Syria took on added urgency. She located two former Marine special operations officers who could do what State had failed to do. In 1998, they began preparations for the rescue, relying in part on intelligence shared with them by their long-established Middle East connections. They learned the father's work schedule, and initiated contact with the children by calling the house when the father was away. After five years apart from their mother, Kevin and Kathleen were eager to flee. At a predetermined time, the two former Marines came to the house and left with the children.

When they crossed over into Lebanon—which is controlled by Syria—Kevin and Kathleen were reunited with their mother. Seeing each other for the first time in five years, the room was filled with "tears, crying, joy—absolute ecstasy," notes Bill Cowan, one of the two rescuers.[22] "But it was mixed with fear, fear that the State

Department wouldn't help them get out of the country." It turns out that the fear was well founded.

Arriving at the embassy in Beirut, the reunited family was greeted by an unusually emotional State Department official. The official was not overjoyed, however, by the miracle that had just occurred. Sara, Kathleen, and Kevin "were met with hostility," explains Cowan. Sara had in hand all the necessary paperwork—from birth certificates to court documents—to prove she was the rightful, legal parent. But embassy staff was not swayed. "They interrogated [Sara] like she was a suspect," observes Cowan. Then they treated her like one, forcing the whole family to leave the embassy—an action that threatened the safety of all three in Syrian-controlled Lebanon. They risked the same fate that befell Monica Stowers and her daughter Amjad in Riyadh, but they were lucky. They survived the night—staying under assumed names at a nearby hotel—and came back to the embassy the next morning.

Because of pressure exerted by Republican congressman Ben Gilman of New York, the embassy begrudgingly accommodated the family on the second day. The children were given the new passports they needed to leave the country—but that was it. As Cowan notes, "[The embassy staff] didn't even use the embassy van to give the family a safer trip to the airport." But by the next day, the entire family was on U.S. soil, breathing freedom, together.

MAHA'S MALAYSIAN MIRACLE

Maha Seramur is a bright, outgoing teenager who shows little sign that she was held against her will in the desert prison of Saudi Arabia for eight years. But behind her warm demeanor and gentle brown eyes lies the pain of knowing her two siblings are still trapped there. That she escaped at all is a testament to her tenacious mother, Sam, and the presence of a CBS television camera crew—*not* any efforts from the State Department.

In 1990, Sam met Mubarak al-Rehaili at a college bar at the University of Dubuque in Iowa, and the two wed a year later in Illinois, when Sam was just nineteen.[23] Shortly after the honeymoon, they moved to Saudi Arabia. They had three children. Safiah was born on Valentine's Day in 1982, and little sister Maha came into the world on September 2, 1985. They welcomed baby brother Faisal on September 15, 1986. Although her husband was not very religious, young Sam says she "found meaning" in Islam, taking to the religion with a passionate devotion soon after arriving in the kingdom. But her husband's increasingly violent behavior made it more and more difficult for Sam to carry on with her everyday life.

In 1991, the family moved to the United States—because al-Rehaili wanted to. In Saudi Arabia, al-Rehaili had raped one of the domestics, which normally wouldn't have been a problem for him, but this time, the rape victim became pregnant. Fearing that the religious police would hunt him down and possibly kill him, al-Rehaili desperately wanted a pre-established escape route, and Sam convinced him that a U.S. green card was his best option. To get his green card, al-Rehaili brought the whole family to America, where Sam filed for divorce just months later. Citing the husband's history of violence, the court awarded Sam a permanent restraining order, granting her sole custody of the children in the process. With no family in America anymore, al-Rehaili went back to Saudi Arabia after receiving his green card.

Because al-Rehaili refused to pay child support and Sam was taking college courses to make up for her decade in Saudi Arabia without an education, Sam was soon on welfare, with barely enough money to feed and clothe her three children. So when she received a call in 1994 from al-Rehaili promising child support payments, Sam was receptive, but leery. Her ex-husband began crying about his father's recent death, saying that he was now a changed man. He pressured her to let him see his children by undermining her self-confidence, calling her a bad mother because she couldn't provide for them. Against her better judgment, Sam reluctantly agreed to his visit. Every day since, she has regretted her decision.

When Sam went to State, she encountered outright hostility. "They told me, 'He'll kill you, and there's nothing we can do to help you,'" says Sam, the disbelief still palpable in her voice.[24] She persisted, and State's response was to tell her that even if she didn't get killed, "You'll get thrown in jail, and then there's nothing we can do."[25] Stunned and saddened, Sam's feelings of helplessness grew over the next eight years. But then, suddenly, her spirits soared— Maha made contact with her.

A friend of Maha's had located Sam's brother through a directory of Hotmail e-mail addresses and sent him a note with a message of "Help, Saudi Arabia." He forwarded the e-mail on to Sam, who was living in Malta at this point. Sam was suspicious—many people knew of her story—but she replied anyway. She quickly was invited to "chat" online. Sam was soon in touch with her daughter. After confirming her identity to her mom by completing a nursery rhyme Sam used to sing to her children, the incredibly astute sixteen-year-old explained that the family was traveling to Malaysia in a few months. The trip to Malaysia—a democratic and relatively open Muslim nation—was the perfect opportunity for Sam to rescue her three children.

Sam informed State that she would need help rescuing her children from Malaysia in August 2002. State's response? Officials there told Sam they had just negotiated some other deals there, so they weren't in a position to "ask for any more favors"—a phone conversation Sam tape-recorded because she was so scared of what State might or might not do. Thinking on her feet, Sam arranged to have a *60 Minutes* camera crew accompany her. Despite some last-minute confusion—al-Rehaili told Maha the family was traveling instead to southern Saudi Arabia, because some unknown person had tipped him off that Maha had been in contact with her mother—Sam traveled to Malaysia, and prepared for the predetermined meeting time: 8 p.m. on August 8, the eighth hour of the eighth day of the eighth month. But because of the father's paranoia, the family stopped at fifteen different hotels in Kuala Lumpur before finally settling on one.

Sam searched all over the city, but couldn't find the hotel where her children were staying. She went back to her hotel, waiting by the phone. In a moment captured on camera, an anxious Sam lunged to the phone the moment it rang—right at eight. She hopped in a taxi and rushed to Maha's hotel. But her daughter came out alone. She couldn't wake up Safiah or Faisal, and with al-Rehaili and his team of servants inside the hotel, it was too dangerous for Maha to go back inside. Sam thought about sending Maha on to the embassy and waiting for her other two children, but she quickly realized *that* was too dangerous as well. "I could not send her to the embassy, because I was afraid that they would interrogate her and send her back to her father," she explains. Filled with a profound mixture of joy and sadness, Sam went with Maha to the embassy. Probably because of the presence of the CBS television crew, State helped the mother and daughter get back to America.

Even with Maha safely back in Florida, not a day goes by that Sam does not think of her two children still held hostage in the desert prison. As of April 2003, Safiah is engaged to be married to a Saudi man, meaning she may never be able to leave Saudi Arabia or see her mother again. And Faisal, although as a male he has better prospects, is regularly beaten by al-Rehaili, according to Sam. Allegedly, his father sometimes strips him naked and locks him in his room, hiding his clothes elsewhere in the house. Sam says softly, "If I had had help from the State Department, Faisal and Safiah would be with me today. I can never forgive them for that."[26]

THE MOST HATED PARENT

As much agony and anguish as State has put so many parents through, none has ever encountered the level or degree of antagonism and devious backstabbing as Patricia (Pat) Roush, whose daughters Alia and Aisha were abducted to Saudi Arabia. Her story has been told many times, but it bears repeating in order to understand the depths to which State will go.[27] After her daughters were kidnapped from their suburban Chicago home by their abusive and alcoholic father, Khalid al-Gheshayan, on January 25, 1986, Pat went to the State Department. Their reaction was harsh, telling her, "Your children are gone. We can't help you. You're never going to see them again."[28] She has worked every day since to prove them wrong.

In 1986, without State's help, a Saudi lawyer on the payroll of the governor of Riyadh negotiated a deal for Pat that would have allowed Alia and Aisha to leave Saudi Arabia. But just before the deal went forward, State refused to allow ambassador Walter Cutler to participate in the final negotiations for the release of the girls. It was the first time State scuttled a done deal that would have saved Alia and Aisha—but it was not the last. Ambassador Wyche Fowler in 1995 scrapped an agreement that had been made by his predecessor, Ray Maebus, for the Saudis to return the girls.

Right after the first double-cross, State ordered one of its officials to "witness" a Saudi propaganda video, where little Alia and Aisha were forced to renounce their mother and proclaim their love for their father and the kingdom. The Riyadh consul general who witnessed the whole affair but said nothing at the time later told Pat that her daughters were distraught and crying, and that they only made the "statements" after more than an hour had passed and they had been taken to a "back room."[29]

In late August 2002, the House of Saud, with State's consent, shuttled the girls (then twenty-three and twenty) to a London hotel teeming with Saudi officials—the very same day that Congressman Burton's delegation was arriving in the kingdom to push for their release. State went one step further, sending a consular officer to "interview" the girls—with an open microphone in the room. State claims that the only person at the other end of the speakerphone was the Arabic translator, but the girls had no way of knowing if that was true. Inside the mini-Saudi Arabia, the consular officer took down the statements of the emotionally stunted young women—who had both been recently married off—saying that they wanted no part of their mother or the United States. State then transmitted the message with no indication of the circumstances under which the girls made it.

With all she's been through, most women might have given up, resigning themselves to a fate they must accept. Not Pat. Because of her persistent and outspoken criticism of State, Foggy Bottom was forced to create the Office of Children's Issues to focus specifically on child abductions. Through Pat, Sam Seramur was able to contact the producers at 60 Minutes. And Pat has served as a source of strength for other left-behind parents, giving them the dogged hope to which she still clings. Although she has only seen her daughters once in seventeen years, Pat dreams of the day when Alia and Aisha will be at her side.

Although State reserves its fiercest venom for people who don't hold their tongues, like Pat Roush and Tom Johnson, even those parents who stay silent receive nothing more from State than kind words and empty reassurances. In some cases, Foggy Bottom expresses dissatisfaction to a foreign government—but does no more.

It would stand to reason that State would want some success stories—and soon. Consular Affairs chief Maura Harty, in fact, traveled to Saudi Arabia in early 2003 to "discuss" child abductions with the government there, although one CA official says Pat Roush's case was not raised.[30] But success would also bring higher expectations from American parents, something State does not want. Pat Roush found this out early on in her struggle. When she kept pressing State to help, an official there snidely remarked, "If we helped you, we'd have to help all the parents." Pat replied with a simple question: "Why don't you help all the parents?"[31]

MARGARET MCCLAIN AND HER DAUGHTER, HEIDI

Heidi was abducted to Saudi Arabia by her father in 1997. The Department of State has never demanded her return.

MICHAEL RIVES, HIS DAUGHTER, LILLY MICHELLE, AND SON, SAMI MICHAEL

Although Michael has full legal custody of his children (even under Saudi law), State has not helped him get the return of his children from his ex-wife, who took them to Saudi Arabia in July of 2001.

Michael Rives and Roua al-Adel

Lilly Michelle

Sami Michael

(from left) Sami Michael, Michael Rives, and Lilly Michelle

LARRY SYNCLAIR SR. AND HIS SON, LARRY JR.

Larry Jr. was taken to Russia by his mother in September 1999. Although Larry has sole legal custody of Larry Jr. under the only final court ruling, State has taken no further action to facilitate Larry Jr.'s return.

Courtesy of Larry Synclair Sr.

Courtesy of Larry Synclair Sr.

MAHA SERAMUR

Although Maha is safely back in the United States after a dramatic rescue, her brother and sister are still in Saudi Arabia.

Courtesy of the Seramur family

ALIA AND AISHA ROUSH

Alia and Aisha Roush were kidnapped and taken to Saudi Arabia by their father in 1986. Their mother, Pat, is still pressing the State Department to help.

Courtesy of Pat Roush

4

Tolerating Tyrants

★ *"THEY HAVE WONDERFUL SENSES OF HUMOR."*[1]

That sentiment was expressed by the assistant secretary of state for South Asia, Robin Rafael, after her first face-to-face meeting with the Taliban in 1996—a session during which, according to an informed source, she sat in a chair with her back facing the radical Islamists.[2] Islamic law, to which the Taliban strictly adhered, forbids any man outside of the immediate family to view a woman's face. Yet the bizarre encounter did not sour Rafael on the Taliban. As history later showed, Rafael's "humor" remark was one of a series of mistaken judgments State made about the political movement that was intertwined with Osama bin Laden's al Qaeda terrorist network.

The Taliban, originally pegged in the international press as a movement of fundamentalist religious students, was met with initial warmth by officials at Foggy Bottom. They believed that not only did the Taliban's capture of Afghanistan's capital city of Kabul in September 1996 bring the promise of "stability," but it also opened up real possibilities for a massive pipeline that might finally allow the resources of the oil and gas fields of Central Asia to reach world markets. These factors—and an unwillingness to confront an increasingly obvious reality—led State at first to embrace, and later to tolerate, after its true nature had become clear, the radical Islamist movement that harbored bin Laden.

"NOTHING OBJECTIONABLE"

The day after the Taliban captured Kabul, State spokesman Glyn Davies announced that officials at Foggy Bottom found "nothing objectionable" about the new rulers of Afghanistan.[3] Nothing objectionable about the complete subjugation of women and girls, the denial of basic freedoms to all, and barbaric military tactics. Indeed, the brutally repressive movement that swept through most of Afghanistan in barely two years had a friend in State—one that was willing to look the other way while atrocities were committed on a regular basis.

Of course it is easy in hindsight to criticize State for cozying up to the Taliban, but it is clear Foggy Bottom officials should have known better. When the Taliban took Kabul in September 1996, State spokesman Glyn Davies stated, "What we haven't had an opportunity to do, of course, is get in touch with the Taliban and discuss with them their intentions."[4] And yet, by its own admission to the *Economist* a few days later, State had had "ongoing contacts for the past couple of years with the Taliban."[5] With the Taliban able to achieve in roughly two years what the Soviet Union could not in a decade—uniting virtually all of Afghanistan—the line about the new regime in Kabul being a movement of "religious students" was absurd on its face.

Still, State's early fawning over the Taliban was, in some respects, understandable. The movement was backed by two nominal U.S.

allies—Saudi Arabia and Pakistan—and even the central government ousted by the Taliban initially supported the new mullah militia. When the Taliban moved to seize Khandahar in 1994, sitting Afghan president Burhanuddin Rabbani (who had been in power since 1992) actually supported its efforts. Khandahar, by all accounts, was a city in chaos. Promising to clean up the city by imposing fundamentalist Islamic law, the Taliban was welcomed by virtually everyone, including the U.S. State Department.

But when the Taliban turned its military machine on its next target, Herat, the same rationale did not apply. "If Khandahar was the worst city in Afghanistan at the time, Herat was the best. Where one was lawless, the other was orderly and a relatively nice place to live," notes former Defense Intelligence Agency official Julie Sirrs, whose portfolio included Afghanistan.[6]

The Rabbani government's support quickly disappeared. The same could not be said for Foggy Bottom. According to Sirrs, the Taliban was able to consolidate control over such a large swath of Afghanistan in a short time because it was assumed to have American backing, which gave it extra legitimacy.[7] All the signals State sent indicated support for the mullah militia.

State's broadcasting arm, the Voice of America (VOA), was fiercely pro-Taliban—a trend that continued nearly unabated for years.[8] A November 1996 Russian press account (which was confirmed by several current and former U.S. officials) found that VOA reporters, "on order from the State Department and the CIA, are doing their best to extol the Taliban's latest achievements in 'establishing peace in the country.' However, so far not one report or news program has ever mentioned the Taliban's harsh treatment not only of their political adversaries, but also of the local population."[9]

When it seemed that the Taliban moved on Kabul, State pressured the Northern Alliance—with whom the United States would fight side-by-side after September 11—to compromise with the Taliban.

But "compromise" with the Taliban meant surrender. With the Taliban shelling Kabul daily, assistant secretary of state Robin Rafael indicated to Ahmad Shah Masoud, second in command and military chief to President Rabbani, that the government should find some way to "work together" with the group trying to capture the capital.[10]

The longtime instability of Afghanistan made the Taliban attractive to State. After multiple coup d'états in the 1970s and war with the Soviets throughout the 1980s, Afghanistan came under the control of the *mujihideen* who had so fiercely battled the Soviets. But even with the ascension of Rabbani in 1992, the situation in Afghanistan remained in flux. State's preference for the stability offered by the Taliban led a *Washington Post* reporter to write: "[A] Taliban-dominated government represents a preferable alternative in some ways to the faction-ridden coalition headed by President Burhanuddin Rabbani, which was unable to impose its authority on the entire country."[11] To the extent that was true, the instability was largely fomented by the series of different militia groups backed by Pakistan, ostensibly an American ally. But while Pakistan was always careful to outwardly position itself as such, the Taliban did not. And with the Taliban's thuggish tactics garnering international attention, State was forced to make excuses in the press. In a *Washington Post* story that quoted "American analysts"—most likely State officials—the potential threat posed by the new rulers in Kabul was downplayed: "American analysts describe the Taliban as 'anti-modern' rather than 'anti-Western,' and note that it seems bent on restoring a traditional society in Afghanistan, rather than exporting an Islamic revolution."[12]

EXPANSIONIST FIREBRANDS

Rafael, still enamored of the Taliban, gave this judgment of the new Afghan rulers to the *Economist*: "[T]he Taliban do not seek to 'export Islam,' just to 'liberate Afghanistan.'"[13] But the same *Economist* article also discussed clear indications that, in fact, the Taliban was looking to "export Islam." It featured the following assessment from an unnamed journalist who had traveled extensively throughout Afghanistan: "They're expansionist. They often talk of their desire to spread their beliefs to Pakistan, Central Asia, the Middle East." In a *Newsweek* article that was published roughly two weeks after the Taliban captured Kabul, a "firebrand" mullah there was quoted spelling out the following grand vision: "We will take Kazakhstan, then Uzbekistan and then, we will take Moscow!"[14]

BLIND EYE

In a *New York Times* story almost two weeks after the fall of Kabul, State spokesman Nicholas Burns said of the Taliban: "We will have to judge them by their actions."[15] But there was already plenty of action to judge very early in the Taliban's reign. In fighting to take the capital city, the Taliban shelled innocents and starved civilians as part of its military strategy.[16] The former Communist dictator of Afghanistan who had preceded President Rabbani and several of his aides were killed, mutilated, and hung in effigy at a busy public intersection.[17] State press flack Glyn Davies, when pressed, would only describe this act of alarming violence as "regrettable."[18] The *Economist*, meanwhile, found that "hands and feet are chopped off for fairly minor offences." Yet State was willfully turning a blind eye to the increasingly gruesome actions of the Taliban and its one-eyed mullah, Mohammed Omar.

In an attempt to cloud the issue, State spokesman Nicholas Burns told reporters at a daily press briefing in October 1996 that what was going on in Afghanistan was "a very complex, complicated situation."[19] It was by no means simple, but the outlines of the conflict were pretty easy to grasp: the ousted Rabbani government represented a more moderate Islamic regime, Pakistan had been causing most of the "unrest" against Rabbani by funding a number of anti-Rabbani forces over the years, the Taliban swept into power in breathtaking fashion employing sometimes brutal tactics, and almost all the countries in the region—save for Pakistan, Saudi Arabia, and the United Arab Emirates (UAE)—were quite fearful about the implications of a Taliban-controlled Afghanistan.

It wasn't as if State was taking its cues from the world community or international organizations such as the United Nations. Indeed, for years after the Taliban's capture of Kabul, most nations continued to recognize the Rabbani government; the Afghanistan seat at the United Nations was filled by a representative of the leader toppled by the Taliban. By the time State forced the Afghan embassy in the United States to shut down in summer 1997, only four nations did not recognize the Rabbani government. Three countries recognized the Taliban: Pakistan, Saudi Arabia, and the UAE. One nation officially recognized neither the Rabbani government nor the Taliban: the United States.

OPIUM, UNINTERRUPTED

Perhaps the most often-repeated reason for State's early support of the Taliban was the pledge its leaders made to curtail, or even eliminate, opium production. But a United Nations study found that opium production increased more than 25 percent in Taliban-controlled areas in the year after the group had taken power.[20] This finding was confirmed by a U.S. Drug Enforcement Agency official who told the *Omaha World-Herald* in 1997, "This [explosion in production] was and is sanctioned by the Taliban, and it accounts for nearly half" of the world's supply of opium, which is the raw material for heroin.[21]

It wasn't until 2000 that the Taliban came to the conclusion that harvesting opium poppies was contrary to Islam—at a time when world prices were quite low, and the reigning mullahs happened to have a two-year stockpile of refined heroin.[22] But the Taliban did not completely ban all things related to opium and heroin. Cultivation was outlawed, but distribution and refinement (the process of converting opium to heroin) were *not*. Not surprisingly, world heroin prices spiked after the Taliban banned opium cultivation—meaning the Taliban profited handsomely. State, however, cheered the move without any apparent cynicism. The *New York Times* headline about the ban on cultivation tells the story of how State viewed the Taliban's change in policy: "Taliban's Ban on Poppy a Success, U.S. Aides Say."[23] The same article also says that because of the Taliban's "dramatic" shift, State was granting $43 million in aid to Afghan farmers.[24]

It was folly at best for State to take the Taliban at its word, given that the group had already lied on a major issue: the handling of opium production. Despite a pledge to eliminate the cultivation and distribution of opium, the levels of opium and refined heroin on the world market surged *after* the Taliban came to power. The *Washington Times* knew this.[25] The *Economist* knew this. Even the United Nations knew this. If journalists and international bureaucrats had figured out that the Taliban was profiting from the drug trade, how could State not have?

PIPELINE DREAMS

The primary reason—at least according to a gaggle of cynics after September 11—that State was so friendly to the Taliban was the potential for a massive oil and gas pipeline. There is a tremendous amount of oil and natural gas sitting in the three former Soviet republics of Turkmenistan, Uzbekistan, and Kazakhstan—but it has little value unless it can be transported to viable markets. That's where Afghanistan comes in. The plan was to have a pipeline run through Afghanistan and then through Pakistan in order to reach other markets, like India.

With Afghanistan finally coming under the control of what seemed to be a "stable" regime, energy conglomerate Unocal saw its best opportunity to build a $1.5 billion pipeline through Afghanistan to transport what some estimates pegged as up to $4 trillion worth of natural resources sitting in Central Asia.[26] State was clearly determined to help Unocal achieve its goal, but State's motivations for its posture toward the Taliban were really about more than just the oil and gas.

FAVORING ISLAMISTS

Starting in the early- to mid-1990s, State had staked out a position favoring "non-violent" fundamentalist Islamists, and consequently saw no harm in radical Islamists like the Taliban. Notice the comment to the *Washington Post* that the Taliban were simply "anti-modern," not "anti-Western." State's embrace of Islamism as an acceptable political movement can be traced back to a speech given by then–assistant secretary of state for Near Eastern Affairs Edward P. Djerejian at the partly Saudi-financed Meridian International Center in June 1992. In the address, he stressed, "If there is one thought I can leave you with tonight, it is this: the U.S. government does not view Islam as the next 'ism' confronting the West or threatening world peace. That is an overly simplistic response to a complex reality."

In 1994, when Algeria was facing the prospect of one-man, one-vote, one-time, with Islamists poised to win a national election, State "pressured the sitting government to give in to the Islamists," notes former State official Richard Schifter.[27] To be sure, the faction competing with the Islamists did not embody Western-style democratic values. But if the examples of South Korea, Taiwan, and Chile show anything, it is that countries ruled by non-ideological strongmen are more likely to give way to free societies than are those headed by ideological dictators, such as Communists—or Islamists. Yet according to Schifter, the attitude at Foggy Bottom from 1992 on was "Islamists are the wave of the future, so why fight it?"[28]

This tolerance bordering on fondness for Islamism explains why, even after the prospects for the oil pipeline all but disappeared in 1998, State kept in close contact with the Taliban—not quite supporting the regime, but not actively opposing it, either.

UNOCAL FACTOR

In 1996, Unocal bet the Taliban would allow it to build a pipeline through Afghanistan. So Unocal went on a spending spree. Unocal lobbyists hit every hot spot in Washington: Congress, the White House, and of course, the State Department. Unocal shelled out $1.7 million in 1996 for lobbying, which continued in full swing throughout 1997, amounting to some $2 million in total lobbying expenditures paid out by the oil conglomerate, according to semi-annual disclosure forms.

Two "consultants"—not technically considered lobbyists—employed by Unocal were Foggy Bottom veterans: Zalmay Khalilzad and Robert Oakley. Khalilzad spent four years working at State in the late 1980s, advising on both the Iran-Iraq and the Soviet-Afghanistan wars.[29] Oakley is the former head of counterterrorism at State with a blemished ethical history. In 1992–1993, Oakley became an agent for Middle East Airlines with the goal of overturning the very regulations he helped draft—something not allowed under the law. Oakley received a wrist-slapping $5,000 fine—and was given permission to "consult" for another company on an international matter under State's purview.

Whereas Oakley played a less visible public role for Unocal—running "diplomacy" efforts from an office in Islamabad, Pakistan[30]—Khalilzad was publicly enthusiastic about his support for the Taliban and the pipeline. On October 7, 1996—when the war clouds over Kabul had barely cleared—Khalilzad wrote a *Washington Post* op-ed piece called "Afghanistan: Time to Reengage," in which he argued that the Taliban leaders were not such bad guys.[31] "The Taliban does not practice the anti-U.S. style of fundamentalism," he wrote, adding that it merely "upholds a mix of traditional Pashtun values and an orthodox interpretation of Islam." He noted that Americans should not fear the Taliban, because Afghanistan's new rulers based themselves on the "Saudi model." At the end of the article, Khalilzad identifies himself only as "a senior strategist at Rand Corp., [who] served in the State and Defense departments in the Reagan and Bush administrations," neglecting to mention his Unocal ties. His "consulting" role might have been of interest to readers, particularly since he offered the following policy prescription: "We should use as a positive incentive the benefits that will accrue to Afghanistan from the construction of oil and gas pipelines across its territory."[32]

OLD COLLEGE TRY

For all the money Unocal lavished on lobbyists and "consultants," the best purchase the oil conglomerate made was a dean at the University of Nebraska at Omaha. But Dean Thomas Gouttierre did not come cheap. In summer 1997, Unocal signed a two-year, $1.8 million contract to help fund the university's Center for Afghanistan Studies program to provide education programs in Afghanistan. Of course, the money was part of Unocal's coordinated efforts to get the oil and gas pipeline built. Why Nebraska? Because the dean is an old friend of Unocal "consultant" Khalilzad[33]—and because Gouttierre missed his true calling as a politician.

The official role Gouttierre's center was to play was to build goodwill in Afghanistan by establishing educational programs in the war-torn nation.[34] Gouttierre, though, went above and beyond the task of setting up educational programs, becoming a stalwart defender of the Taliban regime. When the State Department was in the process of abandoning the Northern Alliance in favor of the Taliban, Gouttierre chimed in that he thought this was a great idea, noting that he supported "anything that can bring them [the warring sides] together."[35] The dean also said—one year after the Taliban took Kabul—that it was a grave misunderstanding to believe that "the Talibs are universally bad."[36]

Gouttierre fondly recalled his initial meeting with the Taliban in Khandahar. They were "surprised" when he spoke to them in their native Dari. He quickly won them over, he said. "They were charmed. By the time I left they were hugging me."[37]

Responding to widespread reports that had poured in during just the first year of Taliban rule, Gouttierre claimed, "The fact is, they are not out there oppressing people."[38] His justification? "We have had sightings of girls [in] schools in Taliban areas," he contended. Gouttierre went so far as to pretend that the Taliban and its supporters were really no different from Americans of the late 1800s and early 1900s who supported three-time Democratic presidential candidate William Jennings Bryan: "They are the same sort of people that spawned William Jennings Bryan. They're populists."[39]

Gouttierre explained to the press that the real reason he began the relationship with Unocal was for the same reason most politicians do almost anything: "the children." "Our emphasis is on children, to educate children," he noted. He may have professed a desire to "educate children," presumably including girls, but Gouttierre did not always feel that way—at least not when he was taking millions from State. In a 1989 briefing report to the U.S. Agency for International Development (USAID, an independent branch of State), Gouttierre argued against educating girls in Afghanistan, for fear of alienating fundamentalist clerics. He wrote, "This type of reform must be left to the Afghans to be solved at their own pace."[40] That report was one of many submitted to USAID as part of a $60 million grant the agency gave to the university between 1986 and 1994.[41] According to the *Chicago Tribune*, "The money was for the university to establish educational programs demonstrating the strengths of a democratic society, but that goal never was realized."

Although the multimillion dollar grant expired in 1994, Gouttierre seemed to be of the same mind as decision-makers at State, as
many of his comments were echoed by top Foggy Bottom officials.
Just as Gouttierre believed in Unocal building the pipeline, so did
Foggy Bottom. In October 1997, an anonymous State Department
official told a reporter, "By Unocal prevailing, our [American] influence will be solidified, the Russians will be weakened, and we can
keep Iran from benefiting."[42]

After the Taliban's reputation became increasingly notorious, praise
and warm words would no longer pass muster. As a result, both Gouttierre and State defended Osama bin Laden's protectors by equating
morally the current and former Afghan leaders. "There are good guys
in both camps and bad guys in both camps," Gouttierre noted to a
reporter in late 1997.[43] About a year later, Robin Rafael (by then the
former head of the South Asia bureau) used a similar tactic, although
she actually disparaged all the parties in the nation—apparently no
longer believing that the Taliban had "wonderful senses of humor." At
a large social function, Rafael had a conversation with John Jennings,
a former Associated Press and *Economist* reporter who did public relations work for the Rabbani forces, during which she remarked,
"They're all bastards. All of them."[44]

PIPELINE PLANS SCRAPPED

In the end, the pipeline across Afghanistan did not come to fruition.
Perhaps the biggest hurdle that Unocal and State could not clear was
mounting feminist objections to the Taliban's horrific treatment of
women. This new feminist push was particularly embarrassing for
Unocal "consultant" Khalilzad, whose wife, Cheryl Bernard, is a
well-known champion of women's rights.[45]

Organizing a campaign assailing "gender apartheid" in Afghanistan, feminist organizations attracted high-profile support from
comedian Jay Leno's wife, Mavis, and most important, First Lady

Hillary Clinton. When Hillary backed the feminist campaign in early 1998—it would have been political suicide if she had not—the writing was on the wall. By late 1998, Unocal abandoned its efforts. It cancelled the second year of the $1.8 million contract with the University of Nebraska at Omaha, leaving Gouttierre's center with a mere $900,000 for all his pro-Taliban shilling.[46]

STILL COZY

Even after plans for a pipeline had been completely abandoned, State continued to meet with the Taliban—up until two months before September 11. Indeed, even after the UN belatedly imposed sanctions on the Taliban in December 2000, Foggy Bottom officials had at least two meetings with Taliban representatives in Germany in March and July 2001.[47] But by this point, even former Unocal "consultant" Khalilzad had changed his tune, condemning the regime in 2000 and recommending that the U.S. pressure Pakistan to stop its support of the Taliban.[48] But State did not share Khalilzad's change of heart.

At a May 2001 conference in Washington, D.C., organized by State, a panel of four speakers had either outright or cautious praise for the Taliban, according to several attendees.[49] The sole State official was actually the least pro-Taliban of the four, but he was quick to point out the "complexity" of the whole situation. He offered some praise for the Taliban's decision to outlaw cultivation of opium, but was generally guarded in his comments.

This was not a new tack for State. From the beginning of the Taliban's reign in Kabul, State had attempted to make things appear far more complicated than they actually were. Witness a comment from an anonymous State official to the *Baltimore Sun* in July 1997: "It's essentially a fuzzy situation, but sometimes that's our way of dealing with things."[50] Fuzziness allowed State to justify backing the

Taliban—whatever its outrages—in the hope that it would support the oil pipeline, or at least ensure "stability" in Afghanistan.

Throughout this time, the Voice of America (VOA) in Afghanistan continued its decidedly pro-Taliban tilt.[51] In the immediate aftermath of the September 11 attacks—while the Twin Towers and the Pentagon were still burning—VOA aired a twelve-minute interview with Taliban leader Mohammed Omar, who told VOA listeners, "America has created the evil that is attacking it."[52] The official line at first was that State disapproved of this broadcast, but barely nine months later, Foggy Bottom officials gave an award to the man responsible for airing the mullah's propaganda. In a lavish June 2002 reception held on the eighth floor of the State Department's main office in Washington, D.C., VOA news director Andre de Nesnera was given an award for "constructive dissent"[53]—State's way of apologizing for having to issue obligatory criticisms back when Americans were actually paying attention.

NO AXIS, NO EVIL

The day after President George W. Bush first uttered the most famous phrase of his public life, "the axis of evil," U.S. embassy staffers in London fanned out across the city with a message: "The president didn't mean 'axis,' and he didn't mean 'evil,'"[54] according to an administration official.

To the foreign policy elites at the State Department, the idea of a "simplistic" categorization of "evil" was not worthy of the highly evolved and "nuanced" view of the world they had achieved—just as they had refused to see Islamism or the Taliban as necessarily "bad." They were embarrassed that the man who was their ultimate boss had, in their minds, an almost child-like view of "reality." It's not that they thought Iran, Iraq, and North Korea were misunderstood or somehow wonderful countries. But they thought the president was doing irreparable harm by vilifying the leaders of three increasingly powerful nations—leaders with whom State officials believed they would need to negotiate before long. A diplomat's job, after all, is to reach agreements, always to "further" the relationship—or at least that's the Foggy Bottom mindset.

No good, in State's view, can come from isolating a nation; "talking" and signing agreements are the solutions to almost any problem. But in order to "talk" to some of the world's most unsavory figures—Gadhafi, the Iranian mullahs, and so on—a diplomat cannot allow himself to think that the person sitting across the table is "evil." That would be too "simplistic." But it is one thing to hold this worldview; it is quite another to adhere to it over the very clear directions provided by the president.

About a month after the president's "axis of evil" speech, director of Policy Planning Richard Haass—who, as head of State's policy shop, is responsible for converting the president's vision and grand design into concrete policy—delivered some shocking news to the Israeli government. Haass told the Israelis that they needed to "engage" Iran, even though the nation had—just a month earlier—been named a member of the "axis of evil."[55] Such apparent insubordination is not unusual, because State's career diplomats often take enormous liberties, and take advantage of a president like George W. Bush, who follows the "delegation" school of management.

Foggy Bottom's culture is so powerful that most employees there eventually adopt the worldview in which "stability" is paramount and agreements become ends in and of themselves—and in which ruthless thugs and terrorists are merely thought of as negotiating partners. This moral relativism is allowed to persist because these diplomats—who, it must be stressed, are not stupid or evil or treasonous—live in a sort of bubble. When they are "talking" with countries like Saudi Arabia, Syria, or even Belgium or France, they mingle not with "the people," but with the rulers or leaders safely ensconced in their palatial estates with ornate chandeliers and marble floors.

During his 1996–1998 stint in Lebanon, for example, former ambassador to Lebanon Richard Jones met with Elie Hobeiqa. Hobeiqa was widely believed to have been responsible for a massacre that claimed the lives of hundreds of Palestinians at the Sabra and Shatila refugee camps in Beirut in 1982.[56] A former bodyguard of his had also accused Hobeiqa of ordering assassinations in the 1980s.[57] Jones was under no illusions about the atrocities Hobeiqa had allegedly committed. He told his professional colleagues in the United States he was under an obligation to meet with the accused war criminal, because Hobeiqa was a minister in the Lebanese government. "Yes," one of those he told remarked, "but you didn't have to go sailing on his yacht."[58]

The self-defined job description of a State Department diplomat almost never includes promoting fundamental change or reform in thoroughly corrupt and abusive regimes, but to secure continually "smooth" relations with foreign governments. Notes the American Enterprise Institute's Danielle Pletka, "As Jesse Helms used to say, 'The State Department is about making the world safe for cocktail parties.'"[59] In a world dominated by high-level contacts and meetings and "talks" with powerful leaders, it is easy to see how elitism can become an occupational hazard. And in this alternate universe, one's sense of reality—not to mention one's moral compass—can become skewed.

SILENT VOICE

On October 19, 1984, a Catholic priest named Jerzy Popieluszko was kidnapped in Warsaw, Poland, and viciously murdered shortly thereafter. He was killed by a mercenary group known as the "Zomo," which was organized by the Communist government's Ministry of Internal Affairs. The Soviet bloc nation was having an increasingly tough time combating the burgeoning Solidarity movement, so it used the exceptionally violent Zomo to impose order. In order to fill the ranks of the Zomo, "the government was literally opening the prisons to get enough criminals to crack innocent people's heads open," notes someone familiar with the situation in Poland at the time.[60] When Popieluszko was murdered, a Voice of America (VOA) writer changed the story to identify the Zomo as "thugs."

After the VOA radio broadcast aired the story identifying the Zomo as "thugs," the embassy in Warsaw cabled Washington. The embassy did not allege a single factual error or misstatement, but it complained that the broadcast was "not helpful."[61] Luckily for VOA at the time, State's political leader in Washington, Secretary George Shultz, was not going to accede to requests to tone down rhetoric against a Soviet puppet regime. But VOA is not always tough on tyrants.

The Voice of America has, at times, become the voice of the despots in a particular region. That's what happened with the Taliban. At other times, the broadcasts are censored so as not to offend the host nation. There was a time when VOA excised all references to Hitler in any broadcast heard in Germany for fear of offending Germans—in the early 1990s.[62] This from the broadcasting entity that is supposed to bring messages of freedom and liberty. Sometimes the hesitance to offend crosses over into State taking orders from repugnant regimes, such as Saddam Hussein's Iraq.

Back in 1990, a Voice of America commentary proclaimed,

> Lasting change can come to the Soviet Union when citizens no longer need to fear massive surveillance—and worse— from the K.G.B. Secret police are also entrenched in other countries, such as China, North Korea, Iran, Iraq, Syria, Libya, Cuba, and Albania. The rulers of these countries hold power by force and fear, not by the consent of the governed. But as East Europeans demonstrated so dramatically in 1989, the tide of history is against such rulers. The 1990s should belong not to the dictators and secret police, but to the people.[63]

This ringing endorsement of freedom was undoubtedly welcomed by oppressed peoples throughout the world—but it was no laughing matter to Iraqi despot Saddam Hussein. Saddam communicated his dissatisfaction with the broadcast—he labeled it a "call to revolution"—and U.S. ambassador to Iraq April Glaspie obligingly sent four cables to NEA bureau chief John Kelly to make sure he understood that Saddam was not happy. Kelly wasted no time. Agreeing with Glaspie—and coincidentally, Saudi Arabia's King Fahd—Kelly told Secretary of State James Baker at a morning meeting that such truthful messages should be stopped. Baker agreed. Policy was changed so that all VOA commentaries had to be cleared *in writing* by State before being aired. All this happened in the span of two days—from the broadcast on February 15, 1990, to the morning meeting on February 17.[64] Less than six months later, Saddam invaded Kuwait.

SYRIA SKATES

In April 2002, a bipartisan group of senators—including avowed liberal senator Barbara Boxer of California and staunch conservative senator Rick Santorum of Pennsylvania—introduced the Syria Accountability Act. On paper, it seemed a sure bet for passage: a total of forty-five of one hundred senators were co-sponsors (far more than the normal handful that co-sponsor bills that *pass*), it would have imposed only mild sanctions against a regime that is officially designated a state sponsor of terrorism, and public sentiment in the aftermath of September 11 appeared to make targeting terrorist-sponsoring states easier than ever. But none of this deterred State from opposing it. Foggy Bottom officials worked their relationships with members and staffers on Capitol Hill to kill a bill that State viewed as "dangerous."[65]

Out of the seven official state sponsors of terrorism, Syria has perhaps done the most to earn its spot on the notorious list. While Iran may be the most active financial backer of terrorism—Saudi Arabia can't technically compete for that title, because it is not one of the official seven state sponsors of terrorism—Syria does the most to support terror by protecting and harboring known terrorists and terrorist organizations within areas it controls. Operating openly within Syria are such terrorist organizations as the Popular Front for the Liberation of Palestine (PFLP), the Popular Front for the Liberation of Palestine-General Command (PFLP-GC), the Palestine Islamic Jihad (PIJ), and the Islamic Resistance Movement (HAMAS).[66] In all, seven terrorist groups have headquarters or offices in the Syrian capital of Damascus, complete with published addresses.[67] The deadliest terrorist group sheltered by Syria is Hezbollah, which until September 11, 2001, held the distinction of being responsible for the deaths of more American citizens than any other terrorist organization in the world.[68]

Syria doesn't simply play host to terrorist organizations; it works closely with them in guiding their actions, and advocates on their behalf to the rest of the world. According to State's annual "Patterns of Global Terrorism" report, Syria actively defends the activities of terrorist organizations. The 2003 edition notes that "at the UN Security Council and in other multilateral fora, Syria has taken a leading role in espousing the view that Palestinian and Lebanese terrorist groups fighting Israel are not terrorist."[69]

But Syria does not limit itself to providing logistical and political support for terrorist organizations. Syria is also a player in the proliferation business, with development of biological and chemical weapons and deployment of short- and medium-range ballistic missiles.[70] Not that any of this seems to matter to State.

Barely a month after the Syria Accountability Act had been introduced in the House and Senate (both versions were nearly identical), State sent to Capitol Hill a written statement opposing the legislation. The top reason cited? That it "appears one-sided to the majority of nations in the Middle East region."[71]

Rather than confront Syria, State believes that it can bring Syria around with "engagement." This was, in fact, the primary thrust of the written statement opposing the Syria Accountability Act. State's letter to Congress stated, "We believe that carefully calibrated engagement, combined with the current sanctions already in place, will be more effective to advance our goals."[72] But State has been "engaging" Syria for years—although not in a "carefully calibrated" manner—to little effect. During the Clinton administration alone, State arranged twenty-eight high-level meetings with the Syrian government.[73] And on the sanctions front, Syria continues to enjoy the least onerous set of sanctions of any of the seven state sponsors of terrorism.[74]

State went all-out to oppose a bill that, in reality, had very little "teeth" in it. Though the Syria Accountability Act accurately documents the particulars of Syria's sponsorship of terrorism and other related activities, it doesn't actually impose any new sanctions. Aside from reinforcing existing law (and to some extent closing loopholes), the bill, if enacted, would have required such "sanctions" as "reducing" diplomatic contact with Syria (whatever that means) and limiting the travel of Syrian diplomats in the United States to a twenty-five-mile radius of Washington, D.C., or the UN headquarters in New York City.[75] But the import of the bill was not the actions it would have triggered, but rather the statement that "engaging" a terror master should no longer be the foreign policy of the United States—which is precisely why State opposed it so aggressively.

One congressional aide recalls a conversation with a Foggy Bottom official in which the aide rattled off just a few of the deadly attacks carried out by Hezbollah, which is given safe haven by Syria in the southern areas of Lebanon it controls:[76] the bombing of the Marine barracks in Beirut in October 1983, which killed 242 Americans; the April 1984 bombing of a restaurant near a U.S. Air Force base in Torrejon,

Spain, that killed eighteen U.S. servicemen and injured eighty-three people; the kidnapping and murder of U.S. Marine Corps Lt. Col. William Higgins in February 1988; the kidnapping and murder of Israelis that continues to the present day. The official from State did not dispute any of the facts—he couldn't, because State's historian provided the reference material used by the aide.

By law, State must issue an annual report on the status of global terrorism. As an official state sponsor of terrorism, Syria is necessarily discussed. But even when State does a perfunctory job of listing some of the terrorist activities perpetrated by groups harbored by Syria, it typically downplays direct ties to Damascus. Incredibly, the 2002 report (released in April 2003) claims, "[T]he Syrian Government has not been implicated directly in an act of terrorism since 1986." Such a statement could only be considered true using semantic acrobatics to define the word "directly." Syria directly harbors and supports terrorists that continue to kill innocent civilians. The Syrian government is no less "directly" responsible for these acts than a husband who hires a hit man to kill his wife.

But State's appeasement does not end there. In order to soften the report's stance toward Syria further, Damascus is given credit on a series of fronts. The report notes: "The Syrian Government has repeatedly assured the United States that it will take every possible measure to protect U.S. citizens and facilities from terrorists in Syria." The "assurance" is taken at face value—though maybe it is genuine, considering that Syria has, since the 1990s, set its sights almost exclusively on terrorist acts aimed at killing Israeli citizens. (But several of the suicide bombing attacks, most notably the one at Hebrew University in Jerusalem, have claimed the lives of Americans.) State is so desperate to portray Damascus in a positive light that it applauds even trivial gestures. Syria is praised, for example, for having "discouraged any signs of public support for al Qaeda, including in the media and at mosques."

In the end, the Syria Accountability Act went nowhere. Certainly not for lack of support, though. According to multiple congressional sources, the bill had more than enough votes to pass—but congressmen and senators never had the chance. Because it was clear that the bill was never going to come to a vote in the Senate, the House didn't bother to vote on it. State's success in the Senate rested in the hands of perhaps the only three senators who opposed the bill: Democrat Joe Biden of Delaware and Republicans Richard Lugar of Indiana and Chuck Hagel of Nebraska. But they are not just any three senators; they are the top three members of the Senate Foreign Relations Committee, the committee with jurisdiction over the bill. And at State's behest, those three congressional enablers killed the Syria Accountability Act.

MORE FREE PASSES

"Iran remained the most active state sponsor of terrorism in 2002." So states Foggy Bottom's 2002 report on Patterns of Global Terrorism, as does the 2001 edition, as do most others in previous years. But when Congress tried to renew a law that would actually do something to combat Iran's (and Libya's) sponsorship of terrorism, State fought. Fiercely.

In summer 2001, the Iran-Libya Sanctions Act (ILSA) came up for a five-year renewal. As sanctions bills go, ILSA is relatively tough, in that it authorizes sanctions not just against the regimes in question, but also against countries and private entities (namely companies) that do business with them. As with almost all sanctions, the president is empowered under ILSA to waive sanctions for reasons of "national security"—if they are even imposed in the first place. All ILSA does is establish a "menu" of sanctions from which the president is supposed to choose. But for practical purposes, such questions of foreign policy are left to the respective experts, meaning the bureaucrats at Foggy Bottom.

Just as with the Syria Accountability Act, State loathed the idea of even voluntary sanctions—sanctions, after all, are "negative," and they interfere with a diplomat's desire to "engage" a foreign country. And even in the cases of Iran and Libya—both of whose governments are responsible for openly sponsoring and harboring terrorists who have murdered Americans—State believes the correct approach consists almost exclusively of "engagement." The mere principle of opening a dialogue with a rogue nation is not necessarily inimical to U.S. interests; compromising America's moral clarity without receiving anything in return, however, clearly is.

In most of the global terrorism reports from 1989–2002, Iran has been listed as the "most active," "most dangerous," or "premier" sponsor of terrorism. According to the 2001 edition of *Patterns of Global Terrorism*, "Iran's Islamic Revolutionary Guard Corps (IRGC) and Ministry of Intelligence and Security (MOIS) continued to be involved in the planning and support of terrorist acts and supported a variety of groups that use terrorism to pursue their goals." Furthermore, the report noted that in 2001, Iran "increase[d] its support for anti-Israeli terrorist groups" and "provided limited support to terrorist groups in the Gulf, Africa, Turkey, and Central Asia." In addition, practically every international observer (including State) agrees that Tehran has not wavered in its efforts to develop chemical, biological, and nuclear weapons. Yet, in spite of this, State remained convinced that the best approach was to reward Iran with "engagement." Even after September 11, this mindset did not change, as evidenced by State's Haass telling Israel to "engage" Iran barely a month after President Bush had designated Tehran a member of the axis of evil.

While State at least acknowledged the general outlines of Iran's support for terrorism in its annual reports, the activities of Moammar Gadhafi's Libya have been airbrushed. In the 2001 report, State claims, "Libya appears to have curtailed its support for international terrorism." If true, then State's opposition to ILSA might make some sense for the Libya half of the equation. But it is simply not true. Aside from maintaining an active program of developing assorted weapons of mass destruction, Libya has continued supporting terrorist organizations over the years, including al Qaeda. In the year prior to the ILSA legislative fight in summer 2001, Gadhafi had given two large payments to Abu Sayyef, an al Qaeda affiliate in the Philippines founded in the late 1980s by a brother-in-law of Osama bin Laden.[77]

Gadhafi funds Abu Sayyef by paying ransoms to release hostages captured by the group, payments that he describes as "humanitarian assistance."[78] The amount of "humanitarian assistance" is sizeable: Gadhafi paid a $20 million bounty in April 2000[79] and another $6 million that September.[80] But according to an administration official who has studied these transactions at length, "the money is given with the full intent of aiding Abu Sayyef's terrorist activities."[81] Before raking in millions in ransoms from the likes of Gadhafi, Abu Sayyef was a small group of some two hundred rebels.[82] Once flush with cash, however, its ranks swelled to over five thousand, and the group became far more violent.[83] Abu Sayyef killed seven people in 1993 by rolling grenades down the aisle of a Catholic church.[84] Two years later, it massacred fifty-three people in a shooting spree in a mostly Catholic village.[85] The al Qaeda affiliate continued making more and more money by kidnapping Westerners, killing some and releasing others.

With full knowledge of the activities funded by Gadhafi's "humanitarian assistance," Foggy Bottom's deputy press flack Philip Reeker said in 2000 that although America doesn't negotiate with or pay ransoms to terrorists such as Abu Sayyef, State would "welcome" mediation by Libya.[86]

Despite the bloody record assembled by Iran and Libya—some of which has been documented by State—Foggy Bottom pulled out all the stops to defeat the Iran-Libya Sanctions Act in summer 2001, making most of the same arguments it would recycle the following year in combating the Syria Accountability Act. Realizing that it would be harder to stop a reauthorization of an existing law from coming to a vote before the full Congress, State focused most of its energies on limiting the time frame of the renewal to a year or two (instead of the five years supported by the bill's sponsors).

According to a source involved in the legislative battle over ILSA, State was making headway in its efforts.[87] But then a powerful Jewish organization, the American-Israeli Political Affairs Committee (AIPAC), decided to make ILSA a top priority. If members voted against re-authorizing ILSA, then they would have received lower scores on AIPAC's annual legislative scorecards—something that can hurt a politician's chances of re-election. Consequently, the tide shifted—much to State's chagrin.

As with many battles in the Senate, if the vote is not going to be close, members switch sides. Thus many who opposed re-authorizing ILSA ended up voting in favor of the full, five-year re-authorization. But on the plus side for Foggy Bottom, the vote was not unanimous. In the more stately Senate, where State had its best chance to get a bill more to its liking, ninety-six senators voted for the full reauthorization of ILSA. Two senators, however, stuck with State: Republicans Richard Lugar and Chuck Hagel, two members of the three-man operation that would later bottle up the Syria Accountability Act.

EMBRACING GADHAFI

After 270 people were killed in the Pam Am Flight 103 bombing in December 1988—all 259 on board died, as did eleven on the ground in Lockerbie, Scotland—Libya's dictator Moamar Gadhafi, who was widely hailed to have sanctioned the attack, became an international pariah. In the following decade and a half, the tyrant of Tripoli continued his support for terrorists and his development of weapons of mass destruction (WMD). Yet according to an administration official, the current head of Near Eastern Affairs, William Burns, "has made it his mission to bring Gadhafi back onto the world stage."[88] Burns' strategy has been more or less to disregard the extensive evidence of Gadhafi's bad behavior and to focus instead on the despot's belated willingness to compensate the families of the Pam Am 103 victims.

After a decade during which almost nothing of substance happened on the Pam Am 103 front, Gadhafi agreed to hand over for trial Libyan intelligence agent Abdel Basset Ali al-Megrahi and Libyan Arab Airlines employee Al-Amin Khalifa Fhima, the two suspects in the bombing.[89] As part of a deal brokered in part by State, Libya was assured in a letter written by UN Secretary-General Kofi Annan that the investigation and trial "will not be used to undermine the Libyan regime."[90] In other words, the tyrant of Tripoli was promised that neither he nor other elements of his government would face any further consequences for participating in the murder of 270 innocents.

Once Gadhafi cooperated by turning over the two Pam Am 103 suspects, State determined that the best way to "engage" Libya was to work out a compensation deal with the families. In 2002–2003, there were at least three publicly announced meetings with Libyan officials—in addition to others that were held in secret—to negotiate both a compensation package and a game plan for bringing Gadhafi's regime back to normalcy. State was the chief architect of a deal to pay $2.7 billion to the families ($10 million each), only half of which was to be paid once the United Nations sanctions—suspended as of 1999—were officially ended.[91] The other $5 million per family was to be paid out if and only if the U.S. sanctions—the ones Libya cares most about—were also lifted. Thus, State had structured an agreement that would have made the families lobbyists to end U.S. sanctions.

Why do Burns and the rest of the NEA bureau want to relegit-imize Gadhafi? Presumably because of State's long-followed prac-tice of "engaging" ruthless regimes, and because Libya is home to billions of dollars worth of oil fields, few of which have been devel-oped since debilitating sanctions were imposed in the late 1980s. There's also the simple factor of bureaucratic convenience. Explains the American Enterprise Institute's Danielle Pletka, "It's not that Burns *likes* Gadhafi or *wants* to re-legitimize him. But having Gad-hafi in the situation he's in now is an annoyance for State, and it makes NEA's life more difficult. They want the annoyance to go away."[92]

As of May 2003, the official lifting of UN sanctions against Libya is considered a done deal. In a closed-door meeting in March 2003 with the victims' families, Burns said that UN action was immi-nent.[93] In the same meeting, Burns acknowledged to the families that Gadhafi possesses weapons of mass destruction, which he merely labeled a matter of "concern."[94] Although the issue did not come up in the meeting, Burns and other Foggy Bottom officials are fully aware that Gadhafi is also actively developing nuclear weapons. What is still something of a mystery, though, is why neither the con-tinued support for terrorism nor the possession and further expan-sion of weapons of mass destruction programs has deterred State from its desire to "engage" and relegitimize Gadhafi's regime.

The victims' families deserve compensation. Many of them understandably support State's efforts to negotiate a deal, even if some do not understand the full implications of the proposed agree-ment. But for State to trade compensation for a repeal of UN sanc-tions and a pledge to fight for the lifting of sanctions makes little sense. Rather than negotiating with an unrepentant and unreformed despot, State could have helped the families collect compensation from the $1.2 billion in blocked Libyan assets sitting inside the United States.

What makes the deal so unsavory, though, is not that it brings Gadhafi to diplomatic normalcy, but that it does so by making the victims' families responsible for redeeming the man ultimately responsible for the murder of their loved ones.

5

Understanding State — To the Extent It's Possible

★ *"YOU HAVE ONE MORE TEST TO PASS."*[1]

That's what then–secretary of state George Shultz would tell newly appointed diplomats after they had finished the obligatory grip-and-grin. The guest in his office would look puzzled, and Shultz would instruct him or her, "You have to go over to the globe on my desk and identify your country." Invariably, the statesman would point to New Zealand or Egypt or some other nation, to which Shultz would reply, "No, point to *your* country," reminding him where his true loyalties lie.

"Originally," Shultz says, "I thought of it as something fun." But when it took several years for someone actually to spin the globe around and point to the United States, the exercise became a potent—and telling—display of the underlying problem of the State Department. Foggy Bottom's inverted priorities—believing that the job of the diplomatic corps is to represent a foreign country's interests in America, not America's interests in the foreign country—can be seen in any number of examples, from easy visas to child abduction cases.

By its own admission, State lobbied against the rather mild Syria Accountability Act in part because Syria and its neighbors would not like the sanctions bill. The intent might not have been to represent Syria's interests—State's standard line is that sanctioning countries hurts "relations"—but the effect is that it did. Saudi Arabia was able to enjoy Visa Express even after September 11 because State believed that ending the program would harm "relations" with the House of Saud. And State does little to help left-behind American parents recover their children abducted to foreign lands because exerting real pressure—in the minds of State officials—would make it more difficult to get other "favors" from the foreign governments.

ENDURING CULTURE

The State Department as an institution has changed little since Shultz's tenure during the Reagan administration, and to the extent it has changed, things have gotten worse. It's the culture. Like any corporation, State has a unique culture to which employees are expected to conform. But it is a culture that most objective observers would view with a combination of bewilderment and disgust.

State cannot be understood in a partisan context. It is neither Republican nor Democrat, and it operates with surprisingly little regard for the sitting president. That's not to say that different presidents and secretaries of state have not had an impact on Foggy Bottom—some have—but fluctuations aside, State operates today as it almost always has. It is the fourth branch of government, in part because of its self-perpetuation, but also because it operates largely independently of the other branches.

To understand State—to the extent possible—one first has to understand what makes the organization tick. Foggy Bottom is driven by three fundamental impulses:

1) an obsession with "stability," even if the "stable" situation is one where terrorists roam free and innocent people are oppressed by ruthless regimes
2) the desire to be liked by foreign leaders, even despots and tyrants, for the purpose of maintaining "smooth relations"
3) the tendency to see agreements as ends in and of themselves

But in a world where evil exists all around us, keeping focus on these goals requires State to employ moral relativism, sometimes even moral equivalence. In other words, the moral relativism and equivalence are occupational hazards that allow State to do what it sees as its "job" with minimal discomfort.

If someone thinks of North Korean leader Kim Jong Il as the murderous thug that he is, it would be impossible to break bread and drink wine with him with a smile on your face—as former secretary of state Madeleine Albright did during a visit there in 1998. And if State hadn't reopened diplomacy with North Korea and made its dictator "happy," then no progress would have been made toward new agreements that would enhance the "stability" of the region. Never mind that North Korea was proliferating weapons and developing nukes the entire time in complete violation of the 1994 accord.[2]

It's not that the State Department is evil or has malicious intent; on some level, State's diplomats think that the U.S. benefits by Foggy Bottom maintaining "stability" and "smooth relations," which is what America "needs" in the long run. But in fact, America's security has been severely undermined by State's misdeeds over the last several decades.

"CRIPPLED INSTITUTION"

In spring 2001, the bipartisan Hart-Rudman commission blasted the State Department as a "crippled institution" in its report on the overall state of national security. Citing mostly structural flaws—as opposed to cultural ones—the commission recommended fixing the "dysfunctional" agency with a series of organizational reforms, such as "revamping" the entrance exams, changing the structure of bureaus, and beefing up ongoing professional education programs for members of the Foreign Service.

Although the report noted that State "suffers in particular from an ineffective organizational structure in which . . . sound management, accountability, and leadership are lacking,"[3] the strongest proposed changes were streamlining bureaucratic processes and increasing the staff of the Foreign Service by ten to fifteen percent in order to allow for more comprehensive initial and ongoing training of officers. Former speaker of the house Newt Gingrich, who served on the commission, based many of his proposed reforms in his much-publicized April 2003 speech and subsequent July 2003 *Foreign Policy* magazine article on the commission report. Just like the commission, though, Gingrich offered stinging criticisms, but paired them with rather modest proposals.

The Hart-Rudman report touched on State's cultural woes only indirectly, but interestingly: "We recommend changing the Foreign Service's name to the U.S. Diplomatic Service. This rhetorical change will serve as a needed reminder that this group of people does not serve the interest of foreign states, but is a pillar of U.S. national security."[4]

BIG DYSFUNCTIONAL FAMILY

In 1967, dismayed by what he saw as an unwieldy bureaucracy, then–secretary of state Dean Rusk commissioned a management consulting study from Yale professor Chris Argyris to determine what was wrong with the Foreign Service, and how those problems could be solved.[5] Though he stopped just short of calling it a "crippled institution," Argyris essentially said that the Foreign Service was so broken, it couldn't be fixed.

The Yale professor's most interesting findings involved his analysis of the nature and dynamics of interpersonal relationships among those in the Foreign Service. What he found was that the social "norms" were cold, clinical detachment and a disdain for anyone who does not conform. Those who are "emotional" or "aggressive," the report concluded, were punished and ostracized. Based on conversations I have had with dozens of current and former State officials, nothing much has changed in thirty-six years.

Argryris' overall portrait is one that resembles what many jaded movies have depicted as the quintessentially repressed 1950s nuclear family, where emotion is hidden from view and communication is limited to phony niceties. The Foreign Service vocabulary is littered with dull-edged words designed to cause minimal turmoil and not upset "relations." It is a reflection of the Foreign Service's self-perceived high-mindedness that it is able to eschew emotion and moral judgment. In a section explaining this mindset, "To be rational is to be effective; to be emotional is to be ineffective,"[6] Argyris quotes a Foreign Service officer (FSO) who states, "Mature people are people who can control their feelings and not let them get in the way of rational discussion."[7] Typical members come across in the report—though the study did not use these words—as both arrogant and elitist. For example, one of the FSOs, in discussing conversations with coworkers, said that he "would much rather use a more civilized form of communication, that is, write it down."[8]

The Yale professor's study did not call for a Foreign Service filled with cowboys constantly picking fights with foreign governments, but seemed to suggest that inability or unwillingness to accept, let alone promote, change hobbled American foreign policy. The cultural sterility and aversion to emotion described by Argyris might help explain the tendency of the Foreign Service to prefer viewing results based on procedure, rather than substance.

Confrontation—the ultimate destabilizing force—elicited contempt and scorn from members of the dominant culture. Argyris wrote, "The appropriate reaction to aggressive fighting or openly competitive behavior was to distrust it and to withdraw from active confrontation," and even if such behavior were "openly pardoned," it would be "covertly condemn[ed]" at the same time.[9] In fact, if someone were the opposite—meaning nice—then that was mistrusted, too. "After all," Argyris noted, "if their own politeness was a facade, then maybe this was true of the others."[10] The golden rule was for no one to upset anyone else, either through confrontational or polite behavior. Typical members were so averse to upsetting other people that they believed that "[a] loyal member should not openly hurt others even in the interests of the organization."[11] This interpersonal dynamic is often played out on a global scale, with State Department officials fearful of offending any nation, whether a free society like Britain or a tyranny like Libya.

The Foreign Service's culture, the report found, continues its vicious cycle because of the people it attracts and then promotes, the people it "converts," and the nonconformists it punishes. The people most likely to apply to the Foreign Service are those who already fit the personality profile of existing members. "Individuals tend to choose consciously (and unconsciously) those professions and those systems whose norms are congruent with their values," meaning that "the values [such as disdain for emotion] were held by the Foreign Service officer long before he entered the Foreign Service."[12] Once there, these like-minded individuals excel within the system because members of the Foreign Service "look for, seek out, reward and encourage Foreign Service personnel who do not violate the norms," which has helped it turn into "its own inbred club."[13]

The "inbred" culture is so powerful, in fact, that even those who don't hold the worldview of a typical FSO coming in stand a high probability of "converting" in due time. The study explains, "The members come to feel entrapped and controlled by the system," which eventually trains them to "write careful and innocuous memos, round the sharp corners off the telegrams . . . [and] fear taking responsibility."[14] People who don't play along and actually try to change policies and practices are typically seen by most of the Foreign Service as "unpredictable" and "somewhat unstable," and eventually are labeled "deviants."[15] Even today, these "deviants" are marginalized, or worse, in order to prevent them from pursuing policies that might upset foreign governments, and thus upset "stability" and harm "smooth relations."

Self-preservation is inherent to the culture, the report found, at least in the sense that members of the Foreign Service will defend their brethren at almost any cost. When faced with the department versus the outside world, the study found that FSOs rallied around the bureaucracy—much like members of a dysfunctional family who relentlessly hound each other but nonetheless forcefully fight any outsider who might attempt to do the same. "Each member of a department focuses more on protecting his department than on making effective decisions."[16]

REFORM IS POSSIBLE, IF FLEETING

It is nearly impossible to fire State Department employees, though some were discharged after felony convictions[17] and State managed to clean house (somewhat) in summer 2002. After a month of intense negative press coverage relating to its handling of Visa Express in Saudi Arabia, Congress was on the verge of stripping the visa authority from State and handing it over to the Department of Homeland Security. Not only would such a move have resulted in a tremendous loss of political power—the ability to determine who does and does not enter the United States—but it would also have meant the loss of an annual $800 million cash cow.[18] Secretary of State Colin Powell went to the mat to save the prized visa power—and to keep the congressional wolves at bay, he offered up four of the top five officials at Consular Affairs (CA), the bureau that oversees consulates, embassies, and visa issuance. Officially, all four "retired"—though State's deputy press secretary Phil Reeker said the head of CA, Mary Ryan, was "asked to retire"[19]—but, notes one senior State Department official, "they gave them up as sacrifices to show Congress things are going to change."[20]

But real reform was snuffed out before it could even begin because State chose as Mary Ryan's successor a woman who is her protégé and clone, Maura Harty. Like Ryan, who headed CA for nine years, Harty is a career diplomat who had spent almost her entire professional career in the Foreign Service. State promoted her as an "agent of change." If only. In previous positions where she could have been an "agent of change," Harty clearly was not. She had two stints heading up the Office of Children's Issues (OCI), the division within CA responsible for recovering American children abducted to foreign lands, and in both tours, she failed miserably. She managed to recover just one percent of kidnapped kids,[21] a record that Foggy Bottom officials actually spun as successful when she was nominated for the CA position. Not surprisingly, very little has changed at CA since Harty's arrival.

INVERTED PRIORITIES

In early 2003, Harty, then the assistant secretary of state for Consular Affairs, was about to accomplish what she thought the White House would love: a deal securing hundreds of billions of dollars in Social Security benefits to millions of new beneficiaries—illegal aliens from Mexico, to be exact. Comments Charles Hill, a former top State official and adviser to Secretary Shultz during the Reagan administration, "It isn't enough to say that these people are venal or stupid."[22] They are neither: they just put the interests of other countries first and assume that this improves "relations."

True to form, the proposed Social Security deal with Mexico was cloaked in red tape and bureaucratic language, making it seem harmless at first glance. It was called a "Totalization Agreement," which is an arrangement the U.S. has with twenty other nations (mostly in Europe) that allows people who split their careers between the U.S. and a foreign country to receive a single "totalized" benefit payment upon retirement. But the Mexico deal was going to be different. Much different. Harty had structured the deal so that illegal aliens from Mexico—unlike in any other deal—could receive Social Security benefits without first having to become a U.S. citizen or legal resident, as the law presently requires. Given the millions of illegal aliens from Mexico who work in the United States, various experts pegged the total cost of the accord at up to $345 billion—or more—over the next two decades.[23] (Congressional outrage has temporarily shelved the deal.)

PERVERSE INCENTIVES

People like Harty rise through State's ranks because they fulfill the priorities of State's institutional culture, which can reward even those who have to be fired because of outside political pressure. The former deputy assistant secretary of Consular Affairs, Georgia Rogers—one of the four top CA executives sacrificed by Colin Powell over the Visa Express scandal—was named by Harty to represent CA on the Iraq Task Force at the start of the war in March 2003. Rogers collected a salary—while still raking in a healthy retirement income from the federal government—for a total annualized sum of more than $200,000.[24]

State's culture is so far removed from reality that it actually gave large cash bonuses to top officials responsible for the lax visa policies that paved the way for the death of three thousand Americans. As noted in an official State Department document, each of the four CA top executives eligible to receive an annual bonus (excepting Georgia Rogers, because she was not a member of the Foreign Service) was awarded $10,000 to $15,000 for "outstanding performance during the period April 16, 2001, through April 15, 2002"—a period that included September 11, and a time frame during which at least five of the terrorists were given visas that should have been denied under the law.[25] If the law had simply been followed, in fact, at least fifteen of the nineteen September 11 terrorists never would have been in the country on September 11. But the people responsible for the policies that created those gaping loopholes in our border security were given bonuses for "outstanding performance."

INBRED INTRANSIGENCE

With State's self-perpetuating culture and its perverse incentives, the most important thing a president could do to reform Foggy Bottom is to shake up the leadership by taking full use of his power to appoint people from the outside to high-ranking positions. While the overwhelming majority of slots at Foggy Bottom must be filled by careerists—either members of the Foreign Service or career civil servants—the president has the ability to fill positions in the top five levels (secretary of state, deputy secretary, undersecretary, assistant secretary, and deputy assistant secretary) as well as some of their support staff. This amounts to a maximum of several hundred people, not counting the ambassadors (who are a mixture of roughly two-thirds career diplomats from the Foreign Service and one-third political appointments), out of an entire department that has some 47,000 employees.[26] (It is important to note that most Foreign Service members hold substantive positions, while most career civil servants hold administrative ones.)

To get a visual sense of this, think of a pyramid. There's one secretary, one deputy secretary, six undersecretaries, thirty-three assistant secretaries (each of whom runs a bureau), and well over one hundred deputy assistant secretaries (roughly three or four under each assistant secretary). And underneath that, you have 47,000 other people, 30,000 of whom are Foreign Service nationals (FSNs) who work in the consulates and embassies.

Even with the placement of the maximum number of true political appointments—meaning people who have not made careers of working at State—changing course at Foggy Bottom would still be a challenge of Herculean proportions. Secretary of State Colin Powell makes a good case study. When appointed, he committed a fatal mistake in deciding that his top priority would be to promote and enhance the role of careerists at State. While Powell may have won the hearts of the Foreign Service, he did not win their minds. The men and women of the Foreign Service do not like—actually, they despise—President Bush. Bush's "jingoism" and thick moralism—that whole "axis of evil" thing showed he lacks the Foreign Service's keen ability for "nuance"—have made him an anathema to the diplomatic corps.

With such open hostility in the ranks, the only way to impose some semblance of order is with determined and skillful political leadership, something that just does not exist in the Powell State Department. Both Powell and the deputy assistant secretary, Richard Armitage, have bought entirely into the Foreign Service culture, and roughly forty percent of the undersecretaries and assistant secretaries are products of Foggy Bottom. But even that understates the problem, because a large number of the "outside" appointments come from the foreign policy establishment inside the Beltway, which was largely created by ex-State Department types and actively promotes the Foggy Bottom worldview. Of course there are many dedicated and even some truly outstanding members of the Foreign Service—some of whom are serving in top roles in the Bush administration—but Foreign Service members filling these slots generally spells trouble.

At the level that really matters—deputy assistant secretaries dominate specific issues and policy fights—the vast majority in the Powell State Department are career members of the Foreign Service. The Powell State Department sadly isn't that much different from its predecessors.

DESK OFFICERS RUN THE SHOW

Even a State Department with the maximum number—and highest caliber—of political appointees would find it tough to actually control the place. Regardless of the leadership at the top, the real power rests many levels down in the hands of the desk officers.

Roughly speaking, there is one desk officer for every country (more important ones can have two or more, and less important ones can be lumped together and assigned to a single desk officer) and anywhere from five to ten desk officers are assigned to each office director. Each desk officer is considered *the* specialist in Washington on his or her country and also serves as the communication go-between—resulting in an enormous amount of power in the hands of a typically low-level FSO. Enhancing that leverage is the fact that all cables and memos that relate to a specific country in any way must be cleared by that country's desk officer before getting official approval.[27] And since all communication from the embassy must go through the filter of the desk officer, what folks in Washington know about the goings-on in a foreign country (particularly those not covered in the American press) largely hinges on what the desk officer chooses to pass on. Notes an administration official with significant desk officer experience: "Desk officers control policy by controlling the flow of information."[28]

The desk officer has that control, the official explained, because he or she "is the conduit through which embassies communicate with the State Department," which means that "if the desk officer has a particular interpretation of a situation, that can seriously color the way it is perceived by officials in Washington."[29]

A desk officer can sometimes significantly alter the relationship with his or her assigned country *unilaterally*. In 1988, then-candidate George Bush and his adviser Brent Scowcroft talked in the campaign about implementing a one-year freeze on relations with the Soviet Union. This caused something of a "freeze" between Reaganites and Bushies in the foreign policy community, because the former group was making real progress in winning the Cold War through hardball diplomacy. But the Soviet desk officer at the end of the Reagan administration, a career FSO, really liked the idea of a freeze, according to the then–assistant secretary for human rights, Richard Schifter. So after Bush won in November, but before he took office, the desk officer implemented the freeze, with only the help of the assistant secretary for the European bureau.

With a few minutes at a word processor and a few minutes sending the cable—which had Secretary of State George Shultz's "signature"—a desk officer and an assistant secretary changed U.S. foreign policy during the Cold War with the world's only other superpower—and against the wishes of still-serving President Reagan.[30] Richard Schifter recalls that when he saw the cable that had already been sent to the Soviets, he couldn't believe that Shultz would have signed off on it. So, he brought the cable into Shultz's office, and handed it to him. As Shultz read it, Schifter says, his face became red with rage. Shifter, who was going to the Soviet Union the following week, asked Shultz if there was any message he should deliver to the Soviets. Shultz simply said, "Tell them I have problems with my bureaucracy, too."[31]

REVOLVING DOOR KEEPS ON REVOLVING

Most decisions at State are driven by the obsession with stability and the twin desires to be liked and to get a deal, any deal. But sometimes, money enters the equation. Not in the sense of bribery—although Chapter 8 will discuss that factor in terms of visa fraud—but in the "legal" sense of State officials feeding from the foreign trough on retirement, often representing the very countries they were charged with handling while at State, which results in another perverse incentive for serving officers looking forward to retirement income. Why would the Yemeni government, hypothetically speaking, want to hire a "tough" former assistant secretary who hurt Yemen's interests in the name of national security while at State? A foreign country is a State Department official's possible future employer.

After serving as ambassador to Tunisia from 1987 to 1991, Robert H. Pelletreau became ambassador to Egypt. Three years later, he got a nice promotion to assistant secretary of state for Near Eastern Affairs (NEA), which oversees the Middle East and is widely considered the most powerful regional bureau in State. (There are two kinds of bureaus: regional and functional. The former is responsible for geographical areas, and the other deals with issues such as economics or arms control, regardless of location.) As the head of NEA, Pelletreau wielded an enormous amount of clout for three years. A little over a year after leaving State, he registered as a foreign agent of Tunisia, providing the Arab nation with "political and legal advice"[32] for a tidy sum of $157,000 per year.[33] Tunisia is most likely one of several of Pelletreau's clients. To show that he is nothing if not an equal opportunity opportunist, Pelletreau now also represents the government of Egypt.[34]

Not everyone who profits from his or her State Department ties does so as a registered foreign agent—and not every profiteer manages to stay within the confines of the law.

Robert Oakley, in his capacity as head of counterterrorism at State from 1984 to 1986, helped draft the regulations that banned Middle East Airlines (MEA) from operating in the United States because of strong evidence of its ties to terrorists.[35] But a few short years later, in 1993, after leaving State, Oakley took MEA on as a client. His goal?

Overturning the very same regulations he helped write. This was no act of a guilty conscience to undo something he later came to see as a mistake, however.

Oakley's agreement with MEA promised him a lucrative payday of $450,000—$300,000 of which he would get only if he succeeded in getting the restrictions lifted.[36] Yet the law in this area is clear: former government officials are under a lifetime ban from trying to influence government action on any matter in which they had participated "personally and substantially." Thus law enforcement did not look too kindly on this, and Oakley was prosecuted. His punishment? A plea bargain in late 1994 down to one civil count and a $5,000 fine.[37] His reward? Then-president Clinton appointed him in 1993—after Oakley had started lobbying on MEA's behalf—to be the U.S. special envoy to Somalia.

Though he did not take money directly from a foreign government or represent a company to overturn a law he helped write, Richard Holbrooke allegedly used State Department resources after retirement to help advance the business interests of his employer.[38] After finishing a long career in the Foreign Service—which included stints as ambassador to Germany and head of East Asian and Pacific Affairs under President Carter and European and Canadian Affairs under President Clinton—Holbrooke became a high-ranking executive at an investment bank and financial services company, Credit Suisse.

According to a former State Department official with intimate knowledge of the investigation, private citizen Holbrooke would call people he knew on staffs of various embassies to set up meetings with foreign officials, and he allegedly used former employees to provide him with office space and drivers.[39] His punishment? A plea bargain down to one civil count and a $5,000 fine. His reward? Then-president Clinton immediately appointed him to be ambassador to the UN.

STATE OF NO CHANGE

State is involved in almost every aspect of the War on Terror. Foreign policy is conducted through the 250 consulates and embassies that State operates, and all international agreements and accords go through State. State handles all interaction with the United Nations and other international bodies, including those whose goal is to restrict the proliferation of arms and weapons of mass destruction. In a time of war when the enemy wants nothing more than to send its operatives into the United States, State determines who does—and does not—get a visa. State is even responsible—along with the Commerce Department and the Pentagon—for "export control," the policy of restricting U.S. technologies with military applications from falling into the wrong hands.

Even in areas that may seem extraneous to the War on Terror, State's actions are important because stopping terrorists is just the short-term objective. The real purpose of the War on Terror is to fashion a world that is inherently inimical to the cultivation of new terrorists, something that is not possible when despots are given free reign to maintain "stability." But for State to fight for freedom in foreign lands seems unlikely given that Foggy Bottom doesn't even fight for Americans who desperately need help—and sometimes actively works against those who are seeking justice from the world's worst tyrants.

"There are two kinds of people in Washington: those who see gray because they know the difference between black and white, and those who see gray because they don't believe in black and white," notes former Defense Department official Henry Sokolski.[40]

The State Department doesn't believe in black and white, which raises the question of how State can help us win the War on Terror when it refuses to engage on a battlefield of right and wrong, of morality.

6

Courting Saddam

★ *"THESE ARE GOING TO BE USED FOR DEFENSIVE PURPOSES."*[1]

That was the refrain that Steve Bryen and his co-workers at the Department of Defense kept hearing over and over again in early 1988. Bryen was the last person needed to sign off on an order for 1.5 million militarized atropine injectors, known as autopens. Unlike his counterparts at the State Department—who had recommended approval of the sale—he was not satisfied that the sizeable order was intended strictly for "defensive" purposes.

Atropine injectors are used to immunize people against the effects of nerve gas. So it is completely understandable that they could be used for truly "defensive" purposes—but only if there is a legitimate threat of an enemy using nerve gas. If the atropine injectors are in the same hands as those controlling the nerve gas, then the injectors become *offensive* weapons, allowing the immunized side to use nerve gas with relative impunity.

Given that the person who had placed the order was Iraqi dictator Saddam Hussein, Bryen was concerned. Although Iraq was considered an ally and had received substantial assistance from the U.S. throughout the 1980s (including military equipment and dual-use technology that enhances military capabilities), many inside the Reagan administration were leery of what they saw as a looming threat.

Despite being pressured from all sides—including some at Defense—Bryen and a handful of others among his staff at the Pentagon decided to dig a little. Bryen asked the Defense Intelligence Agency to find out which countries in the region possessed nerve gas. That would indicate what potential defensive purposes the injectors might serve. The answer? Only Iraq.

Since Iraq faced no such threat from any of its neighbors, Bryen was convinced that the injectors were intended to facilitate an offensive use of nerve gas. As he put it, "They couldn't have been used for defensive purposes, since there was nothing to defend against."[2] Bryen assumed that his counterparts in the other agencies would agree once they saw the same evidence. He assumed wrong.

Since the order fell under the category of "munitions," the State Department had the ultimate authority to approve or refuse the license for Survival Technologies of Rockville, Maryland, to sell the 1.5 million autopens to Iraq. But Bryen believed that even State wouldn't approve a license for something that would allow a foreign nation to unleash a nerve gas attack—something that would be a grave violation of both international law and basic principles of human decency.

Undeterred, State was determined to issue the final license, but as it turned out, the biggest booster was someone at Defense, Richard Armitage. Armitage, who in 2001 became State's number two man, was in 1988 the assistant secretary of defense for international security affairs, and an active supporter of State's position that Saddam was a strong and important U.S. ally. He went to unusual lengths to have the sale of the militarized atropine injectors to Saddam approved.

Scheming with State, Armitage had the Pentagon's general counsel office write a "legal opinion" in favor of the license—a highly unusual move. At around the same time, the head of State's Near Eastern Affairs bureau, Richard Murphy, sent a letter to the White House protesting Bryen's actions. The pressure was mounting—but then the entire situation changed with a single newspaper story.

The *Washington Post* ran an article on the gassing of the Kurds in Halabja—in which Saddam used chemical gas to kill five thousand of his own people—and the general counsel's office quickly changed its opinion. Armitage and State "let the matter drop quietly," explains Bryen. But had it not been for the media attention, there's a very real possibility that Saddam would have obtained 1.5 million militarized atropine injectors. If Iraqi soldiers had been equipped with them during the Persian Gulf War, events could have unfolded much differently.

Survival Technologies did not suffer much economic damage as a result of the license being denied. It later sold the 1.5 million autopens to the U.S. Army for use during the Persian Gulf War.

MELTING PLUTONIUM

On June 27, 1990, a large shipment that was supposed to set sail for Iraq was held back—literally at the last minute.[3] Despite having a valid export license—issued by the Department of Commerce—to sell three large furnaces to an Iraqi industrial company, the American manufacturer voluntarily agreed to delay the transaction. That the furnaces, which could have been instrumental in the development of nuclear weapons, were stopped at all is a testament to the tenacity of several government officials—and an investigative journalist.

From almost the moment it learned of the proposed $10 million transaction in early 1989, the Commerce Department strongly supported it.[4] A representative from Commerce was the biggest cheerleader, pushing hard for it right up until the export license was revoked in July 1990. But because the furnaces were "dual-use" — they were supposedly going to be used for melting down metals to create prosthetics, but could have melted down metals for developing nuclear weapons — U.S. law requires that the Departments of State and Defense also approve such purchases by most foreign entities. They both approved — but Defense later had second thoughts when it received more information in mid-1990.

As the furnaces sat in a dock in Philadelphia, ready to be shipped to Saddam in June 1990, the Pentagon received a tip — from the same Steve Bryen who had stopped the 1.5 million atropine injectors two years earlier. Bryen, who at this point was out of government, learned of the furnaces from a reporter at the *Philadelphia Inquirer*, and according to the *Washington Post*, he alerted his former office at the Pentagon.[5] What followed was a frenzied investigation at Defense, with a number of different people attempting to determine the best approach to halt the transaction. But all the information they needed had actually been given by the company selling the furnaces, Consarc, more than a year earlier.

When Consarc first went to Commerce — the company's point of contact in the government — the manufacturer did not hide the possible military uses of its furnaces, which were described in one news account as "somewhere between the size of a desk and a bus."[6] In fact, the company was quite explicit about it. According to an internal memo written by Consarc president Raymond Roberts on February 15, 1989, "I told him [the Commerce representative] ... there is nothing to stop them from melting zirconium, the main use of which is a cladding material for nuclear fuel rods."[7] Company records also show that one week later, Roberts told a different Commerce representative that the furnaces could be used "without modification" for nuclear applications.[8] These revelations apparently did not faze the folks at Commerce—nor did similar arguments made by officials at Defense the following year.

Commerce officials were apparently satisfied that the furnaces were intended for benign purposes, based on nothing more than a pledge from the Iraqi entity purchasing them that they were going to be used for scientific research and to make prosthetic limbs for handicapped war veterans.[9] But Commerce likely would not have accepted a mere promise had State moved Iraq onto a list of countries with the most restrictions on purchasable items. As matters stood, despite using chemical weapons against both Iran and his own people, Saddam was still allowed to purchase dual-use items up until 1990.

Though it is not entirely clear what officials at State knew when they originally signed off on the transaction, they did not back down once the Pentagon investigation revealed compelling proof that the furnaces had clear capability to assist in making nuclear weapons— and that they were not going to be used to create artificial limbs for handicapped Iraqis.

Among the Pentagon's findings was that the furnaces were bound for a facility south of Baghdad, far from any hospital or medical center.[10] And the Iraqi firm receiving them had previously conducted WMD-related research for the Iraqi government.[11] Officials at Defense then discovered that these furnaces would be absolute overkill for making prosthetics and could be used for developing any number of components for nuclear weapons, including missiles used to deliver them. But perhaps most alarming was that the furnaces were so state-of the-art that they could be used for melting plutonium—something that then creates a nuclear core.[12] (To understand just how powerful a furnace would have to be to do this, note that plutonium's melting point is 1183 degrees Farenheit/640 degrees Celsius.[13]) In short, a Defense official noted to the *Washington Post*, "[T]he U.S. government had ample evidence to believe that the end-use was nuclear."[14]

Acting alone, officials at Defense pushed U.S. Customs agents to stop the shipment temporarily on June 28, 1990. Officials at Commerce and State were not happy. On July 11, a Commerce representative named Michael Manning placed an angry phone call—from Consarc's New Jersey headquarters—to a Customs official. Manning told the Customs official that neither Commerce nor State supported the detention.[15] But just over a week later, State and Commerce were overruled at a highly unusual interagency meeting chaired by White House staff and conducted over closed-circuit television.

On July 19—one day before the temporary detention was to expire—participants at the high-level meeting were presented truly damning evidence. A leading expert on furnace technology from a national weapons lab said that if he wanted to melt plutonium to create a nuclear core, he would want the Consarc furnaces Saddam had ordered.[16] That same day, the transaction was permanently halted.[17]

"STENCH OF DEATH"

On March 16, 1988, the Kurdish village of Halabja in northern Iraq suffered one of the worst chemical gas attacks since the first World War.[18] Lifeless bodies of women, children, and old men were everywhere. Those who did survive were permanently maimed and disfigured. Here's how a Reuters reporter who witnessed it described the scene: "Bodies lay on the streets and in the rubble of smashed buildings. Others sprawled half out of cars. Dead women clutched lifeless children. Doctors said the waxlike appearance of some of the corpses was due to cyanide poisoning. They looked like dolls. The stench of death was overpowering."[19]

When images from Halabja reached the United States nearly a week after the attack, White House spokesman Marlin Fitzwater called the pictures on television "horrible, outrageous, disgusting and should serve as a reminder to all countries of why chemical warfare should be banned."[20] That forceful statement was made on March 23, 1988. Nine days later, its hand forced by the White House, the State Department officially condemned Saddam's gassing of his own people as a "particularly grave violation of the 1925 Geneva Protocol Against Chemical Warfare."[21] But in the next breath, the State Department spokesman tried to take the spotlight off Saddam, noting that "there are indications that Iran may also have used chemical artillery shells in this fighting."[22]

HEMMING AND HAWING

When Saddam ordered a second wave of chemical gas attacks against the Kurds that August, State was still in no hurry to criticize the Iraqi dictator. State eventually did condemn the mass murder of mostly Kurdish civilians, but only because of the efforts of its human rights bureau, headed by Richard Schifter. In a struggle that lasted roughly two weeks, Schifter battled the Near Eastern Affairs (NEA) bureau, which vociferously opposed any direct criticism of Saddam.

Richard Murphy, the head of NEA who earlier that year had written the White House to complain about Steve Bryen's delay of Saddam's order for atropine injectors, argued that castigating Saddam would accomplish nothing more than angering an "ally."[23] Schifter, on the other hand, made the case that the U.S. had a moral obligation to condemn a despicable act. This fight played out several times during preparations for the daily press briefings (which typically occur several times a week).

When the State Department spokesman takes the podium for a press briefing, every answer given is highly scripted. Most of the time, there is general consensus on the appropriate wording. But not always. During the last week of August and first week of September 1988—from the time of the early reports on the latest wave of gas attacks to the official condemnation—representatives from Human

Rights (which had few careerists) and NEA (which was populated mostly with careerists) clashed repeatedly. "There were often fights in the mornings before the press briefings. We were on one side wanting stronger statements, and NEA was on the other side," explains Nathan Kingsley, who was Human Rights' number two official and participated in those morning meetings.[24]

The internal conflict was apparent in the press briefings. The transcripts of the briefings reveal that the official line at first was one of complete ignorance that the attacks had occurred; then it shifted to a general condemnation of the attacks, but official ignorance as to who was responsible for them. But neither was truthful. Schifter notes that Foggy Bottom officials knew full well from almost the moment the slaughter occurred that it was Iraqi forces conducting the gas attacks against largely civilian populations in Kurdish areas.[25]

A reporter first raised the issue of the second round of chemical gas attacks in the briefing on August 25, 1988, which was discussed shortly after the spokeswoman, Phyllis Oakley, had reiterated State's concern about the expulsion of several Palestinians from the West Bank. The exchange went as follows:

> *Question:* Could I ask one question—another one, please, on the Middle East? There's a report to the effect that the Iraqis are conducting an offensive against Kurdish strongholds in the triangle between Iraq, Iran, and Turkey. Some 150,000 Kurds are trapped, and the Iraqis are supposedly using chemical weapons against them. What do you have on that?
>
> *Ms. Oakley:* I don't have anything on that situation; our general information has been that the cease-fire has been holding, that there have been a few incidents. But on this specific concern about Kurds, I simply have nothing on it.

Question: Well, can we get something on this, where 150,000 people may be involved under chemical attack by Iraqi military forces? Isn't that something a little more important than deporting one or two "Palestinians," as you call them, from the West Bank?

Ms. Oakley: Yes? [as in asking for the next question]

Question: You're not answering the question.

Ms. Oakley: That's correct. Yes?[26]

Nearly a week later, nothing had changed. On August 31, Oakley told a reporter asking for new information of the situation in northern Iraq, "No, I don't have anything new on that question."[27] The next day, September 1, the official line changed—but only after it had become nearly universally accepted that the gassings had occurred and that Iraq was responsible. State belatedly acknowledged the obvious—that thousands of Kurds had been gassed—but then refused to assign blame to any particular party. Oakley said, "If the reports are accurate, this is a grave violation of international human rights standards."[28] What she didn't mention was that State had already known for roughly a week that the reports were accurate.

State continued to plead ignorance about the perpetrator of the attacks for the entire first week of September. At a briefing on September 6, spokesman Charles Redman commented, "We, of course, have seen these same reports that you're referring to [about the chemical gas attacks], but we don't have any information to confirm whether or not those reports are true."[29] When pressed if State had talked directly with Iraq about its involvement in gassing the Kurds, the following exchange ensued:

Question: Chuck, have you asked them whether they're [the reports] true or not?

Mr. Redman: We've been in touch with a variety of sources. I don't want to go down the list, but just let me leave it that we've been in touch.

Question: Well, I mean, I don't want to go down the list with you either. It's Iraq that's accused, not a list of countries. And you're on pretty good terms with Iraq these days. So I wonder if the U.S. has asked Iraq, and if Iraq has refused to provide information, or given you evasive or ambiguous information?

Mr. Redman: That invites me to go into all kinds of diplomatic exchanges, which I won't do.

Question: So you can't say if the U.S. government has asked Iraq if these reports are true?

Mr. Redman: I think it's obvious that when we go into these kinds of issues, anybody who has information, we're talking to.

Question: Do you intend to convey any displeasure directly to Iraq?

Mr. Redman: I don't think there's any secret. We've said it before. We've publicly condemned the use of CW [chemical weapons] by Iraq on occasions, by other countries when they have used it, so that there's no doubt that if any report on the use of chemical weapons proves true, we'll express our displeasure. But as I say, in this case it's hypothetical in the sense that we don't know whether these reports are true.[30]

By the next day, on September 7, it was clear that the two-step State had come up with—admitting that the attacks occurred, but feigning ignorance as to who was responsible—was becoming nearly impossible to maintain. Witness the following give-and-take with a reporter:

Question: Chuck, there seems to be some very vivid eyewitness testimony about the use of gas against the Kurds by the Iraqis. Do you have any firmer grasp on whether in fact there has been such happening?

Mr. Redman: No, I don't have anything that would go beyond what I said yesterday. But because we have seen reports, you note that I went on ahead to say yesterday how we felt about this issue, regardless of whether or not we can pin with any precision this latest incident.[31]

The strain on Redman of sustaining State's absurd position of official ignorance became apparent a few moments later:

Question: Chuck, if I could go back to the Kurds a little bit. When the United States first noted that Iraq was using chemical weapons in the Iran-Iraq war, I think it was back in '84, the evidence was fairly sketchy, it was based largely on Western journalists' eyewitness reports. It seems that there's a reluctance this time to make any sort of judgment call from this podium as to whether the same conclusion can be drawn. And it just strikes me as odd that at this late date there isn't some sort of firmer evidence, intelligence sources—

Mr. Redman: My only job is to give you the best assessment that I can give you, consistent with the facts. That's what I'm doing. There is certainly no hesitation to draw judgments about the use of chemical weapons wherever they occur, and if they have occurred in this case, as I said yesterday, we condemn it with the strongest possible terms. But all I'm trying to do is stay with the facts. That's our job.[32]

The following day, State "magically" discovered that Iraq was, in fact, responsible for gassing thousands of Kurds. What actually happened was that Schifter had finally won his fight to have State officially condemn Iraq's actions. Over the strenuous objections of NEA and its bureau chief, Richard Murphy, John Whitehead (who was acting secretary of state while his boss, George Shultz, was out of the country) sided with Schifter. State spokesman Redman started off the September 8 briefing by announcing, "As a result of our evaluation of the situation, the United States government is convinced that Iraq has used chemical weapons in its military campaign against Kurdish guerrillas. . . . We condemn this use of chemical weapons."[33]

It didn't take long, however, for State to backtrack from any appearance that it was taking a tough stance against Iraq. Within a week of the official condemnation, the Senate had already unanimously approved legislation that would have imposed wide-ranging sanctions, and the House was preparing to vote on a similar bill. But when asked about the proposed sanctions at the September 14 briefing, Redman explained, "[W]e believe that the sweeping sanctions in the House legislation are premature." He justified State's position by noting, "We've been working strenuously to convince the Iraqis of the unacceptable nature of this practice"[34]—meaning the "practice" of mass murdering its own civilians with chemical weapons. But despite State's strong opposition to the sanctions, the House passed its bill overwhelmingly, 388–16.[35]

Officials from State managed to delay final passage by the Senate until the session ended that October. And so the sanctions were not imposed.

Part of the argument that State used to persuade the Senate to hold off final passage of the sanctions legislation was pointing out that Iraq had agreed that using chemical weapons would be wrong. State made this same argument publicly, with Redman announcing at the September 20 press briefing, "[O]n this question of the use of chemical weapons, we welcome the announcement by Iraqi Foreign Minister Tariq Aziz in Baghdad on September 17, that Iraq respects and abides by all the provisions of international law, including the 1925 Geneva Protocol and other agreements within the framework of international humanitarian law. This is a positive step."[36]

As with the atropine injectors and the Consarc furnaces, State was content to take Saddam's word. As Redman concluded, "We take this statement to mean that Iraq foreswears [sic] the use of chemical weapons."[37]

GETTING CLOSER

The United States forged an increasingly close alliance with Saddam Hussein in the mid-1980s during the Iran-Iraq war, viewing the secular Iraqi despot as a counterbalance to Iran's Ayatollah. Despite growing discomfort in some circles in the U.S. government, that relationship intensified in those areas overseen by the State Department. State, particularly its Near Eastern Affairs (NEA) bureau, had to go to greater and greater lengths during the 1988–1990 period to maintain ties with Saddam in the face of mounting opposition from many in Congress and others inside the administration.

The NEA's efforts to build up Saddam kicked into high gear only after the end of the Iran-Iraq war in August 1988, explains Schifter, who was the head of the human rights bureau at that time.[38] Those efforts coincided with a massive outcry—in the United States and around the world—over Saddam's mass murder of some 100,000 Kurds and widespread, indiscriminate use of chemical weapons. Barely two months later, however, NEA forcefully backed U.S. taxpayer-guaranteed Export-Import Bank loans to Iraq.[39] By the end of December, the issue became a pitched battle between NEA chief Murphy and Schifter.

When Schifter was asked to sign off on the recommendation for Iraq to receive medium-term export credit guarantees (putting U.S. taxpayers on the hook for any loan defaults), he strenuously objected to rewarding Saddam financially just months after his killing spree. In an internal memo, Schifter wrote that Saddam's regime was "one of the most brutal and repressive in the world" and that "its actions in 1988 outdid its previous performance. They probably constitute the most serious violations of the 1980s."[40] He pointed out that the chemical weapons attacks against the Kurds "were ordered from the very top, in a cold calculated manner. . . . If the general American public was aware of Iraq's human rights violations, as it is aware of human rights violations in countries covered more fully by the media, there would indeed be a great public outcry against U.S. assistance to that country. Even though the facts about Iraq's deplorable human rights record are not generally known, they are known to us and should be taken into full account."

Murphy took strong exception to Schifter's characterization of Saddam. He dismissed Schifter's concerns, and wrote that the U.S. needed to be "hard-headed" about the situation. He argued that the U.S. would lose its ability to apply economic pressure to influence Iraq's behavior. The Bureau of Economic Affairs sided with Murphy, but with less than a month remaining in Reagan's term, Secretary Shultz decided to leave the decision to the incoming Bush administration. The credits were eventually approved.

Shultz was involved in the fight over the Export-Import Bank credit guarantees, but by the end of 1988 he was becoming increasingly withdrawn from day-to-day operations. With Shultz preoccupied with the end of the Reagan administration, a turning point in the U.S.-Soviet relationship, and a handoff of power to the incoming Bush administration, NEA more or less had free rein to pursue its strategy of courting Saddam.

"MODERATING FORCE"

As the administration changed over from Reagan to Bush in January 1989, NEA exploited the transition period to "engage" Saddam further. It was then that State coined its argument that Saddam was a "moderating force" in the Middle East, though at the time it was only the tertiary reason offered for forging closer ties with Iraq. The first two reasons? First, that Iraq has the largest unproved oil resources, and second, it has a large, educated population.[41] To advance its goal of a tighter alliance with Saddam, NEA asked Schifter in January 1989 to go to Baghdad that spring for a human rights conference it wanted to hold there—an odd request, Schifter believed, given the atrocities the despot had committed just months earlier. He even received pressure from Richard Haass, then the Middle East specialist at the National Security Council in the White House. "I felt like I was going to be used as a prop in a big lie," explains Schifter.[42] He refused.

In what was perhaps the first briefing James Baker received on Iraq as secretary of state, it is clear that NEA wanted broader and deeper ties with Saddam. The acting head of NEA, Paul Hare, in a March 1989 memo to Baker, wrote matter-of-factly, "Iraq is the strongest state in a region vital to our interest, with a powerful army and oil reserves second only to the Saudis."[43] The memo paints a picture of a moderate Arab state, continuing, "During the [Iran-Iraq] war, Iraq drew closer to our friends among the Arab moderates, getting financial support from Saudi Arabia and Kuwait."

Hare at least acknowledged that Iraq "is working hard at chemical and biological weapons and new missiles" and that it "used CW as part of a campaign to suppress a Kurdish rebellion last August." But Hare did not discuss the death toll and, in fact, tried to downplay Iraq's flagrant violation of international law by pointing out that it "participated constructively in the Paris CW Conference" in January 1989. Hare repeatedly stressed the importance of forging a stronger alliance with Saddam.

The acting head of NEA informed Baker that the purpose of his upcoming meeting with a top Iraqi official, Nizar Hamdun, was "to express our interest in broadening U.S.-Iraq ties." The memo concluded with the following points: "We are committed to expansion of trade and U.S. exports around the world. We believe reconstruction and development projects in Iraq will present significant opportunities for U.S. exporters."

Finding a receptive audience in Baker, NEA pressed ahead with its pro-Saddam agenda—culminating in a huge victory that fall. After months of intense lobbying (which included the enthusiastic support of Richard Haass, who handled the Middle East for the National Security Council in the White House), NEA won the president's signature on National Security Directive 26 (NSD-26) in October 1989, which called for the "pursuit of improved economic and political ties with Iraq," according to an internal State Department memo written shortly after it was enacted.[44] NEA would soon bootstrap off NSD-26—which never would have been signed without pressure—to fight for stronger ties to Saddam in the face of stiffening opposition elsewhere in the U.S. government.

ARMING SADDAM

With Iraq fighting Iran during the 1980s, the United States approved the sale of various dual-use items and a whole host of materials that considerably boosted Saddam's biological and chemical weapons capabilities. For each such transaction, U.S. companies had to receive export licenses from the Commerce Department, though State and Defense also had to approve transfers before Commerce could issue valid licenses. Commerce was often the biggest supporter of the exports, but State was rarely in disagreement. Defense was more skeptical, particularly starting in 1985. While each party deserves some of the blame for approving the licenses, State was undoubtedly the driving force behind an increasingly close U.S. alliance with Saddam.

The official policy on dual-use items—those with both civilian and military end-uses—was spelled out in a November 1989 internal State Department memo: "[E]xports of dual-use commodities for conventional military use may be approved."[45] And approved they were. As the numbers show, Saddam had little trouble getting his hands on everything he needed to build up his war machine. From 1985–1990, U.S. companies applied for 810 licenses to sell Iraq chemical or biological agents and high-technology items with military capabilities; 771 licenses were issued; only 39 applications were denied.[46] The grand total spent by Iraq to buy these items was more than $1.5 billion.[47]

The chemical and biological transfers to Iraq were by no means benign. According to a congressional study, "These exported biological materials were not attenuated or weakened and were capable of reproduction."[48] Undoubtedly aided by the U.S. exports, Iraq had developed substantial bio-warfare capability. According to an April 1992 Department of Defense report to Congress, "By the time of the invasion of Kuwait, Iraq had developed biological weapons. It's [sic] advanced and aggressive biological warfare program was the most advanced in the Arab world."[49]

Included among the approved biological agents that Saddam acquired from State Department-approved transactions were the following toxins:

- *Clostridium botulinum*, the bacterial source of botulinum toxin. It is often fatal, causing headache, fever, dizziness, vomiting, dilation of the pupils, and paralysis of the muscles involved in swallowing.[50]
- *Histoplasma capsulatum*, which causes a disease that superficially resembles tuberculosis and may itself cause pneumonia. Other symptoms include enlargement of the liver and spleen, anemia, an influenza-like illness and an acute inflammatory skin disease.[51]
- *Clostridium perfringens*, a highly toxic bacteria that causes gas gangrene. A congressional report describes its effects: "The bacteria produce toxins that move along muscle bundles in the body, killing cells and producing necrotic tissue that is then favorable for further growth of the bacteria itself. Eventually, these toxins and bacteria enter the bloodstream and cause systemic illness."[52]

Also on Saddam's shopping list was *Bacillus anthracis*, or anthrax. As noted in a congressional report, anthrax "begins abruptly with high fever, difficulty in breathing, and chest pain. The disease eventually results in septicemia (blood poisoning), and the mortality is high."[53] The main supplier of these products for Iraq was the American Type Culture Collection, which made seventy separate shipments of anthrax and other deadly toxins.[54]

State often used two justifications for the licensing of dual-use items and biological and chemical agents for export to Iraq. First, with U.S. companies supplying the products, State would be better positioned to monitor and control how items were used, and second, if the U.S. companies stopped supplying Saddam, other countries would simply fill the void. But a congressional inquiry revealed that out of the 771 approved licenses, only one resulted in a follow-up to determine how the item purchased was being used.[55] In other words, the U.S. had no way of knowing how the other 770 purchases were being used, or if they had been utilized to bolster Iraq's military capabilities.

State's other justification was just as flawed. Richard Murphy, head of NEA for most of the Reagan administration, explained in 1990 how this logic led him to have State push for approval of almost every license application: "If an item was in dispute, my attitude was if they were readily available from other markets, I didn't see why we should deprive American markets."[56] In congressional testimony in June 1990, Murphy's successor, John Kelly, stated flatly, "None of our friends and allies among the industrial countries is willing to impose either sanctions or an export embargo against Iraq."[57] But the "problem" indicated by Kelly is actually of State's design.

In a November 1989 classified cable from Washington to the U.S. ambassador in Jakarta, Indonesia—apparently to counter a previous cable that indicated the U.S. discouraged military sales to Iraq—the policy regarding arms sales by U.S. allies to Iraq was made explicitly clear:

Department *does not repeat not* clear on proposed talking point for use during the ambassador's meeting with minister of state for research and technology. Although the U.S. severely limits the sale of our own munitions list items to Iraq. We have *not* had a policy of discouraging other countries' arms sales to Iraq.[58] (emphasis added)

SIGNS EVERYWHERE

From the moment he took power, there should have been little doubt that Saddam was a madman. Shortly after becoming president in 1979, Saddam videotaped a session of his party's legislature, where he had several party members executed on the spot.[59] "The message, carefully conveyed to the Arab press," observed *Newsweek* in a 2002 article, "was not that these men were executed for plotting against Saddam, but rather for thinking about plotting against him."[60] Saddam's depravity became even more clear when he began using chemical weapons against Iran in 1984.

By 1985, many officials at Defense were sending warning signals about Iraq. Although not pegging him as an enemy, the officials were leery of what they considered an increasingly worrisome war machine. In an internal Pentagon memo dated July 1, 1985, to Secretary of Defense Caspar Weinberger, Richard Perle (whose office managed Defense's role in export licensing) wrote, "[W]e have a number of legitimate national security concerns in regard to high technology exports to Iraq that must continue to be addressed." He justified those concerns by noting, "[T]here is a body of evidence indicating that Iraq continues to actively pursue an interest in nuclear weapons . . . and that, in the past, Iraq has been somewhat less than honest in regard to the intended end-use of high technology equipment."[61]

State did not give much merit to Defense's reservations about Iraq, and, in fact, appeared annoyed at delays in license approvals.

In a letter to Weinberger dated April 30, 1985, then–secretary of state George Shultz stated that the U.S. should expand "our political and commercial influence in Iraq," and further, "my main concern is to prevent future delays in technology transfer to Iraq."[62] Shultz argued that Defense should work with State to ensure "timely review of applications to export advanced U.S. technology to Iraq."[63] He explained that this was necessary because "[u]nwarranted denial or further delay in pending and future cases would set back our political, commercial, nonproliferation, and technology transfer interests."[64]

In many respects, the alliance with Iraq during the Iran-Iraq war made strategic sense. American policy placed a clear priority on containing the Iranian mullahs. As *Washington Post* columnist Charles Krauthammer, by way of analogy, remarks, "When you have Hitler and Stalin, you choose Stalin."[65] But counterbalancing is a dangerous game, especially when the "ally" becomes increasingly depraved.

On May 17, 1987, nearly a year before Iraq unleashed chemical weapons on Kurdish civilians in Halabja, an Iraqi fighter jet bombed the U.S.S. *Stark*, which was in international waters in the Persian Gulf, killing thirty-seven Americans.[66] Two missiles hit the *Stark*, with the second one sparking a fire that trapped sailors sleeping in their bunks.[67] Both the U.S. and Iraq labeled the attack an accident, and Iraq claimed its pilot believed he was attacking an Iranian ship.[68] But the Pentagon soon discovered that the ship was twelve nautical miles outside of the so-called "exclusion zone" where Iranian ships were normally found.[69] The incident should have put Saddam's later call for U.S. forces to leave the Gulf[70] in a different light.

Saddam gave still more cause for worry in April 1990, when he threatened to use his chemical weapons arsenal to "burn half of Israel."[71] The statement didn't sway State to back away from Saddam.

State was not acting entirely on its own accord, to be sure; President Bush personally signed NSD-26 in October 1989, mandating closer ties with Iraq, and did so with full knowledge of Saddam's gassing of the Kurds. But the professional diplomats at Foggy Bottom should have tried to push foreign policy in a far different direction.

Though State was unwilling to confront the reality about Saddam, plenty of others were. In the press, *Washington Post* columnist Jim Hoagland and *New York Times* columnist William Safire were sounding alarms about Saddam for months before the August 1990 invasion of Kuwait. In Congress, a bipartisan group of legislators — from liberal senator Claiborne Pell of Rhode Island to conservative senator Jesse Helms of North Carolina — were highly critical of the Iraqi despot. Several sanctions bills were introduced in 1988 and again in 1989 and 1990, all of which State helped to squash. And in the administration, a growing number of officials, particularly at the Department of Defense, were concerned about Saddam's despicable behavior. Even inside the State Department, opposition to the idea of considering Saddam an ally grew.

TALE OF TWO HEARINGS

Iraq was the best of allies. Iraq was the worst of allies. It depended on who was asked — even within the State Department. Although the NEA bureau was still a strong supporter of Saddam, by summer 1990, the Human Rights bureau was not. The division within State played out in remarkably dissimilar testimonies to Congress by officials from the respective bureaus in June 1990.

First up was NEA's chief, John Kelly. Six weeks before Iraqi tanks rolled into Kuwait, he opened his testimony for the Senate Foreign Relations Committee by stating, "In the 1990s, we expect the Persian Gulf and Iraq to increase in importance to U.S. national security and interests. Now and in the future, Iraq will play a major role in the Gulf."[72] He hedged his bets somewhat by noting Saddam's well-known erratic behavior, but he did his best to put a positive spin on it. He claimed, "In recent years Iraq has taken some steps the

United States has wanted in an effort to improve bilateral relations for its own benefit."[73] But the first example he cited—Iraq's expulsion of Abu Nidal's terrorist organization—was at best a half-truth, for the *New York Times* had reported more than a month earlier that Nidal's group had reopened offices in Baghdad.[74]

Since Congress was understandably most concerned about Saddam's past use of chemical weapons, Kelly downplayed such fears. He rattled off the following litany of good deeds on chemical weapons:

> Iraq had participated in the January 1989 Paris Review Conference of the 1925 Geneva Chemical Weapons Protocol. Iraq participated in the September '89 Canberra Government/ Industry Chemical Weapons Conference. Iraq had joined as an observer the Conference on Disarmament in Geneva, where we are working towards a comprehensive ban on chemical weapons.[75]

Kelly did not even make a passing reference to Saddam's mass murder of some 100,000 Kurds.

Immediately after Kelly finished, the number two official at Human Rights, Joshua Gilder, testified. Wasting no time, Gilder opened his remarks by stating flatly, "Once again this year, we've found Iraq's human rights practices were abysmal. Human rights, as such, are not recognized in Iraq."[76] He continued:

> [T]he ordinary Iraqi citizen knows no personal security against government violence. Disappearances followed by secret executions appear to be common. In some cases the family only learns that one of its loved-ones has been executed when the security services return the body and, in line with the Iraqi regime's view of justice, require the family to pay a fine. The penalty for expressing opinions deemed objectionable by the regime is swift and brutal.[77]

Gilder, who had a heated argument with Kelly in private before the hearing,[78] did what the NEA chief did not—he directly addressed Saddam's slaughter of thousands of innocent Kurds. He stated, "Perhaps the most shocking demonstration of this was the use of chemical weapons against parts of the Kurdish population suspected by the regime. Thousands of defenseless men, women, and infants died as a result. Many more thousands fled across the border into neighboring nations."[79]

RUNNING INTERFERENCE

Kelly's statements to the Senate committee were similar to arguments State made behind the scenes to counter congressional efforts to impose sanctions on Iraq. After the sanctions legislation died in 1988, several new bills were introduced in 1989 and 1990. State opposed all of them. Realizing that the sanctions legislation would face long odds, Representative Gus Yatron, a Democrat from Pennsylvania, introduced a non-binding resolution that would have condemned "the deliberate and systematic human rights violations by the Government of Iraq."[80] State vociferously opposed it.[81]

Although the bill wouldn't have imposed sanctions, it did expose State's coddling of Saddam. In the House, State drafted Representative Lee Hamilton, a Democrat from Indiana, to stop the bipartisan resolution from moving forward. He was successful in preventing the full Committee of Foreign Affairs from even voting on it. On August 2, 1990—the day Saddam's tanks rolled into Kuwait—he was still blocking the resolution.

SCANDAL ERUPTS

On August 4, 1989, FBI agents and officials from the U.S. Attorneys' office in Atlanta, Georgia, raided the Atlanta office of Italian-owned Banco Nazionale de Lavoro (BNL). According to press accounts from the time, BNL was the subject of a federal investigation for making off-the-books loans to Iraq that financed "[a]n Iraqi shopping list of sensitive equipment and technology worth more than [$600 million] and up to [$1 billion.]"[82] BNL had made a total of $4 billion in loan commitments to Iraq, more than $3 billion of which were off-ledger transactions, though only $1.85 billion of the covert funds had actually been transferred to Baghdad.[83]

BNL was not just Italy's largest bank, it was also a major player in U.S.-backed loan programs for foreign governments, including Iraq. So when investigators revealed to the press that Iraq had used the money for nefarious purposes, it appeared that the scandal might damage State's latest campaign to secure $1 billion in agricultural "assistance" for Saddam for fiscal year 1990 (which started on October 1, 1989). Investigators faced a daunting task: completely untangling the tangled web of transactions made using the billions of dollars of BNL loans, with a special challenge posed by Iraq's consolidation in 1988 of its civilian and defense industries.[84]

According to the *Financial Times*, BNL started providing the under-the-table loans to Iraq in February 1988, and before that, "Iraq and its procurement agents had begun to indentify [sic] companies and technologies for machine tools, computers, and composite materials manufacturing."[85] The same September 1989 article also noted that Saddam's regime had used $620 million worth "of direct loans by BNL Atlanta to the Iraqi central bank...to buy items on Iraq's shopping list."[86] A congressional investigation in 1992 revealed that "Iraq's Ministry of Industry and Military Industrialization [MIMI], which was headed by Saddam Hussein's son-in-law, Hussein Kamil, eventually utilized over $2 billion in BNL loans for its ambitious military industrialization effort."[87]

UNDER AMERICA'S NOSE

On September 11 and 12, 1989, an Iraqi named Sam Naman visited State Department officials in Washington.[88] Naman worked in the 1980s for a known Iraqi intelligence official, Safa al Habobi, in the United Kingdom.[89] Given the business activities of Naman and al Habobi, it was most likely no coincidence that the "visit" to Washington came just five weeks after the raid of BNL's Atlanta branch.

Al Habobi ran the procurement division for the Al-Arabi Trading Company, which operated in Europe and the United States. A 1992 congressional investigation found that: "Al-Arabi was headquartered in Baghdad and appears to have been under the control of Iraq's main weapons complex, the Nassr State Enterprise for Mechanical Industries [NASSR]. NASSR was the key producer of Iraqi missiles and was heavily involved in clandestine nuclear and chemical weapons programs and some aerial bombs."[90]

In 1987, under al Habobi's leadership, Al-Arabi made a major purchase, buying (through a holding company) the British machine tool manufacturer Matrix-Churchill Ltd. and its Cleveland, Ohio, affiliate, Matrix-Churchill Corporation. Machine tools are devices that can be used to make desks, chairs, refrigerators, or ovens. But machine tools can also be used to make almost anything mechanical necessary for a war machine, from military equipment to ballistic missiles. Matrix-Churchill was a leading machine tool maker, in operation since 1923 and employing roughly seven hundred people.[91] Its Cleveland, Ohio, subsidiary had been open since 1967.

Matrix-Churchill was a good purchase, at least from Iraq's perspective. According to the congressional investigation: "Sometimes Matrix-Churchill would purchase the equipment directly from the United States firm and then ship it to Iraq. However, the Iraqi end-user usually purchased the goods directly from the United States firm."[92] One of the biggest and most disturbing transactions was the sale of a fiberglass factory to Iraq, which could have been used to make missile casings.[93] The man who oversaw these shipments to Iraq was Naman. And the funding for Al-Arabi's Matrix-Churchill acquisition came from BNL loans. Which begs the question: What did Naman discuss with State Department officials in his visit to Washington five weeks after the BNL raid?

Naman's confab with State in September 1989 appears to have paid dividends. Matrix-Churchill's Ohio subsidiary was not shut down until a year later—six weeks after Iraq's invasion of Kuwait.

BILLION-DOLLAR JEOPARDY

The emerging BNL scandal had the potential to scuttle $1 billion in agricultural credits—through what was known as the Commodity Credit Corporation (CCC) program—that were scheduled to be given to Iraq for the twelve-month period beginning October 1, 1989, for two reasons. One was the possibility that senior Iraqi officials would be implicated, and the other was that CCC funds were tied up with the funds Saddam used for illicit military purchases. BNL had already provided over $800 million in CCC credits—money that is supposed to be used solely to purchase U.S. agricultural exports—to Iraq alone over the past several years. And out of the $267 million in Export-Import Bank loans that Iraq had received between 1985 and 1990, some $50 million came directly from BNL.

State saw the $1 billion credit guarantees as central to its efforts to "engage" Saddam, and was consequently determined to do everything possible to salvage the CCC disbursements scheduled to be handed over sometime in late 1989.

In early October 1989, the Agriculture Department—concerned about the allegations of CCC malfeasance and the potential for Iraqi complicity in the BNL scandal—offered Iraq a modified CCC package of $400 million, with an opportunity to revisit further credit guarantees after the investigation had been given more time to unfold. Iraq flatly refused.[94] The reasoning, as noted in an internal State Department memo addressed to Secretary of State James Baker, was that the Iraqis believed that "so large a reduction would be widely viewed as a

U.S. vote of no-confidence in their economy."[95] State's response to Iraq refusing America's generosity? To fight for the full $1 billion program.

FURIOUS LOBBYING

Despite opposition from the Federal Reserve, the Treasury, and the Agriculture Department, State made a full-court press in October and November 1989 to have the full $1 billion CCC program approved. In an October 26, 1989, memo briefing him on the CCC matter, Secretary of State Baker was informed that "[o]ur ability to influence Iraqi policies in areas important to us, from Lebanon to the Middle East peace process, will be heavily influenced by the outcome of the CCC negotiations."[96] Baker was told that the CCC loans were vitally important to maintain the high level of trade that had "become the central factor in this relationship."[97] In short, "Offering a program of up to $1 billion would strengthen relations with Iraq, in line with NSD-26, and help U.S. exporters."[98] Baker complied with the request to lobby for the full $1 billion in CCC credits, placing several calls to other high-ranking administration officials.

Despite claiming otherwise, State knew that taxpayers would likely pick up at least a substantial portion of the tab for the CCC loans. After a long and debilitating war with Iran, Iraq's economy was in shambles. The October 26 memo to Baker indicated that Iraq was "$30–40 billion [in] debt to non-Arab creditors,"[99] though it didn't mention that Iraq was at that moment unable to make even a $12 million repayment to the Export-Import Bank.[100] When a November 3, 1989, interagency meeting delayed resolution of the CCC loans in large part because of those credit concerns (although the BNL scandal also factored in), State dug in its heels. Since an October 31 phone call from Baker to the secretary of agriculture did not achieve the desired result, NEA wrote a memo to deputy secretary of state Lawrence Eagleburger urging him to "telephone Treasury and OMB and urge that an alternates meeting take place as soon as possible to approve USDA's [United States Department of Agriculture] proposed full program of CCC credit guarantees." He complied, and an additional interagency meeting was held just two days later, on November 8, 1989.[101]

At the November 8 meeting of the National Advisors Council, a representative from State delivered the following message: "The CCC program is crucially important to our bilateral relationship with Iraq. State strongly supports immediate action by the NAC Deputies to approve the new program proposed by USDA."[102] State's representative then warned that terminating or reducing the CCC program would "cause a deterioration in our relationship with the Iraqis."[103] Addressing the concerns that several participants raised about the BNL scandal, State's representative "noted that the Iraqi Foreign Minister had given assurances that Iraq would cooperate fully with the investigation."[104] The Federal Reserve representative expressed the same sentiment as other participants when he said that his agency "did not want to be obstructionist."[105]

State's pressure paid off. At the end of the NAC meeting, a "consensus" was reached that Iraq would receive the full $1 billion, but it would be disbursed in two payments of $500 million each as a precautionary measure in case more damaging evidence from the BNL investigation emerged.

WHAT STATE KNEW—AND WHEN

In the October 26 memo to Baker on the CCC program, the secretary of state was informed that it was "unclear" whether or not Iraqi officials were involved in the massive web of wrongdoing in the BNL scandal. This was simply not true.

Among the "talking points" given to Baker in the October 26 meeting—meaning the arguments he was supposed to make with other high-ranking administration officials in pushing for the full

$1 billion—was the following: "Obviously we should not go forward with the program if we have substantial evidence of a pattern of serious violations of U.S. law by high-ranking Iraqi officials. Our information about the investigation indicates that the prosecutor does not now intend to indict Iraqi officials."[106] But in fact, prosecutors were very much interested in indicting Iraqi officials, having amassed substantial evidence by the time the memo was written that top Iraqi government officials were involved.

In a May 1990 letter from the U.S. Attorney's office in Atlanta, the prosecutors expressed frustration that the Iraqis received the CCC loans despite the fact that prosecutors had shared examples of Iraqi complicity prior to the release of the first $500 million.[107] And two days before the November 8 interagency meeting, the CIA gave State a report that detailed Iraqi involvement in the BNL scandal—and even warned State about the BNL connection to Matrix-Churchill.

In a November 6, 1989, memo titled, "Iraq-Italy: Repercussions of the BNL-Atlanta Scandal," the CIA wrote, "Baghdad has created complex procurement networks of holding companies in Western Europe to acquire technology for its chemical, biological, nuclear, and ballistic missile development programs."[108] It further informed State, "One such network begins in Baghdad with the Al-Arabi Trading Company.... In 1987, TMG (an Al-Arabi holding company) gained control of Matrix-Churchill, Ltd., the United Kingdom's leading producer of computer-controlled machine tools that can be used in the production of sophisticated armaments."[109] The CIA made clear the involvement of the Iraqi government, even indirectly referencing the roles of al Habobi and Naman in Matrix-Churchill: "We believe that Iraqi intelligence is directly involved in the activities of many holding companies funnelling [sic] technology to Iraq."[110]

IN A HAZE

When deputy assistant secretary of state for Near Eastern Affairs Skip Gnehm traveled to Baghdad in December 1989 to meet with Iraqi officials, he told the Iraqi trade minister that after investigating BNL, prosecutors "concluded on the basis of information available that the allegations were baseless. Hence, we went ahead with the CCC program." To the Iraqi trade minister—who had to have known of his government's extensive involvement in BNL-related illegal activities—this message must have come as a relief. Though it is not clear what Gnehm personally knew, the people who cleared that specific talking point knew better—both from the November CIA report and the October warnings from Atlanta prosecutors.

An internal State Department memo from January 4, 1990, shows that State was again informed that evidence from the BNL investigation was increasingly likely to implicate Iraqi officials, noting, "Last month, USDA undersecretary Richard Crowder told Richard McCormack that new allegations of Iraqi wrongdoing had arisen from the investigation" into BNL, "which could jeopardize the second $500 million tranche [installment] of FY90 CCC guarantees for Iraq."[111] The same memo concluded, "However, our foreign policy interests in Iraq would be better served by moving ahead on the second tranche this month. . . . If it appears that USDA is holding back, we may want to force the issue by bringing it before a meeting of the the [sic] NAC Deputies."[112]

After the first $500 million payment was made in November 1989, others in the administration started getting cold feet about sending Iraq the rest. The Agriculture Department was refusing to release the second $500 million because of the BNL scandal. Yet State seemed to be in a parallel universe, repeatedly claiming that there was no Iraqi malfeasance in the BNL affair.

An internal State Department memo dated March 5, 1990, states, "[T]here is no apparent justification for continued delay in the release of the second tranche of CCC guarantees for Iraq. The BNL investigation has not brought to light any evidence of official Iraqi misconduct in connection with the CCC program."[113] The memo, from the acting head of NEA (probably because John Kelly was out of the country), Jack Covey, stressed, "The Iraqis need the second tranche now."[114] But the BNL investigation had, in fact, "brought to light" evidence of "official Iraqi misconduct"—and State knew it. Prosecutors in Atlanta had informed State directly on several occasions, including telling USDA (which quickly told State) on February 23, 1990, that "various Iraqi officials are implicated in a scheme to defraud BNL, to demand after-sale services from exporters receiving CCC guarantees, and to collect payments from non-CCC exporters."[115]

Two months later, State was still downplaying the likelihood that there was any Iraqi involvement in BNL. In an internal May 18, 1990, memo titled "Weekly Report," NEA staff (no individual signed it) claimed, "[W]e have seen little evidence to support such charges" against Iraqi officials "for conspiracy to defraud BNL."[116] But just two weeks earlier, the prosecutors sent a letter to Washington with a message that was both direct and clear: "Please be advised that the Department of Justice has developed credible evidence in connection with the Banco Nazionale del Lavoro (BNL) Atlanta investigation which shows criminal complicity of certain Iraqis who were also involved in the CCC program."[117]

By this point, State knew that indictments were imminent. In an internal State Department memo from May 22, 1990, a reference to "consultations" that would take place before any indictments would be handed down was followed by the recommendation, "In such consultations, it would be entirely appropriate for us to to [sic] point out that there are foreign policy concerns in this case which must be taken into account."[118] The NEA-prepared memo to NEA chief Kelly further advised, "At the appropriate time, you may want to intervene to ensure that our concerns are taken fully into account in any decision regarding indictments." State, in fact, did "intervene," not just in the decisions relating to the $1 billion CCC program, but also in the BNL investigation itself—and not on behalf of the prosecutors seeking justice.

OBSTRUCTION OF JUSTICE

Secretary of State Baker, parroting the talking points given to him by NEA, told other high-ranking administration officials in late October 1989, "Obviously we should not go forward with the program if we have substantial evidence of a pattern of serious violations of U.S. law by high-ranking Iraqi officials."[119] What he did not tell them—perhaps because he did not fully know himself—was that State itself was proving the biggest obstacle to prosecutors' ability to gather "substantial evidence of a pattern of serious violations of U.S. law by high-ranking Iraqi officials." And in the same memo, when it was written that it was "unclear" if Iraqi officials were involved, it was only "unclear"—to the extent that that was true—because State did everything it could to thwart the investigation. Even without any cooperation from State, though, prosecutors were prepared to issue an indictment by October 1989—until State prevented it.[120]

Central to the development of any criminal case is interviewing key figures and other witnesses. Prosecutors wanted to do this, but the Iraqis involved could only be interviewed overseas. When prosecutors had arranged to interview several Iraqi figures in Turkey in fall 1989, State nixed it. State refused to allow prosecutors to travel abroad to interview key witnesses and suspects, using its broad authority to prevent U.S. officials from conducting certain government business overseas.[121] State's "compromise" was for prosecutors to submit written questions to it, which Foggy Bottom officials would then pass on to the Iraqi figures.[122] When that procedure yielded few results, prosecutors made the highly unusual move in March 1990 of offering the Iraqi witnesses and suspects the option of flying to

America, all expenses paid, to be interviewed. The Iraqis were even given assurances that they would not be arrested while in the United States.[123]

No Iraqis accepted.

In the minds of prosecutors, State had also dealt a tremendous blow to their efforts by pushing through the first CCC program payment of $500 million in late 1989. A letter written by prosecutors in May 1990 states:

> In November 1989, when BNL was attempting to negotiate at least partial collateralization of the over $2 billion of credit extended through the Drogoul/Iraqi scheme to defraud, the Iraqis simply laughed. They cited the "clean bill of health" just provided by the United States government through the October, 1989 extension of $500 million in CCC guarantees.[124]

As the months wore on, and spring turned to summer in 1990, State still managed to hold indictments at bay. The *New York Times*, in a 1992 article, uncovered internal documents showing that prosecutors on several occasions in 1990 had planned to issue indictments imminently, but none came that year.[125] The internal State Department memo from May 1990 demonstrates that State was painfully aware how close prosecutors were to handing out indictments, and that it was prepared to stop that from happening. State succeeded; no indictments were issued until after the end of the Gulf War.

END RESULT

Perhaps because State was willing to give $500 million in CCC credits to Iraq after the BNL scandal had come to light, BNL executives in Rome believed they should honor the commitments made by the Atlanta branch. In January 1990, BNL officials in Rome—for the stated purpose listed on the signed contract of "improving and strengthening the relationship and cooperation between the Parties" — released $1.5 billion that its Atlanta office had previously promised.[126]

But despite all its bad actions and questionable judgment, BNL did not fully suffer the consequences of its actions. In February 1995, BNL received $400 million from U.S. taxpayers to cover its losses related to CCC loans to Iraq.[127] Because Iraq defaulted on all bank loans through the CCC program the moment the Gulf War started, U.S. taxpayers ended up on the hook for a total of $2 billion in paying back defaulted loans.[128]

U.S. taxpayers would have been hit for another $500 million if State had had its way. The Agriculture Department formally stopped the second $500 million payment in May 1990, infuriating Foggy Bottom officials. When word reached the U.S. embassy in Baghdad, ambassador April Glaspie wrote in a cable back to Washington, "Turning down the CCC credits would send the signal that the administration had decided to join forces with those in the Congress who had already reached the conclusion that the U.S. had no option but to pursue a policy of sanctions and containment."[129] State, in fact, continued lobbying for the release of the other $500 million until shortly before the Iraqi invasion of Kuwait.[130]

Despite State's obstruction, prosecutors were finally able to issue indictments in the BNL scandal on February 28, 1991, one day after the end of the Gulf War.[131] Although some Iraqi officials and some BNL executives from the Atlanta branch were indicted,[132] there were some conspicuous omissions. Not indicted was any executive from BNL-Rome — not even the officials who issued the $1.5 billion to Iraq five months *after* the raid on the Atlanta office. But there's more to the story.

Prosecutors wanted to indict the Central Bank of Iraq because it had $1 billion in assets that could be frozen to pay back damages resulting from fraud. They also wanted to indict a powerful Jordanian shipper and businessman named Wafai Dajani.[133] But while the war was still going on, State argued that indicting the bank would set a bad "legal precedent" since the bank was essentially a government agency.[134] (Never mind the "precedent" this created of encouraging foreign governments to use state-controlled banks to commit fraud or fund arms smuggling.) And as for Dajani, the *New York Times* in a 1992 article discussed State's lobbying on his behalf, quoting from a State Department memo sent to prosecutors:

> Mr. Dajani is a powerful figure in Jordan, and his brother, it pointed out, "is a former Minister of the Interior, and Wafai himself is considered well connected to the King and to U.S. grain exporters." It continued, "His indictment would be seen as a further U.S. attempt to 'punish' Jordan" for its support of Iraq.[135]

That memo was drafted just days before the indictment was handed down. Neither the Central Bank of Iraq nor Dajani was indicted.

7

Crushing Freedom

 "NEA WOULD APPRECIATE ANY ASSISTANCE [TO HELP] SHUT DOWN THE INC."[1]

That was what a **State Department** official from the Near Eastern Affairs (NEA) bureau told auditors from the Inspector General's office, according to minutes of a May 17, 2002, meeting. The "INC" in question is the Iraqi National Congress, at the time an umbrella organization for anti-Saddam Hussein, pro-democracy groups. Having done everything it could to thwart the INC through bureaucratic chicanery and by badmouthing the group and its leader, Ahmad Chalabi, in the press, NEA was determined to drive a stake through the INC's heart by having auditors help them "shut down" the INC. The auditors refused.

INC was created in the aftermath of the Gulf War by Chalabi, a secular and Western-educated Shiite who had lived in exile for several decades, to coordinate the various groups opposing the rule of Saddam Hussein. Based for the first several years in the Kurdish-controlled areas of northern Iraq, the INC was forced to move to London in 1996 following a crackdown by Saddam Hussein.

For reasons that are not entirely clear, State hated the INC and Chalabi. Some point to Chalabi's unheeded warnings against a doomed CIA-backed coup attempt in Iraq 1996. State and CIA were no doubt embarrassed that the coup failed, as he predicted it would. But the real reason probably stems from the fact that, as one administration official observes, "More than anything, State hates that it can't control Chalabi."[2]

Congress, however, authorized $97 million in funding for "Iraqi opposition" groups—with the clear intent that most of the money go to the INC.[3] But within weeks of the president signing the Iraq Liberation Act on October 31, 1998, officials from State were telling the media—"anonymously," of course—that funds were not necessarily going to flow to the INC.

So when State Department official Yael Lempert asked the auditors to provide "any assistance" they could to help "shut down the INC," she was doing exactly as she was told. Richard Armitage—State's number two man under Colin Powell since 2001, became the driving force at Foggy Bottom to "shut down the INC."[4] Armitage's name appears throughout the auditors' notes about their interactions with NEA over audits of the INC. That the audits were ordered at all is a result of the NEA's strong desire to "shut down the INC." More on that later.

FURIOUS LOBBYING

Before State sicced auditors on the INC—twice—it did its best to keep Congress from approving funding for the pro-democracy group. While Congress was working on the Iraqi Liberation Act in 1998, lobbyists from State fought the measure. But despite State's best efforts, Congress overwhelmingly endorsed the bill. The House passed the bill 360-38, and in the Senate, there was not a single "no" vote.

State was at it again in 2000, trying to get Congress to drop the "earmark" for the INC. After failing in that effort, State in spring 2002 fought congressional efforts to provide an additional $30 million to the INC. Armitage burned up the phone lines, calling all his trusted allies on Capitol Hill.[5] This time, State succeeded. Congress did not authorize the additional $30 million.[6]

"FINE-TOOTHED COMB"

With most of its lobbying efforts on Capitol Hill ending in defeat, State had to look for other ways to realize its dream of "shutting down the INC." So NEA—which had oversight over the INC's grant program and the grant officer—had State's Inspector General's office conduct an audit in May 2001. The auditors examined every payroll stub, every receipt, every expense report, and every budget line item. As one administration official notes, "They went over everything with a fine-toothed comb."[7]

With such exacting scrutiny, the auditors found some irregularities—but not many. The INC was in some respects a rag-tag operation that did not have the best administrative practices, though, as one administration official remarks, "it was nothing on the scale of an Enron."[8] The auditors found $113,000 as "unallowable" and questioned some $2 million spent as "unsupported," meaning improper accounting and administrative procedures were used. This represented roughly ten percent of the group's annual budget. But as audits go—an auditor's *job* is to find problems—the report released in October 2001 was relatively benign. And according to multiple administration officials, the INC implemented each recommendation suggested by the auditors. Even State had to acknowledge the INC's administrative improvements, with spokesman Richard Boucher commenting at a daily press briefing in January 2002 that the INC was making a "good faith effort...to address the weaknesses that were identified by the Inspector General."[9]

But despite its public pronouncements, State was not pleased that the INC was becoming better organized. With the INC implementing each of the auditor's proposals, State had lost its main excuse for holding back on giving the INC the full funding called for by Congress. To fix that "problem," State ordered a second audit, which was conducted in May 2002. The audit was ordered for the sole purpose of killing the INC once and for all. That was why Yael Lempert asked the auditors that time around for "any assistance" in helping NEA "shut down the INC."

Not only did the auditors give the INC a clean bill of health the second time around—only $10,000 total (or less than 1 percent of the annual budget) was even questioned—but they also noted that it was "impossible" for the pro-democracy group to fully comply with all of State's various requirements. The auditors did, however, find fault with the operations of another party: the Near Eastern Affairs (NEA) bureau. The inspectors wrote that NEA was "violating" government rules with some of its actions,[10] and further criticized the entire structure of placing the grant program under NEA's authority. The auditors might as well have been talking about the actions of Ms. Lempert when they cited "the possible lack of independence and conflict of interest that can occur when the grants officers report to (NEA) Bureau management."[11]

The overarching problem the INC faced was that State essentially wanted to manage the group. But with government grants, the oversight organization only has the power to disallow costs and possibly to decide not to renew funding. Yet NEA wanted the power to hire and fire staff, for example, and to approve expenditures on a case-by-case basis, often forcing the INC to go above and beyond what is required of almost any other group. While State mostly failed to "shut down the INC," it did its best to hobble the group through the bureaucratic process.

DEATH BY PAPERWORK

A little over two weeks before Yael Lempert—most likely on direct orders—asked the auditors to "help" the NEA, State press flack Richard Boucher stated flatly, "We continue to support the activities of the INC."[12]

Once the auditors refused to do NEA's dirty work, State did a masterful job manipulating bureaucratic minutiae to shave off every dollar it could from the INC's budget, to prevent the INC from paying its bills (and even its employees), and to shut down programs it didn't like—even though it didn't have the authority to do so. But rather than make drastic moves that would raise the ire of many on Capitol Hill, State contorted the system to inflict maximum damage on INC—while attracting minimal attention. State's basic approach was to delay approval of funding and then pay out several weeks or months late—and when payment was finally made, the payments were conspicuously made out for less than what was supposed to go to the INC.

Most agencies or groups funded by government grants work out budgets on an annual basis, and funds are dispensed at monthly intervals, with little question as to how much is going to be paid and when. No such luck for the INC, however. Going into any given month, the INC did not know how much money it would receive for that month's expenses or when it would receive it. State kept the INC on a precarious financial footing, unable to proceed with its activities with any certainty as to whether full funding would later be received.

In a typical example, the INC operated throughout November and December 2001 without receiving any of the $1.2 million it was supposed to receive each month. Only on December 31, 2001, did State cut a check—but the amount was only for $1.7 million, $700,000 shy of the $2.4 million total budget INC had been operating under for those two months.[13]

As anyone who's ever worked in a small business can attest, paying bills late can annoy creditors, and paying salaries late hurts morale. INC employees never knew when to expect paychecks, or if they would have to be suddenly laid off. Consider the experience of someone the INC was forced to hire after the first audit, a financial controller. The controller, who was hired in October 2001, got his first paycheck on time, but didn't get another one on time until 2003.[14] Luckily for him, he couldn't be fired. In April and May 2002, State provided money for both months midway through May, but the funding was short by over $100,000. To make up the shortfall, the INC had to lay off two of its employees in London.[15]

PIECE BY PIECE

Since State was unsuccessful in killing the Iraqi National Congress outright, Foggy Bottom officials sought to shut down various INC programs, one at a time. Sometimes State was able to keep programs from being launched in the first place by withholding funding. Congress wanted to give humanitarian relief to the people of Iraq—and lawmakers wanted the INC to be at the center of those actions. But State had other ideas, putting the $12 million Congress appropriated out for bid to other non-governmental organizations—not giving even a penny of that sum to the INC, which unsuccessfully bid for grant funding.[16]

One of the attacks Foggy Bottom officials would use in "anonymous" conversations with reporters and staff and lawmakers on Capitol Hill was that the INC was run by exiles with no real ties to Iraq. The INC was, in fact, created by exiles, but every time it tried to forge ties with people in Iraq to help lay the groundwork for a post-Saddam democracy, State became an obstacle. Every time the INC included travel expenses in its budgets—which State was supposed to approve in advance—those line items were deleted.[17] In other words, by refusing to allow the INC to use funds for travel expenses,

State was trying to relegate the pro-democracy group to being an armchair observer from London and Washington, where its two main offices were.

But INC officials did have a significant intelligence presence inside Iraq with its Intelligence Collection Program (ICP). Staffed by former intelligence officials and Iraqi defectors, the ICP was very successful, often more successful than U.S. officials in search of the same types of information. The INC's intelligence officials were the ones, for example, who discovered Salman Pak, the training facility just outside Baghdad where Saddam's henchmen instructed would-be terrorists on how to hijack an airplane.[18] As part of the mission of finding evidence for future trials on human rights abuses, those same intelligence agents also uncovered ties between Iraq and al Qaeda—some of which the U.S. revealed after the war—and provided substantial information on Saddam's WMD capabilities.[19] No wonder State spokesman Richard Boucher said in January 2002, "We continue to provide funding, for example, to groups that collect information for possible war crimes prosecutions."[20] A mere four months after Boucher expressed support for the ICP, State tried to end all funding for the program.[21]

The INC was also supposed to be funded and assisted by State in recruiting people for non-lethal training—everything from computer systems to logistics—that would be provided by the Pentagon. Instead, State did its best to prevent this effort.

The INC needed sixty days' worth of advance funding commitments to cover medical exams and visas and the like to participate in the Pentagon program. But the INC never knew if it would have money sixty days out. And so the pro-democracy group had to stop recruiting for non-lethal training. It simply couldn't make commitments to people, putting its reputation on the line, without a firm pledge from Foggy Bottom that the funding for that particular program would continue uninterrupted. State refused to give any such assurance.[22] Shortly after the INC stopped recruiting due to uncertain funding, State cancelled the program *because* the INC had stopped recruiting.

In February 2002, State informed the INC that it would fund nonlethal training again if recruiting started back up. In April, the INC resumed its recruitment efforts, making commitments to individuals and detailed preparations for their travel to the U.S. But in July 2002, State again started withholding funding. By the time the money finally did arrive in October, the INC had had to cancel plans for all but the first round of people who had signed up for the program.[23] And when President Bush signed off on lethal training for people recruited by the INC—at a time when the U.S. was gearing up for war—State prevented the directive from being fulfilled by simply not providing the necessary professional staff to administer it.[24]

CATCH-22

In order to effectively build a political base in Iraq to prepare for the end of Saddam's regime, the INC operated an office in Iran's capital of Tehran. Because Iran is an official state sponsor of terrorism, the INC had to get a license from the Office of Foreign Asset Control (OFAC) to send money to its Tehran office. It had a license for calendar year 2001, which meant that it could only wire money there until the close of business on December 31. But as previously noted, State didn't provide funding for November and December until December 31. Because of the lead-time necessary for wire transfers, the money came exactly one day too late—something about which Foggy Bottom officials were well aware.

Since the Tehran office would close down without funds, the INC sent a small amount of money in the new year. INC officially applied for a new OFAC license on February 1, 2002.[25] But State delayed approval for months, which it can do since State is typically given deference on "foreign policy" matters relating to issuance of

OFAC licenses. When the INC tried to collect funding for its Tehran office, a source close to the situation observes, "State kept telling the INC, 'We'd fund you [for the office], if only you had an OFAC license.'"[26] But State was *the reason* the INC didn't have an OFAC license, so Foggy Bottom had created a catch-22. As a result, the Tehran office operated with a skeleton staff for the rest of 2002. The OFAC license didn't get approved until the very end of that year, on December 27, 2002—nearly eleven months after the INC application was submitted.

OFF-THE-AIR

State was able to get away with most of its bureaucratic machinations in large part because of the ethical cloud created by two consecutive audits. It didn't matter that the second one seemed designed for the sole purpose of getting auditors to help "shut down the INC"—an audit (particularly a second one) often has the same effect on a group's reputation that criminal charges have on an individual. Even though the auditors provided a glowing report for the INC following the second audit, State exploited the year between the release of the results of the first and second audits to blame the INC for the financial difficulties—almost all of which stemmed from State's pattern of paying late and reducing funding levels after the fact. But when the INC was forced to shut down Liberty TV—which it broadcast into Iraq—in May 2002, many in Congress took notice, although it took the imminent start of the war in Iraq for lawmakers to pressure Foggy Bottom on the issue effectively.

As part of the Iraq Liberation Act, the INC had started Liberty TV in August 2001. It was essentially an INC-run television version of Voice of America, broadcasting messages of freedom and liberty, in Arabic, to the Iraqi people. It started in makeshift offices, with plans to move into a professional studio later on. But rather than upgrading facilities and improving the quality of programming, the INC was forced to shut down Liberty TV entirely. The satellite company needed $25,000 for an uplink from Liberty TV's studios to the satellite. But because it hadn't received money for April 2002 by the end of that month, the INC didn't have the money to give the company. Being flexible, the satellite company told the INC that it would settle for a commitment by State to pay $25,000 at a later date. State refused. Liberty TV went off the air for a lack of $25,000.[27]

Even though U.S. and British forces would have been aided considerably by pro-freedom and anti-Saddam broadcasts to the Iraqi people during the war, Liberty TV was still not on the air by the time the conflict began. Primarily driven by their concern for Liberty TV, five Republican senators wrote a letter to President Bush in late March 2003 asking that he "personally clear the bureaucratic road blocks from within the State Department" and get funding and other support to the INC.[28] The letter called for a full and prompt payment of the $7 million State owed—but had refused to pay—the INC. The same day the letter was sent, State announced that it would release funds for the INC—but only $4 million. No indication was given about the fate of the remaining $3 million.[29]

THE REPLACEMENTS

For years, State pursued an A-B-C strategy for developing a post-Saddam transition government: Anyone But Chalabi. It went to great lengths to cultivate alternatives to Chalabi, including recruiting someone openly backed by the House of Saud and trying to protect reputed war criminals from prosecution.

One of the main figures angling to become Iraq's first post-Saddam leader was Laith Kubba, a man who happened to be on the U.S. taxpayer payroll. A one-time member of the INC, Kubba founded the Iraqi National Group in early 2003 to enhance his profile—and his chances for a top role in the post-Saddam leadership.[30] When he was not participating in this struggle, Kubba worked for the

National Endowment for Democracy (NED), a taxpayer-funded organization ostensibly providing grants to groups that help further the cause of democracy. NED provides grants in Iraq as well, and Kubba is the project manager overseeing the issuance of those grants.

Kubba used his perch at NED to further his own political interests by supporting a group that strongly criticized the INC—all at U.S. taxpayer expense. One of the first NED grants Kubba issued was to the misleadingly named Iraqi Institute for Democracy (IID). Based in the Kurdish-controlled north, IID openly disparaged the INC in the press and conducted several polls purporting to show that Chalabi and the INC had little support in the region.[31] Several months before the start of the war in Iraq, IID president Hussein Sinjari lobbied administration officials in support of Kubba for president of a post-Saddam Iraq.[32] (Sinjari denied this in an e-mail to the author on April 15, 2003: "That IID lobbies for Dr. Laith Kubba is simply not the truth.") Although there is no indication that Kubba asked or pressured Sinjari to lobby on his behalf, Kubba's interests were nevertheless still promoted by a recipient of an NED grant.

Aside from the conflict of interest, there are other reasons State should not have embraced Kubba. Until 1988, Kubba was a member of the Dawa party,[33] which was responsible for the 1983 bombing of the embassy in Kuwait that killed six and injured dozens.[34] Kubba, who remains an Islamist as of 2003,[35] opposed the Iraq Liberation Act in 1998.[36] Two years later, he opposed sanctions against Saddam's Iraqi regime as "morally unacceptable."[37] And at the Chicago Council on Foreign Relations meeting in early March 2003, Kubba voiced opposition to the war.[38]

Apparently believing that he could not become the leader of a post-Saddam Iraq, Kubba, while still employed by NED, had his Iraqi National Group join forces with an octogenarian former foreign minister of Iraq, Adnan Pachachi, who is openly backed by the

House of Saud. State actively courted Pachachi well into 2003, encouraging his efforts to build political support in order to compete with Chalabi and the INC. One administration official says that the special envoy to Iraq, Zalmay Khalilzad (the former Unocal lobbyist who initially supported the Taliban), is "so obsessed with Pachachi that he forced Jalal Talibani [leader of the Patriotic Union of Kurdistan, an INC member organization] to put Mr. Pachachi on the Iraqi opposition leadership council."[39] Pachachi didn't want to be on the council because Chalabi was also on it, and said as much in a *Financial Times* column in March 2003. Pachachi's column was no secret to Foggy Bottom; it was posted on State's website. (Interestingly, State's website did not have any of the high-profile columns written by Chalabi.) Yet to many Foggy Bottom officials, Pachachi remained the top choice to lead a post-Saddam Iraq.

State even lobbied Denmark to overlook the alleged crimes against humanity of another alternative to Chalabi. Nazir Khazraji was a general in the Iraqi military during the 1980s, and was reportedly a leader of the attacks that resulted in the slaughter of some 100,000 Kurds in 1988, including the chemical gas attacks in Halabja that March. According to the *Washington Post*, "He was formally accused of murder, pillage, and the wanton destruction of property in violation of the Geneva Conventions."[40] Danish prosecutors gathered firsthand accounts from over one hundred witnesses,[41] but according to an administration official, "State begged Denmark not to prosecute Khazraji, because they wanted him to be a leader of the Iraqi opposition."[42]

Danish authorities apparently were not swayed by State's lobbying on Khazraji's behalf. In November 2002, the former Iraqi general was placed under house arrest, pending trial.[43] But after going outside to smoke a cigarette one day in March 2003, Khazraji disappeared.[44] There was some speculation that he was killed, but as of May 2003, nothing definitive has been reported.

FRIENDS OF BA'ATH

As soon as the war in Iraq ended, the transition to a new government began. Despite a clear goal of de-Ba'athification—akin to de-Nazification in Germany after World War II—laid out by President Bush, the State Department had other ideas. Because the Ba'athists had been in control of Iraq for thirty-five years—nearly twenty-five of which were under Saddam Hussein's leadership—State wanted to phase out senior Ba'ath party officials from the transition government over time.

Considering some of the people at the center of U.S. efforts in Iraq, this belief should not come as a surprise.

The special envoy to Iraq, who coordinated plans for a post-Saddam Iraq until he was officially placed under the command of Paul Bremer in May 2003, was Zalmay Khalilzad—the former Unocal representative who argued for quick acceptance of the Taliban in 1996. (Although he was technically a National Security Council representative in Iraq, State strongly supported his appointment there.) Another key figure in Iraq immediately following the war was Robin Rafael, the former head of the South Asia bureau who originally sought closer ties with the Taliban, even commenting on their "wonderful senses of humor." Rather than being banned from Foggy Bottom for their track record of extremely questionable judgment, Rafael and Khalilzad were handed two of the top positions in the selection of new leaders for a post-Saddam transition government.

Under Khalilzad's guidance, several senior Ba'ath party officials were given plum posts in the transitional authority. The new minister of health, Dr. Ali al-Janabi, was formerly the number three official in the health ministry in Saddam's regime.[45] The State Department gave him a promotion to the top spot, even though he refused to renounce the Ba'ath party.[46] State Department official Stephen Browning actually praised al-Janabi, telling the Associated Press that the new minister of health was a "Ba'ath party member who is not associated with criminal activities."[47] But others evidently disagreed: after a wave of protests from Iraqi doctors and nurses, al-Janabi resigned a mere ten days after accepting the appointment. Perhaps even more amazing, Rafael personally reinstated as president of Baghdad University Saddam Hussein's personal physician, Dr. Muhammad al-Rawi.[48] Like Dr. al-Janabi, Dr. al-Rawi was still loyal to Saddam, even refusing after the war to remove a statue of the deposed despot from the school's grounds.[49]

The looting and rioting that followed the end of the war, which received considerable attention in the international media, was largely coordinated by Ba'athists. According to several administration officials, significant evidence showed that the Ba'athists were behind much of the criminal unrest as well as the "vandalism" that struck strategic locations, such as the electrical grid.[50] When U.S. officials were attempting to repair the grid in the aftermath of the war, the "vandals" repeatedly sabotaged the transformers, something that required a detailed knowledge of the grid, which only the senior Ba'ath party officials who previously maintained and operated the grid would have.

With Ba'athists organizing much of the disorder, the State Department's bias toward "stability" was actually responsible for destabilizing Iraq after the fall of Saddam Hussein's regime.

"UNHELPFUL REACTIONS"

In early 2003, when Senator Sam Brownback attempted to create an Iran Democracy Foundation to help foment freedom in the nation that the State Department's annual reports on terrorism consistently name the "most active state sponsor of terrorism," State strongly objected. At what is known as a mark-up (where committee members review and "mark up," or edit and amend, a bill), Brownback attempted to amend the Foreign Relations Authorization bill in April 2003 with a simple provision establishing a foundation. State's top congressional lobbyist, Paul Kelly, attended this session for the sole purpose of persuading senators on the committee to vote against the Brownback amendment. This was significant because administration officials almost never attend committee mark-ups. They do so only if the issue is considered particularly important.

Kelly explained to the senators that creating the Iran Democracy Foundation "could provoke unhelpful reactions from Iran."[51] What was so "unhelpful" about Brownback's proposal? The conservative Republican senator from Kansas wanted to establish a center that would be endowed with $50 million to give grants to groups dedicated to the cause of bringing freedom and democracy to Iran. The bulk of the money was designed to go to groups that would broadcast messages of liberty, which was probably State's main concern. Broadcasts reminding Iranians of their God-given right to be free of tyranny and oppression would not sit well with the tyrants oppressing them. Which is why Kelly reminded the senators, "Finally, the department is also concerned that under the Algiers Accord, the Iranians could make a convincing claim based on our interference in their internal matters. Again, there could be litigation."[52]

The "Algiers Accord" Kelly referred to is the agreement President Carter signed in late 1980 that set the terms of release for the hostages at the U.S. Embassy in Tehran. The agreement did, in fact, call for the U.S. to stay out of Iran's internal affairs. But aside from being legally meaningless (according to an attorney in the Justice Department),[53] agreements to tolerate tyrannies permanently are morally bankrupt on their face. And if Iran does sue, American Enterprise Institute's Michael Ledeen remarks, "So what?"[54] If anything, Iran suing the U.S. for promoting freedom and basic human rights would only enhance America's moral standing on the world stage.

Brownback should not have been surprised that State opposed—and successfully blocked (at least temporarily)—his amendment. The previous summer, in 2002, he had introduced a non-binding resolution condemning "the continuous repression of freedoms within Iran and of individual human rights abuses, particularly with regard to women."[55] Despite being co-sponsored by a bipartisan group of eight senators—including Democrat Barbara Boxer of California, who is as liberal as Brownback is conservative—one of State's strongest Senate allies, Foreign Relations Committee chairman Joe Biden, prevented the resolution from even coming to a vote.

NO MESSAGE

On July 9, 2002, thousands of demonstrators took to the streets of Iran to protest the mullah dominance of the country's Islamist government. They were marking the third anniversary of a brutal police crackdown on peaceful protestors at Tehran University, when armed security forces stormed dormitories and beat and arrested hundreds of students.[56] In the days following the 1999 incident, some fifteen thousand dissidents protested the government's crackdown, in what the New York Times described as the largest demonstration since the fall of the shah in 1979.[57] As the Iranian people increasingly decry the mullahs, they mount a demonstration each year on the anniversary of the crackdown. The 2002 demonstration came less than six months after Bush's "axis of evil" speech; many of the protestors probably assumed that the United States would openly support them. They would have been wrong—at least concerning the State Department.

When asked at the daily press briefing on July 8, 2002, if the U.S. had a message for the Iranian protestors, State spokesman Boucher flatly replied, "No."[58] State didn't want to offer even words of sympathy, notes an administration official, because doing so would have "angered" the Iranian mullahs.[59] President Bush himself had to intervene for the U.S. to voice any support.

Later that week, on July 12, 2002, Bush issued the following statement: "We have seen throughout history the power of one simple idea: when given a choice, people will choose freedom. As we have witnessed over the past few days, the people of Iran want the same freedoms, human rights, and opportunities as people around the world. Their government should listen to their hopes."[60] He concluded his statement, which State lobbied to stop, by telling the demonstrators, "As Iran's people move towards a future defined by greater freedom, greater tolerance, they will have no better friend than the United States of America."

Particularly revealing about State's attitudes toward those literally risking their lives to protest for the freedoms that Americans enjoy was Boucher's initial, cavalier response to the question at the July 8 press briefing. This was the exchange:

> *Question:* Scheduled for tomorrow, there are supposedly going to be major demonstrations in Tehran. Does the State Department have a message for the demonstrators, given U.S. interest in this recently?
> *Mr. Boucher:* No.
> *Question:* You have no message?
> *Mr. Boucher:* We don't. We don't.
> *Question:* It's supposed to be a really big demonstration.
> *Mr. Boucher:* Cool. (Laughter)[61]

"IRAN IS A DEMOCRACY"

Seven months later, in February 2003, State had a message, of sorts, for the Iranians risking their lives in the fight for freedom: "Iran is a democracy." Those were the words uttered by State's number two official, Richard Armitage, who had spearheaded efforts to shut down the INC.[62] This is, at best, a bizarre statement given that President Bush had repeatedly referred to the leaders of Iran as the "unelected few," with good reason, since the Iranian mullahs are no more democratically elected than the leaders of the Soviet Union were.

Although Iran has several positions that are elected, the ballots that are cast are essentially meaningless. The Council of Guardians, a group of twelve mullahs, vets all candidates for president and the Parliament before voters even step into polling places. President Mohammad Khatami, for example, was able to appeal to the voters only after the Council of Guardians had rejected 234 of the 237 other candidates.[63] Khatami was likely deemed acceptable by the mullahs because he served as minister of Culture and Islamic Guidance from 1982–1992, where he censored over six hundred publications. But even if Khatami and the other so-called "reformers" wanted to reform Iran, they couldn't. The unelected "Supreme Leader," Ayatollah Ali Khamenei, controls the judiciary, the press, the police, and the military.

"REDEFINING" AMERICA

Five months after September 11, a top State Department official explained to a reporter the new U.S. strategy of improving the image of the United States overseas. "We have to be as good at listening as we are at proposing our point of view," in order, she continued, to bring Muslims to an "understanding that they don't need to kill us to get our attention."[64] The person making the statement was not a State Department careerist, but rather famed advertising executive Charlotte Beers, whom Powell hired, as he testified to Congress, at least in part because "she got me to buy Uncle Ben's rice."[65] The Madison Avenue prodigy produced commercials that told Muslims around the world that Muslims in the United States were free to practice their religion—as if that was the source of the hatred many Muslims harbor for the U.S. Absent from the campaign was any effort to promote American ideals of freedom and individual liberty.

Although the strategy was designed by Beers, it was embraced by Foggy Bottom's careerists. They sincerely believed that the "image problems" the United States suffered could be fixed with television and radio commercials and glossy publications. But looking at the treatment of the Iraqi National Congress and the Iranian dissidents—comparing that to State's embrace of Saddam Hussein in the late 1980s or its handling of the early years of the Taliban—it is not hard to surmise that at least part of why the United States is despised in many quarters is because it often fails to embody its own values.

For State Department bureaucrats who lobby Congress on behalf of ruthless regimes wishing to avoid sanctions, while at the same time obstructing the efforts of American parents to recover their children who have been abducted to foreign lands, American principles of liberty and justice are but a distant memory, mere obstacles to maintaining "stability." No wonder Foggy Bottom's top executives and career staff didn't raise any eyebrows after Beers explained that her quest to "rebrand" the United States was "almost as though we have to redefine what America is."[66] The real problem, of course, is that State long ago "redefined" what America is—at least in the minds of people around the world who have seen the results of State's stability-driven foreign policy.

8

Visas: Everywhere Terrorists Want Them to Be

★ *"THE 'BLACK' ONE IS EASIER."*[1]

I n an April 1996 article in the *Beijing Chronicle* about the visa section at the U.S. embassy in Beijing, the "'black' one" was not identified by name, but every embassy employee who read the article knew exactly which worker the story described: Charles Parish, the only African-American working in the visa section at the time.

Parish, an athletic and engaging former Marine in his fifties, was possibly the most popular American in Beijing. He was constantly invited to banquets, made regular trips to the United States with Chinese citizens, was known for always having a comely Chinese woman twenty or thirty years his junior on his arm—and received hundreds of e-mails in his two years in China from Chinese nationals grateful for receiving visas to the U.S.

Although Parish was never charged with any crime, his alleged behavior was so egregious that an accounting of it will leave almost

161

any reader breathless. When a congressional committee—a small handful of staffers, actually—conducted a several-month-long investigation in 1999, the evidence unearthed was startling. The resulting 328-page report—whose details have never been reported by a major media outlet—paints a picture of a State Department that wasn't simply inept, but reckless. (Parish himself took the Fifth.) It is a case that goes beyond mere money but encompasses sex, lies, and threats to national security. But the scariest aspect of the story is how well it captures the inner workings of Foggy Bottom's culture.

The *Beijing Chronicle* article, of which all the officers at the embassy were aware,[2] was not the first indication that something was amiss. Junior Foreign Service officers (FSOs) who worked under Parish, the head of the nonimmigrant visa division, told congressional investigators that Parish overturned, on average, three to four refusals per week—and that was for *each* of his subordinates. (FSOs are in charge of determining who does and does not receive a visa to come to the United States.) While superiors overturning refusals issued by junior FSOs is not unheard of, it is uncommon. But when it does happen, the supervisor usually cites a reason for doing so on the visa application. Parish never did.

Parish's inability to follow accepted practice became so problematic that the embassy started requiring a written explanation for each refusal that was overturned, implemented solely because "Parish so frequently overturned junior officers' rejections without explanation."[3] And Parish's habit of granting visas to young, attractive women—some of whom had been earlier rejected by a different FSO—only to then engage in "personal relations with them"[4] also became something of a sticking point for workers at the embassy.

The complaints about Parish came early, and were repeated often. Barely two months into Parish's tenure—in early 1995—junior FSOs conveyed their concerns to the consul general, Parish's direct supervisor. But those warnings went unheeded. Far from being merely ignored, the congressional report noted, "People who tried to complain about Parish were 'squashed.'"[5] Donald Schurman, who eventually conducted a half-hearted and ham-handed investigation of Parish, admitted to congressional investigators that "he heard early on in his tenure [he started in February 1995] that Parish was easy to get visas from, especially if you were a young, attractive woman."[6] He also conceded that he was aware of the allegations against Parish and even about the *Beijing Chronicle* article in April 1996, but "he did not find these matters troubling, and he did not look into them."[7] This was curious, especially considering that Parish had been suspected of fraud at his two previous postings in the early 1990s in Bangladesh and Nepal.[8]

After a while, it became harder and harder to ignore Parish's actions. David Chen of the Chinese-American Association wrote a letter to ambassador James Sasser on September 28, 1995, urging him to investigate and stop the selling of visas in the embassy.[9] Parish's habit of receiving gifts had become so notorious that "junior officers would joke that Parish's office looked like a gift shop. Parish was quite open about receiving gifts from the Chinese," the report noted. Concerns about Parish finally found a receptive audience in the deputy chief of mission (DCM), Scott Hallford, the embassy's number two official. Junior FSOs—who generally have no effective contact with someone so much higher in the hierarchy—had dinner with Hallford in April 1996 (the same month of the *Beijing Chronicle* article), where they aired their laundry list of grievances.[10]

Hallford had no choice but to act. He ordered Donald Schurman, the embassy's regional security officer (RSO), who is primarily responsible for protection of embassy personnel, to conduct an investigation. While Parish was away on one of his many vacations, Schurman sealed Parish's office and changed the locks.[11] He sent a cable to Diplomatic Security—State's law enforcement division—in Washington requesting assistance. None came. Schurman—who was also responsible for overseeing protection of personnel at four consulates and two embassies between China and Mongolia—spent a "few weekends" and "some evenings" working on the investigation, but it was far from thorough. He didn't formally interview embassy staff—and consequently missed some rather important clues, such as the witnesses who told Congress that "Parish had been in his office shortly before the investigation began, shredding documents."[12] Asked by congressional investigators why he never searched Parish's apartment as part of his investigation, Schurman told them that it was too much of a "touchy matter."[13]

Schurman discovered a treasure trove of goodies in Parish's office, from e-mails sent by various Chinese citizens thanking him for his "help" in obtaining visas to the vast array of gifts he had received from grateful locals. But the RSO got frustrated investigating a case no one in Washington seemed to care much about. Such neglect made it easier for him to give in to demands from embassy staff to free up Parish's office space. So, aside from a huge stack of e-mail correspondence between Parish and visa recipients, some original visa applications, and a few other items, the RSO threw everything else out.[14] The visa applications Parish had kept in his office ended up being destroyed as well because, Schurman told congressional investigators, "the investigation appeared to be going nowhere."[15] Since most of the evidence was trashed, any future investigation seemed useless. Schurman "never conducted an inventory of what was in the office, and he never photographed the office."[16]

Using his renowned gift for understatement, Peter Bergin—then the director of Diplomatic Security—testified at a congressional hearing, "In my view, with 20/20 hindsight, this was not a model investigation."[17] But the blame is not just Schurman's. Nobody else seemed to want the case to go anywhere, either. Shortly before Schurman left the embassy in October 1997, officials from the Office of the Inspector General, the auditing arm of State, were visiting as part of a regular check-up. The RSO decided to show the visitors the documents he had collected the previous year. "They recoiled when [Schurman] showed them a box of documents."[18]

It was unfortunate that State's internal watchdog division—which is home to some dogged investigators—was so averse to the prospect of looking into Parish's conduct. If OIG auditors had done so, they probably would have uncovered something Congress did in the course of its investigation: when Parish was staying at a posh hotel in Norwalk, California—owned by a major Chinese (state-owned) corporation whose employees Parish often helped receive visas—a cleaning lady found stacks of cash in the room totaling approximately $10,000.[19] This from a man who at the time was making less than $70,000 per year. Though it is possible the money could have belonged to one of the two young, attractive Chinese women staying with him in the same room, Congress found no such evidence.

In the past, Parish had managed to wriggle out of tough spots with bizarre excuses. He tried a few when Schurman began his investigation. When he was questioned by Schurman about his many "contacts" in the local community, he explained that it was his way of "saying that he was interested in Chinese students, photography, art, and was trying to keep in touch with what was going on in Chinese history."[20] As for the gifts, Parish told Schurman that, yes, he had accepted gifts, but he justified doing so by saying that he *had* to accept them.[21] It was a little tougher to explain away his storage of hundreds of original visa applications—a serious violation of protocol. Parish's excuse for the ethical no-no was that he was holding on to the files as a "kind of anti-fraud tracking device."[22] Which might make sense, because Parish, as the cat guarding the mouse cage, was in charge of the embassy's anti-fraud unit, and according to a performance evaluation, his job was to "reinvigorate the anti-fraud program."[23]

But his lucky streak finally came to an end—temporarily, anyway. Even with the bungled investigation, Parish was too much of a liability to stay at the embassy. Though he was reluctant at first to fire Parish, ambassador Sasser was convinced by Hallford and Schurman that he had no other option.[24] But firing a member of the Foreign Service can only be done by the Foreign Service Grievance Board, an administrative panel in Washington consisting of high-ranking Foreign Service officials. So Sasser did the only thing he could do: he forced Parish to "curtail" his assignment in May 1996.

"Curtailing" is peculiar to the Foreign Service, wherein someone who voluntarily leaves a posting or is forced out has three months to find a new assignment. Parish told the Los Angeles Times—one of the only newspapers to write about the Parish affair in any depth, though it did not cover in any detail the 328-page congressional report—that he thought his diplomatic career was over.[25] While in the real world his prediction would have been correct, not so at State. Parish, in fact, got a promotion. And he would get four more raises before he voluntarily retired three years later.

Parish probably shouldn't have been that surprised that he landed a plush new job in Washington less than a month after leaving Beijing. He was, after all, a true believer in State's "courtesy culture." As one of his former co-workers told Congress, "Parish generally thought that leniency was the best policy with visa issuance."[26] The internal forces at Foggy Bottom are such that those who conform get promoted, and those who do not get punished—almost irrespective of other factors, such as allegations of rampant fraud.

But almost from the moment Parish started his new gig in Washington, the allegations kept pouring in. At a May 30, 1996, dinner just outside of Beijing, a parade of Chinese government officials and businessmen told an embassy official that "'everyone knew' that it was 'very easy' to get a nonimmigrant visa from U.S. embassy Beijing," according to an unclassified June 5 memo addressed to

Hallford, the deputy chief of mission. The memo continued, "The Chinese said that if... you were applying for a visa allowing you to work in the United States but you did not speak English — you simply took 'the black official' in the embassy to dinner, gave him a 'gift,' and you were guaranteed a visa."[27] Parish was the only African-American in the visa section.

In March 1998, Cynthia Bushman of the Chinese firm Velur Investments visited Parish's successor, Dennis Halpin. She told him that she wanted to work with the embassy on getting visas for Velur employees, but she wanted to do everything "above board and follow proper procedures, especially after what happened with your predecessor [Parish]."[28] The confused embassy official pressed Bushman about what she meant. After she sensed he still didn't understand what she was getting at, she spelled it out for him, literally: "visas for S-E-X."[29] The memo in which Halpin informed his superiors of the incident had an interesting subject line: "*Another* Report on Past Visa Malfeasance."[30] (emphasis added) But even the flurry of new allegations did not damage Parish's career.

Yet Parish was not just promoted — he was exalted. And he was showered in glory even in Beijing while being the subject of widespread accusations of fraud.

In an April 1996 performance evaluation, Parish's direct supervisor gushed, "Mr. Parish understands the nonimmigrant visa process as well as any officer in the Foreign Service."[31] In a nod to the many Chinese girlfriends Parish was known to have — a violation of embassy rules if such relationships are unreported, which his were — the same superior simply wrote, "Mr. Parish has a wide circle of friends and contacts in the Chinese community."[32] This official had been the one to whom the junior FSOs had complained for sixteen months about Parish's conduct, but there was no mention of those concerns.

At around the same time as Hallford, the DCM, had learned of the specific allegations of fraud and malfeasance, he penned a glowing performance review of Parish. Hallford praised the former Marine for his "deft diplomatic touch" and wrote that a "significant portion" of visa applications were now met with "same-day issuance."[33] The only negative information in the otherwise exemplary evaluation was an oblique reference to the allegations of rampant fraud, something he oddly characterized as merely a "distinct difference in philosophy on visa issuance."[34] Parish, for his part, noted in his self-evaluation that his "greatest accomplishment was to continue to [sic] the process of improving service to the Chinese public."

As thousands of Foreign Service officials have learned over the years, performance evaluations—the marker by which careers are catapulted or killed—are frequently extremely polarized. The evaluations are either exceedingly bland (the equivalent of dismal in a world where no reviewer wants to risk being subjected to a grievance complaint) or, as in Parish's case, sterling. Halpin, Parish's successor in Beijing, found out what life could be like for someone who did not willingly comply with the edicts of the "courtesy culture."

After he implemented a number of reforms aimed at cleaning up his predecessor's mess, Halpin was threatened with the possibility of early retirement (of the involuntary variety).[35] At around the same time—and days before the "visas for S-E-X" allegation was made—Parish was nominated for a "Meritorious Honor Award" for his "exceptional teamwork, dedication, and achievement."[36] Two months later, he was given the award.

In Washington, where he worked in the visa office, Parish received yet another immaculate review, this time on April 15, 1997. The reviewer explains, "Parish indeed deserves high praise" for his "innovative solutions" and his ability to "use relationships to get what we need."[37] The reviewer further lauds Parish, noting that the man who had operated under a cloud of suspicion for years was in fact a man with "a strength of character that is unusual." Parish is described as a "swamp-drainer," a man who attacks "fundamental management problems" rather than "the symptoms—the alligators." "Problems are reduced," the reviewer writes, "when 'Crocodile' Parish is running the show."[38]

What was this job in the visa office where Parish earned such accolades?

In the opinion of the then-head of Consular Affairs, Mary Ryan, it was one in which "there was no way he could do anything wrong."[39] But according to that April 1997 performance review, Parish was in "an office fraught with sensitive issues and cases, the Middle East account," which the reviewer noted is the "region that has more active terrorist threats than any other." Parish's specific duties in this office were remarkable given the torrent of accusations and charges of fraud. He was responsible for "the handling of the most sensitive visa applications, those from persons suspected of terrorism, espionage, or other serious threats to U.S. national interests."[40]

VISA FRAUD, UNINTERRUPTED

As outlandish as the Parish case is, it is by no means an isolated example of visa fraud going unpunished. In most of those cases, embassies or consulates are only interested in making the problems go away—literally. According to an administration official, visa fraud investigations regularly result in transfers or retirements, not prosecutions.[41] In 1999, an *L.A. Times* study came to the same conclusion.[42] That article found that in the decade between 1989–1999, only one U.S. diplomat was prosecuted for visa fraud—and that resulted in a 1997 acquittal. Sometimes the suspected perpetrator is an American like Parish, but often a foreigner working at the post is involved—and then the hands of Diplomatic Security (DS) are tied. According to a former top DS official, Foreign Service Nationals (FSNs)—foreigners who work at U.S. embassies or consulates in the countries where they live—who commit visa fraud are generally only fired. Prosecution is left up to local authorities, who often choose not to pursue the cases.[43]

Even with particularly rampant fraud, perpetrators can operate undetected for years. Over a period of two years, Thomas Carroll, an American, ran a massive fraud racket in Guyana, one that was enforced by "death squads" used to intimidate witnesses. Handling some 3,600 visas, Carroll sold up to eight hundred visas for $10,000–$15,000 each, netting over $4 million in profit.[44] At least twenty-six of the people who received visas from Carroll committed crimes in the United States, ranging from disorderly conduct to gang rape. The only reason Carroll was caught is that he attempted to recruit his successor, Benedict Wolfe, to carry on his scheme. Unfortunately for Carroll, Wolfe chose instead to work with the authorities. Carroll was sentenced in June 2002 to twenty-one years in jail.

Operating out of the Jeddah consulate in Saudi Arabia, Abdullah Noman sold some fifty to one hundred visas to local residents. A Yemeni national and Saudi resident, Noman managed to sell visas for five years—from September 1996 until November 2001—before getting caught. Because he was arrested while on vacation in Las Vegas—where he was still busy selling visas—Noman had to face his punishment in the U.S. court system. He pleaded guilty in May 2002 to accepting bribes.[45] Although prosecutors adamantly deny that Noman sold visas to anyone connected with terrorism, officials were not able to track down every person to whom Noman issued a visa. His sentence? Noman received only two years of "supervised release."[46]

Visa fraud is often allowed to continue unabated because of the "see no evil" approach of top officials at some consulates and embassies. Each post can vary considerably in terms of willingness to look into potential malfeasance, and in many stations, fraud is something not to confront, but to ignore. Upon arriving at his new assignment at the U.S. consulate in Montreal, Canada, in 2000, a consular officer was disturbed by the lack of procedures to ferret out possible fraud. When he went to his superior and asked why, the supervisor responded, "There's no fraud in Montreal." The new consular officer agreed that none had been detected, but he pointed out there were no checks in the process to determine if fraud had occurred. The supervisor, not amused, repeated his response: "There's no fraud in Montreal." The frustrated Foreign Service officer persisted for a few more minutes, but to no avail. His boss closed the conversation by reiterating, "There's no fraud in Montreal."[47]

AN AMERICAN IN QATAR

U.S. officials in the embassy in Doha, Qatar, faced allegations of fraud occurring right under their noses, and they responded—by doing nothing. DS officials later learned that over seventy visas were sold in Qatar from July 2000 to May 2001. But a formal investigation was not launched until two months after September 11—six months after the fraud had ended. The buyers were mostly Jordanians and Pakistanis, and three of them had ties to the September 11 terrorists. Had DS known earlier, those ties to al Qaeda might have yielded important clues about the September 11 attacks. But DS didn't know until later. The same cannot be said, however, for officials at the embassy.

Word on the street—in the cafés, actually, where the best "chatter" in Qatar can be found—was that visas were for sale at the embassy in Doha. Locals in the cafés claimed people were getting their visas for 50,000 Qatari riyals, or about 13,000 American dollars. One American, John Aalders—an entrepreneur who had become quite successful in his decade living in Qatar—didn't believe the rumors when he first heard them in March 2001.[48] But a contact of his in the Qatari Ministry of the Interior told Aalders that it was "common knowledge" that such fraud was going on.

As a former soldier and law enforcement officer, Aalders knew that embassy officials would be grateful to receive a warning about possible fraud, or so he thought. Aalders tried five times to contact three different U.S. officials over the course of two months. When he did get a response—from an official secretary—Aalders was told, "There's no corruption at the embassy." The last time he tried to warn the embassy was in late May 2001, but he finally gave up. Aalders eventually spoke with DS officials after their investigation became public, but he is frustrated he couldn't do more, sooner. "I feel like I let my country down. But what was I supposed to do?" he asks.[49]

THE TERROR VISAS

Although he had received a visa in 1997 to study English at the ELS Language Center in Melbourne, Florida, Hani Honjour was denied a visa in September 2000. Considering how he filled in the application, the refusal should not have come as a surprise. Hanjour requested a travel visa for a "visit," for three years. An unidentified employee at the U.S. consulate in Jeddah, Saudi Arabia, likely a Foreign Service national (a Saudi resident), highlighted the obvious problem: Honjour had stated a desire to overstay his visa—the maximum length for a travel visa is twenty-four months—with a three-year "visit." The unknown employee wrote in the comment box: "like to stay three years or more!" and circled the remark. That employee or a different one also scribbled something underneath about Hanjour's wish to find a flight school during the trip.

Determined to get a visa, Hanjour filed a second application two weeks later, and this time he came prepared with all the right answers. He gave a specific address, complete with a house number and street name in Oakland, California. This time, Hanjour applied for a twelve-month student visa, and changed the purpose of his visit to "study" and the desired length of stay to a more appropriate "one year." So many changes, all of which "fixed" the problem areas on the original application, should have raised red flags. They didn't. On September 25, 2000, Hanjour got his visa to come to the United States. Almost a year later, on September 11, 2001, Honjour helped hijack American Airlines Flight 77, which he then piloted into the Pentagon.

Honjour was not the only September 11 terrorist who should not have been in the United States on September 11, 2001. Six different current and former consular officers who analyzed the visa applications—obtained exclusively by this author—of fifteen of the nineteen hijackers (the forms of the other four had been destroyed) all agreed that not one of them should have qualified for a visa. The reasons varied, but mostly, the applications were lacking basic necessary information. Without that information—such as employment, financial resources, U.S. destination, and purpose for travel—a consular officer cannot, under the law, issue the visa because all applicants are considered ineligible until they prove otherwise. But that didn't stop consular officers in Saudi Arabia from issuing legal visas to people whose applications should have been denied.

The consular officers who granted the visas to the September 11 terrorists, however, were simply following orders. From 1993 on, under the direction of then-head of Consular Affairs Mary Ryan, consular officers were indoctrinated in the "courtesy culture," which—in the name of "customer service"—generated relentless pressure, both from Washington and their direct supervisors, to issue as many visas as quickly as possible. The consular officers, in other words, were strongly discouraged from strictly enforcing the law, particularly in a "preferred" country like Saudi Arabia. Mary Ryan personally wanted Saudis to receive quick and easy visas,[50] leading her to appoint a trusted ally, Thomas P. Furey, as consul general in Riyadh. Furey was known by colleagues for his catchphrase, "People gotta have their visas." During Furey's tenure heading up the consular function in Saudi Arabia from summer 2000 to fall 2001, fourteen of the September 11 terrorists got their visas.

The terrorists' visas should have been denied because of a provision in the law known as 214(b), which holds that almost all non-immigrant visa applicants are presumed to be would-be immigrants. In other words, the law says the burden to prove eligibility is on the applicant, who must convince the consular officer that he is qualified to receive one. The law is clear: "Every alien [except in narrowly exempted subcategories] shall be presumed to be an immigrant until he establishes to the satisfaction of the consular officer, at the time of application for a visa...that he is entitled to a nonimmigrant [visa]." Around the world, 214(b) is the most common reason cited for visa refusals, accounting for roughly three-quarters of all denials. It is intended to be a high threshold to overcome. An applicant must prove he has the financial means (so that he isn't using the visa to get a better job in the United States), ties to his country of residence (house, spouse, and/or employment), and that the stated purpose is both legitimate and the actual reason for the trek to the U.S. But despite falling short on any or all of those requirements, all of the September 11 terrorists—aside from Honjour—received their visas without a hitch on their first attempt.

Although applicants are required to demonstrate means of financial support—through employment or bank statements—few of the terrorists did so. Most listed their present occupation as "student." Salem al Hamzi simply wrote "unemployed," while Khalid al Midhar cryptically referred to himself as a "businessman." For the question, "Who will furnish financial support?" most of them answered, "myself," while the rest listed family—but none offered any proof, as required by law, that they actually could afford the intended travel.

More startling is the utter lack of specific U.S. destinations provided by the terrorists, save for Honjour on his second attempt. Applicants theoretically are supposed to list this information to help the Immigration and Naturalization Service to track someone down in the United States, but the practical purpose is to help consular officers determine the legitimacy of the stated purpose for the visa. But aside from Honjour on his second try, the terrorists listed such destinations as "California," "New York," "Hotel D.C.," and "Hotel." Amazingly, one terrorist listed his U.S. destination as "No." Even more amazingly, he got his visa.

Some of the applications were simply undecipherable. Take, for example, the applications of the brothers Wail and Waleed al-Shehri. Wail listed his occupation as "teater," while his brother claimed to be a "student," and both declared the name and address of their employer or school as simply "South City." Each also wrote a U.S. destination of "Wasantwn." It was not clear if Wail was a "teacher" or in "theater" and it was likewise unclear whether he and his brother were headed to Washington State, Washington, D.C., or some small town actually named "Wasantwn." Neither made clear how a student and his nominally employed brother were embarking on a four-to-six-month vacation, paid for by Wail's "teater" salary, which he presumably would be foregoing while on holiday. And because standard operating procedure in Saudi Arabia was not to request financial statements or other supplementary proof, the consular officer likely did not even attempt to determine whether Wail in fact had the financial means to fund the "vacation."

According to a study from the General Accounting Office (GAO)—an independent government auditor—the September 11 terrorists received the same red carpet treatment that was extended to other Saudi visa applicants before and *after* September 11, 2001. GAO investigators, who investigated the same visa applications of the September 11 terrorists as this author, found that the law putting the burden of proof on applicants had been turned on its head in Saudi Arabia. "Consular officers in Saudi Arabia issued visas to most Saudi applicants [before September 11] without interviewing them, requiring them to complete their applications, or providing supporting documentation," the report states.[51] Even after September 11, State did very little to change the visa procedures. This was glaringly obvious with State's insistence on keeping Visa Express open until July 2002—and only shutting it down then because of tremendous public pressure.

The GAO report also caught State in a lie. Throughout summer 2002, State had insisted to any reporter who would listen that twelve of the fifteen Saudi terrorists had in fact been interviewed before receiving their visas. It was a bizarre argument to make, but the point State was trying to get across was that even interviews don't help screen out terrorists—although the real lesson from such a "fact" is that interviews as conducted by employees of State don't work. But in the end, twelve of the fifteen Saudis were *not* interviewed. In fact, the GAO report found that "Consular officers granted visas to thirteen of these fifteen Saudi and Emirati hijackers without an interview."[52] (One of the fifteen visa applications reviewed by this author and GAO was that of someone from the UAE, and the other fourteen were those of Saudis.) Under the law, consular officers were required to call the applicants in for an interview, if for no other reason than to fill in missing, incomplete, or vague information on the applications. The GAO report, however, found that none of the eighteen applications completed by the fifteen terrorists had even been properly filled out.[53]

COURTESY CULTURE

The reason why actions that should attract tremendous attention don't—think of the Parish affair or of how easily Saudis slipped into the U.S. prior to September 11—is that they don't seem that unusual in light of how the whole system operates. Visa Express is a telling illustration. Although there was justifiable public uproar after the details of the program came to light, the GAO report shows that the standards before Visa Express were almost as lax.

More than anything else, what Visa Express did was insert a new opportunity for fraud and other mischief, such as travel agents helping applicants beat the system. Standards were already so low they effectively couldn't have been lowered any more. The consular officer who issued visas to ten of the terrorists—she was stationed in Jeddah—told government investigators that she would not have issued visas to most, if any, of them had she not been instructed to presume that all Saudi applicants were eligible to receive a visa.[54]

It wasn't just Saudi Arabia where the law was inverted so that applicants were presumed eligible; it happened at posts throughout the world. In some countries—poor countries, to be exact—visa refusal rates are quite high, and getting a visa is notoriously difficult. But in countries where oil flows freely or there's wealth for other reasons, visas are surprisingly easy to obtain. That's not speculation or conjecture—that was State's written policy. Referring to the role of travel agents in programs like Visa Express, Consular Affairs (CA) issued a regulation stating, "If the travel agency is reasonably satisfied that the traveler has the means to buy a tour 'package,' there will be little further evaluation of the applicant's qualifications."[55]

Becoming confused about whom the Foreign Service was supposed to be serving, Mary Ryan directed CA to focus primarily on "customer service." The "customer" in question, of course, was not the U.S. taxpayer, but the foreign visa applicants. More specifically, the real "customers" State sought to serve were those with money. "If you're a drug smuggler from Sweden, your chances of getting in are almost one hundred percent. If you're a perfectly responsible, God-fearing person from Guatemala, your chances of getting in are maybe ten percent," says Wayne Merry, a former consular officer.

Part of the motivation was State's inherent desire to please its "clients"—nothing makes a foreign government happier than easy access for its citizens to the United States—as well as to do the same for U.S. commercial interests, which directly benefit from enhanced travel and tourism in America. In a post–September 11 world, however, it became quickly apparent that al Qaeda typically recruited people from relatively well-off backgrounds with no criminal records—precisely the people who would gain de facto automatic admission under the "courtesy culture." That State wanted to expand business and commerce pre–September 11 is in many respects understandable, inasmuch as so many other sections of the U.S. government had the same goal. But that State violated the law in order to do so is much less forgivable. That State did not change its reckless policies after the worst terrorist attacks in U.S. history, though, is unforgivable.

The courtesy culture was so deeply ingrained in the Foggy Bottom psyche that even after State realized that all nineteen of the September 11 terrorists came to the U.S. on legal visas, very little changed—and that's according to State's own watchdog agency, the Office of the Inspector General. In a December 2002 report, the OIG wrote, "The post-September 11 era should have witnessed immediate and dramatic changes in CA's direction of the visa process. This has not happened."[56] All applicants before and after September 11 had their names run through the applicable terrorist watch lists, but that is little protection when the applicants have clean records. A program called Visas Viper was designed to identify possible terrorists or other criminal types who do not have rap sheets. It was virtually non-existent at many posts before September 11, including in Saudi Arabia. Even after September 11, CA has sent out many cables to consulates and embassies expressing concern that Visas Viper has not been fully implemented at posts around the world.[57]

Not only is State doing a lackluster job of identifying possible terrorists, it is actually fighting for the rights of both suspected terrorists and advocates of terrorism to get visas to come to the United States.

VISAS FOR SUSPECTED TERRORISTS

Deputy Secretary of State Richard Armitage wrote a letter to his counterpart at the Justice Department, Larry D. Thompson, arguing that finding that a visa applicant was a possible terrorist was, in some cases, not enough to deny that person a visa. The Justice Department's Foreign Terrorist Tracking Task Force (FTTTF) had made what it probably considered a common-sense recommendation: deny visas to those who are suspected terrorists. State, Armitage pointed out, didn't see things quite the same way. His response: "Unfortunately, the information we have received from FTTTF so far has been insufficient to permit a consular officer to deny a visa. The information we have received states only that the FTTTF believes the applicants may pose a threat to national security and therefore the FTTTF recommends against issuance."[58] Armitage further explained, "[believing that] an applicant may pose a threat to national security... is insufficient [grounds] for a consular officer to deny a visa." This letter was on June 10, 2002—one day shy of the nine-month anniversary of the September 11 attacks.

State won the initial rounds of this fight with Justice. According to the GAO report discussed earlier, consular officers issued visas—intentionally—to seventy-nine people in fiscal year 2001 whose names were "true matches" to those on the TIPOFF terrorist watch list (which has a comparably lower threshold by which names are added), because State "determined there was insufficient information linking [the applicants] to terrorism."[59]

Those visas, however, should never have been issued. As noted above, the law is very clear that all applicants for visas are presumed ineligible, until they prove their own eligibility. Those who favor looser interpretations of 214(b), however, argue that the law should be read to apply only for socio-economic purposes—meaning to keep out those people who are likely to "overstay" their visas and become immigrants to the United States. So, the theory goes, once someone is eligible on those grounds, the ball is back in State's court. If there is no reason grounded in the law at that point to keep out an applicant, State's argument continues, that person must be issued the visa. Hence Armitage wrote, "[I]f there are no grounds under the law on which to deny an alien a visa, the consular officer is required to issue a visa." But even if that were true—which it is not—State could still keep out anyone it wants to, because denials of visas cannot be appealed in court. That said, the law is obviously on Justice's side. Suspected terrorists can—not to mention should—be denied visas simply for being suspected of having ties to terrorism.

A quick glance at the law debunks Armitage's disturbing argument. The Immigration and Naturalization Act clearly states: "[If] a consular officer knows, or has reasonable ground to believe, [an alien] is engaged in, or is likely to engage after entry, in any terrorist activity," the officer can deny the visa to the alien. Of course, State's legal theory uses as fig leaf cover the notion that "suspicion" of terrorism is not a "reasonable ground" for belief that a visa applicant might engage in terrorist activity. But if September 11 was not enough to make such suspicion reasonable, what is?

IDEOLOGICAL EXCLUSION

If someone is not necessarily a suspected terrorist, but is known as a fiery advocate of terrorism who hurls choice catchphrases such as "Death to America," he *cannot* be denied a visa for his "speech." The glaring loophole has a surprisingly innocuous name: "Ideological Exclusion." To be fair, it was slipped in by Senator Ted Kennedy in 1990 to ensure a visa for the political leader of the Irish Republican Army, but State does have the power under that very provision to shut the door on advocates of terrorism. For more than a year after September 11, State has refused to do so.

Under "Ideological Exclusion," someone cannot be denied a visa unless he has actively aided a terrorist organization or if he gives the consular officer a reason—aside from actually advocating terrorism—to believe that he might commit a terrorist act once in the United States. This is written into State's regulations based on the Immigration and Nationality Act. Under the shocking subheading, "Advocacy of Terrorism Not Generally Exclusionary" is this: "Advocating terrorism through oral or written statements is usually not a sufficient ground for finding an applicant ineligible" for a visa, "no matter how offensive [that support of terrorism] may be." That chilling passage is not law as written by Congress, but regulations as written by State.

It is instructive of State's mindset that even after three thousand Americans were killed in one day, State still considers advocacy of terrorism merely "offensive."

INTRANSIGENCE

Every institution, whether governmental or otherwise, is driven, to a certain extent, by inertia. But what distinguishes Foggy Bottom is the degree to which it dominates the culture. Just as State wants the world to look as it always has, it wants to act as it always has. In short, State is in denial that the world forever changed the moment four hijacked planes were the instruments of the murders of three thousand innocent Americans. It should have shut down Visa Express on September 12, 2001. It didn't. State could have simply acceded to the wishes of the Justice Department that all suspected terrorists be denied visas. It didn't. State could have used its authority under the law to end the dangerous loophole that allows advocates of terrorism—under the cover of "free speech"—to get visas. It didn't.

Even in the face of intense congressional criticism, State stood firm in its defense of Visa Express throughout the post–September 11 period until mid-July 2002. It only caved when Congress was about to take away State's cherished visa power altogether—so State cut off its finger to save its hand. But State never admitted it was wrong to establish and maintain Visa Express.

Ignoring ongoing problems is the first step; pretending the problems don't exist completes the cycle of intransigence. Consular officers in Saudi Arabia followed orders to presume all Saudi nationals eligible for visas, and consequently ignored the scores of red flags. When those visa applications were sitting in Washington, the head of CA didn't even care to look at them. For at least three months after she was tapped to replace Mary Ryan as CA chief, Maura Harty had not read the visa applications of the September 11 terrorists.[60] Harty was acting in accordance with State's overall approach to September 11. The GAO report found that State never formally interviewed the consular officers who issued visas to the terrorists, including the one who issued visas to ten of the hijackers.

Not only does State show no remorse for its actions in granting visas to the September 11 terrorists, it seems to think those actions merit praise—and bonuses. In October 2002, after State announced bonuses of $10,000–$15,000 each for four of the top five officials at Consular Affairs for "outstanding performance" in a twelve-month period that included September 11, State's spokesman lost his cool when this author raised the issue at a daily press briefing. When asked, "What exactly about that constitutes a track record of outstanding performance worthy of these bonuses?" the following exchange ensued:

> *Mr. Boucher:* I want to stop this right here. You've said things that I disagree with and I've said things that you disagree with. I have not gone after your paycheck.
>
> *Question:* I'm not going after yours.
>
> *Mr. Boucher:* I have not gone after—I got one of these bonuses.
>
> *Question:* Congratulations.
>
> *Mr. Boucher:* Thank you.
>
> *Question:* I wasn't questioning whether you deserved one.

Mr. Boucher: I have not said that you didn't deserve to be paid for your services. I didn't say that you didn't deserve to be paid for your articles or your appearances.

Question: Now, Richard, I'm not making this personal.

Mr. Boucher: And I'm not going to do it now.

Question: I did not go after you—

Mr. Boucher: You're attacking friends of mine, people who dedicate their lives to their government and their country.

Question: They are government officials. They owe a certain responsibility to the country.

Mr. Boucher: People who dedicate their lives to their government and their country.

Question: That's fine, but they don't have—they don't owe accountability?

Mr. Boucher: If you want to talk about the GAO report, we'll talk about the GAO report, but I'm not going to talk about whether or not they deserve their bonuses. It's an established procedure. It's done very carefully by the government. It's done under an open set of rules that have been around for a long time. If you want to question those rules, you can go question those rules. *But don't question whether these individuals deserved them or not.* (emphasis added)

When backed into a corner after news broke in October 2002 that at least fifteen, if not all, of the nineteen September 11 terrorists never should have gotten their visas if the law had been followed, Boucher reluctantly acknowledged, "Mistakes were made." That was the public face, as conciliatory a tone as State used when discussing the terrorists' visas. Behind closed doors, however, State officials tried to justify the steadfast refusal to follow the law before September 11. At a briefing for approximately two dozen congressional staffers in the midst of the controversy, officials from State stressed that the "mistakes" were "understandable."[61] One wonders what part of intentionally violating the law State considers "understandable."

9

Justice Denied

★ *"YOU SAW WHAT WE DID TO CHIMINYA."*

D uring the run-up to the June 2000 elections in Zimbabwe, Minister of Defense Moven Mahachi repeated this reference over and over again in his campaign stump speeches. He would further explain to the crowds, "That's what will happen to you if you vote against ZANU-PF." Tapfuma Chiminya was the national youth organizer for the upstart political party the Movement for Democratic Change (MDC), and his efforts to rouse young voters to oust the sitting government made him a target for the ruling party, the Zimbabwe African National Union Patriotic Front (ZANU-PF).

On April 15, 2000, Chiminya was campaigning for Morgan Tsvangirai, the leader of the MDC—and chief political rival to President Robert Mugabe. Mugabe had ruled Zimbabwe with an iron fist for twenty years, but since the Constitution was still in place, parliamentary elections had to be held—and the MDC was on the verge of defeating the ZANU-PF for control of the legislature. And so Mugabe resorted to the preferred tool of tyrants throughout time: violence. When he was traveling home that day, Chiminya became yet another victim in Mugabe's campaign of terror.

Driving in a red Mazda pickup with two assistants, Talent Mabika and Sanderson Makombe, Chiminya stopped at a gas station as they were heading home after a day of campaigning. Moments later, they noticed a white Nissan—with "ZANU-PF" emblazoned on the side—pull up nearby. Several of the ZANU-PF men approached, and one of them, a Central Intelligence Organization member named Mwale, ripped off Chiminya's shirt. Looking at the MDC logo on the garment he had just grabbed, the ZANU-PF thug indignantly asked, "Who do you think you are?" Then he announced, "Today it is over!" The gang of ZANU-PF operatives began beating Chiminya, Makombe, and Mabika. But the MDC members were lucky; they managed to escape.

After going to the hospital for treatment of their wounds, the three went to the police station to report the crime. Once the report had been filed, Chimanya and his two assistants drove toward home. But because of what had happened earlier, they were followed by a police escort. Just outside of Buhera, in the southeast portion of Zimbabwe, the red Mazda pickup was stopped by a ZANU-PF roadblock. Several MDC supporters who had been stopped there were able to escape—but Chiminya, Makombe, and Mabika did not. They were forced from the vehicle and all three were savagely beaten with metal bars, stones, clenched fists, and booted feet.

As Chiminya was lying on the ground, unconscious, the ZANU-PF squad doused him in gasoline and set him on fire. Mabika was also doused with gasoline and set on fire—while she was conscious. Enveloped in flames, Mabika ran a few yards, and then collapsed. The police officers who had escorted the MDC activists watched the entire event unfold. They did nothing. Both Chiminya and Mabika died that day, though Makombe was able to break free and escape into a bushy area off the road. It is because of his sworn testimony that the story of his friends' deaths can be told.

So when Defense Minister Mahachi warned crowds that if they didn't vote for ZANU-PF candidates that they'd end up like Chiminya, the message was unequivocally clear. At least thirty people died during the ZANU-PF's campaign, yet ZANU-PF barely retained its parliamentary majority. The U.S. State Department, however, condemned the election as neither free nor fair, expressing "concern" about pre-election "violence, intimidation, and harassment."[1] And most of the international community agreed.

But when the time came for the State Department to choose sides in a legal battle between Mugabe and Chiminya's widow, State chose the wrong side.

With Mugabe's iron fist controlling the huge swaths of the police force and the courts, Chiminya's widow, Adella, knew that she could never get justice in Zimbabwe. So she and seven other plaintiffs came to the United States, a land where people enjoy the freedom they desire for their homeland. Using a law that Congress enacted in 1992, the Torture Victim Prevention Act (itself based on the Alien Tort Claims Act of 1789), Adella and seven others—four survivors of Mugabe's torture and three estates of those killed by ZANU-PF—filed a civil suit in federal court in New York. But even though the court was a proper venue to hear the case, Mugabe needed to be served notice—what lawyers call "service of process"—in order for the court to have jurisdiction over the strongman personally.

When it became public that Mugabe was coming to the United Nations' Millennium Celebration in September 2000, the lawyer for Adella and the other family members and victims went before a judge to order the Secret Service—which was providing security for the foreign leader—to serve papers to Mugabe. Arguing on the other side were not lawyers for the tyrant, but lawyers on the payroll of the

U.S. government. At the behest of the State Department, the Justice Department sent its lawyers to convince the judge that the Secret Service should not serve process.[2] In fairness, State had some justification for this move, because of potential problems with deputizing Secret Service agents as process servers. But a direct legal precedent existed, in which a judge ordered the Secret Service to serve court papers to alleged war criminal Radovan Karadzic in 1993.

The judge initially ruled that the Secret Service would have to serve the court notice to Mugabe, but after hours of debate, the judge reversed his decision. Undeterred, Adella and the other plaintiffs hired a private process server, former NYPD officer Larry Martin, who faced the daunting task of physically handing a document to someone surrounded by a Secret Service security detail.

On September 8, 2000, Robert Mugabe—escorted by Nation of Islam leader Minister Louis Farrakhan—was going to Mt. Olivet Baptist Church in Harlem to give a speech soliciting support for the ZANU-PF. In a classic service of process, Martin made his way up to Mugabe, confirmed the Zimbabwean's identity, and announced, "Robert Mugabe, you have been served." Mugabe was handed two different court documents—one for him personally, and one for the political party he heads, ZANU-PF.

Less than two months later, the Zimbabwean Embassy asked State to file an immunity recommendation on behalf of the defendants. State complied. Even though the U.S. Attorneys office in New York would officially file briefs with the court—just as Justice had formally done in the Secret Service hearing—State is granted deference on almost all legal matters involving international issues or foreign parties. In February 2001, State provided the court a "Suggestion of Immunity" letter, which was officially submitted by the U.S. Attorneys office for the southern district of New York.

State offered two different, but related, reasons why both civil lawsuits should be dismissed: head of state immunity and diplomatic immunity. The argument crafted by Foggy Bottom attorneys was that Mugabe enjoyed absolute immunity, meaning that not only could he not sit as a defendant in a civil case in the U.S., but he couldn't even be handed court papers to notify the political party he leads—which everyone agreed did not enjoy immunity—that it was being sued. State had some footing with the former argument, given that Mugabe is, in fact, a head of state. But the notion that he couldn't even receive notice for his political party was without precedent, and considering history, shaky at best.

The doctrine of foreign sovereign immunity—that foreign governments and their leaders cannot be sued in U.S. courts—had long shielded foreign regimes. But in 1952, a year after a landmark British case in the same vein, Jack Tate, the acting legal adviser to the secretary of state, penned the now-famous Tate Letter, which stated that the United States should no longer adhere to absolute immunity for foreign sovereigns in the U.S. Tate noted that the United States had for some time no longer claimed absolute immunity for itself in foreign court systems, so foreign governments and their leaders should not enjoy unqualified protection from lawsuits in the U.S. The letter was an anti-Communist political tool designed to strip Soviet- and Soviet bloc-owned corporations of immunity from lawsuits in the U.S., but it set a new legal course.

More than two decades after the Tate Letter, Congress codified the notion that immunity for foreign sovereigns should be restrictive rather than absolute. At the time, State supported the Foreign Sovereign Immunities Act, and even pushed Congress to take decisions out of its hands. A former State Department official familiar with the history of the sovereign immunity doctrine noted, "Throughout the 1950s and 60s, State would pick and choose who got immunity on the basis of pure politics."[3] By having Congress make immunity a legal rather than a political question, State would no longer face political backlash from an ally for deciding that it did not enjoy immunity in a particular case.

Fast-forward to the year 2001, and State was urging the court to side with Robert Mugabe, even though Mugabe himself didn't present any defense of any kind. It was not that State wanted to curry favor with an increasingly unstable and ruthless despot. Foggy Bottom sincerely believed that a court holding that Mugabe could be sued personally or could be served papers on behalf of his political party would set an unwanted precedent. State claims that it doesn't want U.S. officials being served court papers when they are overseas on diplomatic missions. But this is a hollow argument, a current State Department official points out, given that the U.S. already often pays off foreign victims when there is even a potential lawsuit, and State is constantly prepared for lawsuits against the U.S. in foreign courts.[4]

On July 3, 1988, the USS *Vincennes* mistakenly shot down an Iranian commercial airliner over the Persian Gulf, killing all 290 aboard.[5] It was a profound human tragedy, one for which—despite U.S. claims that the Iranian pilot didn't respond to requests for identification—the U.S. at least appeared to be somewhat responsible. In 1996, on the eve of the eight-year anniversary of the attacks, the U.S. made a payment of $62 million directly to the families.[6] This was not an isolated incident. In November 2002, the U.S. Navy agreed to pay $13 million to the families of thirty-three people on board a Japanese fishing trawler that collided with a submarine that was ascending to surface level.[7] The accident had resulted in the deaths of nine men and boys on February 9, 2001.[8] The November settlement was in addition to $11.47 million the navy had paid in April to a Japanese government entity for the costs of a new ship and other items, such as mental health counseling for the survivors and victims' families.[9]

Knowing that legal issues can arise at any time in any part of the world, State has attorneys on retainer in almost every country, and lawyers on speed dial in the few countries not big enough to warrant retainers.[10] In other words, the United States willingly pays money

to settle civil lawsuits—sometimes doing so before a court case is initiated—on a regular basis. So when State argues that exposing a
tyrant like Mugabe to civil liability—where the only risk is a fine
since it is separate from criminal law—harms U.S. interests overseas,
the claim carries little merit. The real reason, notes a former State
Department official, is that State doesn't want foreign governments
and their leaders exposed to lawsuits in the U.S., so they protect
Mugabe to prevent a legal precedent that might in the future harm
a different foreign sovereign.[11]

In a long, drawn-out opinion that exceeded fifty pages, trial court
judge Victor Marrero gave great weight to the arguments of the survivors and victims' families that said Mugabe was not personally
immune. In the end, however, he ruled in favor of State on that
question, though the tone can generously be described as cautious.

While he found Mugabe couldn't be personally sued by the victims of the torture campaign he directed, Judge Marrero ruled that
the process served on Mugabe was valid as service on ZANU-PF,
meaning that ZANU-PF could be held liable for any damages determined in a trial. The judge noted that even if Mugabe was personally immune, he was not absolutely immune from anything relating
to the U.S. court system. ZANU-PF, everyone agreed, was not
immune from lawsuits, so the only legal question was whether
Mugabe receiving service of process could be considered acceptable
given that he was immune from any potential judgments against him
personally. But since being served papers is procedural—meaning
there's no substantive result to receiving documents—there is no
immunity from being handed documents. In other words, Adella
Chiminya could sue ZANU-PF in U.S. courts to seek justice for her
husband's death.

Alarmed that it had actually lost on one of the two legal issues,
State—through the U.S. Attorneys office—asked the judge to reconsider. But Judge Marrero, himself a State Department veteran having

served as U.S. ambassador to the Organization of American States, upheld his initial ruling. The U.S. government, at State's prompting, then asked to be officially joined as a party to the case, not on behalf of the victims of torture, but on the side of the torturers. State made this move because only a formal party to a case has the right to appeal to a higher court and ZANU-PF had no plans to appeal. In February 2002, Judge Marrero granted the motion to join the U.S. government as a party to the case. According to a former State Department official and a current one, this case marked the first time that the United States government has asked to be added as a party to a case involving a foreign sovereign defendant in U.S. courts.[12]

Because the judge ruled the case against ZANU-PF could go forward, Adella and the other plaintiffs had their day in court—exactly one day, as it happened. During the short trial—ZANU-PF defaulted, so all that had to be done was determine what the political party would have to pay in damages—a series of witnesses took the stand to tell of the horrors they had witnessed or endured.

The court considered Efridah Pfebve's written testimony about a night she will never forget: April 29, 2000. At 6:00 p.m., her mother was preparing dinner for Efridah, her brother Metthew, and her father. They heard the sounds of a large group approaching the house. Looking outside, they saw a lynch mob of some three hundred people wearing ZANU-PF shirts. The Pfebve family knew that the ZANU-PF members were leading the mob because Efridah's brother Elliot was an MDC candidate for Parliament. Armed with axes, spears, sticks, and stones, the group's intentions were clear. The family tried to flee, but the house was quickly surrounded. Efridah's mother escaped to the outhouse out back, but a number of thugs started hurling stones at her. They stopped before the old woman died, however, but only because they thought she was dead. Metthew was punched and hit with stones and sticks, as was his seventy-year-old father. The mob then dragged both men away from the home. When the old man become unconscious, they dropped him; he suffered deep lacerations to his head and two broken fingers. But Metthew was not as fortunate.

The day after the attack, on April 30, 2000, Metthew's lifeless, naked body was found nearly a mile down the road.

The court ordered a $71.6 million damage payment in July 2002, and it was affirmed as the final judgment in December. But State was not content to let this decision stand. At State's urging, the Justice Department filed a notice in February 2003, before the deadline expired, to preserve the U.S. government's right to appeal the ruling. In June 2003, the U.S. government formally appealed on behalf of Mugabe, marking the first time in history that the U.S. government has represented a foreign government or leader in an appeal in U.S. courts.[13] Asks a State Department official, "Isn't the United States supposed to be defending human rights, not human rights abusers?"[14]

DEFENDING CASTRO

A stretch black limo pulled up outside a courthouse in Jacksonville, Florida. Two lawyers stepped out. They were lawyers on the U.S. government's payroll—one worked for the Justice Department and the other for State—and they had come to take part in a case involving international issues. They walked to the courtroom where family members of three Cuban-Americans who had been killed by Cuban dictator Fidel Castro were seeking justice for the 1996 tragedy that claimed the lives of three U.S. citizens and one Cuban national who had not yet become a U.S. citizen.

The lawyers representing the U.S. entered the courtroom, walked up the aisle, and pushed through the mini-door into the area where the court participants sit. They undoubtedly saw the lawyers for the victims sitting on the right side of the aisle, but the U.S. government lawyers sat not on the side of the U.S. citizens, but on the other side.[15]

On February 24, 1996, two small Cessna planes operated by the group Brothers to the Rescue were flying over the treacherous Florida straits searching for Cuban refugees when they were shot down—in international waters—by Cuban MiG fighter jets. All three men aboard the two planes died, and their remains were never found. President Clinton called Castro's act a "flagrant violation of international law."[16] Clinton also called on Congress to allow the victims' families to collect damages from the $180 million in frozen Cuban assets in the United States.[17] Congress sent unmistakable signals that it would do as the president had asked. The United States government was fully behind the families of the men killed by Castro's air force. But that was then.

After Congress cleared the way for the families to sue Castro's regime (more on this later), a federal court in Miami held a three-day trial in 1997. After hearing evidence that the two planes were indeed over international waters—a fact confirmed by a United Nations investigation—the trial then focused on the victims: Armando Alejandre Jr., Carlos Alberto Costa, and Mario Manuel de la Peña. Alejandre was a forty-five-year-old writer who idolized Ernest Hemingway.[18] Costa was a twenty-nine-year-old student of airport operations, described in court papers as a "self-starter." Pena, at twenty-four, was the youngest of the three, and according to court papers, he "never deviated from his goal" of becoming an airline pilot.

The families asked the court for $79.9 million, but Judge James Lawrence King exceeded that request and ordered the Cuban government to pay $187.6 million.[19] But when the victims' families went to collect on the judgments they had won, they ran into a series of dead ends.

After initial attempts to collect money from Castro's frozen assets held by the U.S. Treasury were rebuffed, the families were forced to look elsewhere. Their lawyers were encouraged by Treasury officials to collect from funds that U.S. phone companies pay to Castro as part of a business relationship that started back in 1992.[20] They followed the advice. At the district court—the lowest level in the federal court system—the plaintiffs successfully persuaded the court to release money owed to Castro, and have some of those funds go instead to the victims' families. State, however, did not support the action and appealed. Which brings the story back to the Tallahassee courthouse with the black stretch limo parked out front.

U.S. government attorneys argued to the Eleventh Circuit Court of Appeals that the law did not allow for the plaintiffs to collect money that was owed to Castro—even though U.S. Treasury officials had instructed the families' lawyers to go after those very funds. State, in conjunction with the Justice Department, wanted the money to go directly to Castro, not to the families whose lives had been devastated by the dictator. The U.S. government position prevailed.

The victims' families eventually collected from Castro's frozen assets, but only after overcoming the State Department.

CONGRESS ACTS

The Brothers to the Rescue case galvanized Congress to act. In a legislative body in which even bills with widespread support can languish for years, Congress passed two amendments in 1996 to help not just the Cuban-Americans, but all victims of terrorism. Throughout the 1980s and 1990s, terrorism victims' families and the fortunate ones who survived ran into repeated roadblocks in legal struggles to win judgments against the terror sponsors. The main legal hurdle was that even ruthless regimes enjoyed immunity from lawsuits in U.S. courts under the Foreign Sovereign Immunities Act. But the two 1996 amendments, which State *supported*, revised the Foreign Sovereign Immunities Act to strip immunity from countries officially named state sponsors of terrorism (of which there are seven as of 2003) for terrorist actions committed against U.S. citizens.[21]

In the immediate aftermath of the legislative action, State was extremely helpful to many of the families, encouraging some to sue and even providing classified information in certain instances.[22] Often, with credit owed to State, a number of families started winning judgments. That's when the trouble began. With judgments in hand, families pursued the only reasonable option: the blocked assets of the various state sponsors of terrorism. (After a nation is declared an official state sponsor of terrorism—a list that includes Iran, Cuba, Syria, Sudan, Libya, North Korea, and Saddam Hussein's Iraq[23]—all their government-owned and -controlled assets, such as bank accounts, real estate, and companies, are seized by the U.S. and "blocked" so that the terror sponsor cannot access them.)

Given that official state sponsors of terror obviously do not respect the rulings of U.S. courts, it is something of a mystery what State thought would happen after U.S. citizens won judgments against the despots. It should have been clear that the only way plaintiffs would be able to force the regimes found liable to pay up would be by accessing frozen assets. (It is not clear why Foggy Bottom had a change of heart, but it could be because plaintiffs collecting from the blocked assets would threaten State's own plans for using those funds.) Regardless, State fiercely opposed any and all efforts of victims and families to collect from the frozen assets of Saddam Hussein, Fidel Castro, Moammar Gadhafi, and the Iranian mullahs.

Another legislative battle ensued, but this time State did not support new legislation. Congress further amended the Foreign Sovereign Immunities Act to clarify that frozen assets were, in fact, fair game. But at the last minute, an unknown ally of State sneaked in a provision allowing the president to waive the new amendment in the interest of "national security." Taking State's advice, President Clinton immediately invoked the new waiver the moment he signed the bill—resulting in an effective veto—declaring that any collection from the frozen assets of state sponsors of terrorism would harm United States "national security."

CONGRESS ACTS, YET AGAIN

Frustrated that it had acted twice and seen its clear intent thwarted each time, Congress decided to tackle the issue once again in 2000. In that year's bill, Congress specifically designated families of sixteen victims of Iranian terrorism who were to receive compensation and reiterated that those who win judgments against state sponsors of terrorism can collect from the blocked assets. State managed to convince a somewhat bewildered Congress to set up a matching fund scheme for those who were explicitly listed. In a design that is every bit as complicated as it sounds, those families were paid by U.S. taxpayer funds that were earmarked to represent blocked Iranian assets—the upshot being that the families were paid not by the Iranian mullahs (as they wanted), but by U.S. taxpayers. State did, however, relent on the Cuban case, allowing the Brothers to the Rescue to collect some $96 million from blocked Cuban assets.

Although a waiver provision was again included, the legislation stressed that it was not to be used as a blanket denial of compensation.[24] Clinton once again ignored Congress and did as State wanted, leaving all but the sixteen listed families and the Brothers to the Rescue plaintiffs out of luck. In his final days in office—around the same time as his infamous pardon spree—Clinton invoked the new waiver, again citing "national security."[25]

Yet another legislative battle started in 2001. Congress was determined to have its original intent carried out, even if that meant passing *another* bill. In a letter to Republican senator George Allen of Virginia, deputy secretary of state Richard Armitage laid out the rationale behind denying victims and families access to blocked assets: "There is no better example [of protecting national security] than the critical role blocked assets played in obtaining the release of the U.S. hostages in Tehran in 1981."[26] In other words, Armitage believed that those who have suffered should not access the blocked assets so that the U.S. can give the funds back to those tyrants who are smart enough to kidnap Americans and demand their blocked assets back as ransom.

Though it does not appear that blocked assets went to pay ransoms anytime in the decade before Armitage wrote the letter, those funds have been drawn down for a number of purposes.

VANISHING ACT

Blocked assets are routinely paid out to companies who apply for "licenses" on the funds. Typically, a company has an outstanding debt with the country that hasn't been paid, so it applies for a "license." If approved, the company receives money directly from the blocked assets. State has no problems with this arrangement. It is probably the likeliest explanation for the substantial depletion of frozen Iranian assets, which totaled approximately $350 million at the end of 2000, but only around $200 million one year later. Before policy on trade with Iran became far more restrictive, private companies collected more than $700 million in frozen Iranian assets from 1991–1994.[27] None of that money, however, went to those victimized by terrorism.

But the most amazing arrangement for the use of frozen funds involves blocked Cuban assets. Pursuant to a law enacted by Congress in 1992, U.S. telecom companies provide phone service to Cubans as a way of undermining the dictator by allowing his subjects to hear messages of freedom from friends and relatives in the United States (or at least that was the theory). But since Castro would not pay for phone service—and his suffering people are too poor to do so—the funding comes from blocked Cuban assets. More than $100 million is paid out annually to U.S. corporations such as AT&T and

WorldCom, roughly $50 million of which is then funneled back to Castro so he'll allow the phone service to continue.[28] (It was out of that stream of $50 million annually heading back to Castro that the families of the Brothers to the Rescue were originally attempting to collect on their judgment.)

In whose pockets disappearing frozen assets end up is something of a mystery—to the public, anyway. The Office of Foreign Assets Control (OFAC), which operates out of the Treasury Department but takes most of its international policy cues from the State Department, does not make specific licenses publicly available. Not that such information is classified. When a license is granted, a whole host of people without security clearance view at least the basic facts about the transaction—and it can't be classified if it is shown to people not authorized to view classified material. The bank actually holding the blocked assets receives notice of the license, as does the entity that made the original payment frozen by the U.S. and converted into blocked assets. The same procedure holds for every bank from which money exits or through which it passes. (These transactions can be very complex, often involving several banks.) All these various parties know about specific payments that draw down the blocked assets—but the families trying to collect on judgments are prevented from seeing that information.

CONGRESS ACTS, TAKE FOUR

Perhaps because it realized that many other parties were able to receive money from blocked assets, Congress acted yet again, reiterating the same intent from the three previous laws. Congress for the third time explicitly made it clear that victims of terrorism and their relatives could collect from the blocked assets of the state sponsors of terrorism. A 2002 bill attached to legislation on terrorism insurance still had a waiver, but it could only be used to shield diplomatic properties.

State wanted Congress to do for remaining victims' families what it had done two years earlier with the complex taxpayer matching funds that were given to the specifically designated families of sixteen victims of Iranian terrorism. But because of the opposition of the families, the idea was rejected. Victims' families wanted to be paid by those responsible for the terrorism, not by the U.S. taxpayer. This time around, Congress better understood the taxpayer-funded mechanism State had established in 2000, and lawmakers decided that the terrorists must be held to account. The original idea behind suing the terrorists, in fact, came from a desire to bankrupt them, to make terrorism expensive. It may be idealistic, and it may not even work—blocked assets, after all, have probably already been written off by the likes of Gadhafi and the Iranian mullahs—but it does hold the evildoer directly responsible for the evil done.

In lobbying on Capitol Hill over the years, State has repeatedly made the argument that if it were to open the floodgates and allow those with judgments to collect from the blocked assets, the funds would vanish almost instantly. In some instances this may be true—there's only $237.5 million in Iranian assets, for example, but far more than that has already been won—but it should not result in simply denying all the families access to the frozen funds. In situations where one defendant is being sued by many plaintiffs in separate cases, there is often a "rush to the courtroom," people racing to file suit so they can be first in line to collect before the defendant goes broke. But to make the leap that since not everyone can get the full amount owed, everyone must be denied is simply illogical.

TERRORISM WIDOWS

At the White House signing ceremony on November 26, 2002, President George W. Bush had two women who had long done battle with State standing right behind him: Edwina Hegna and Deanna

Frazier, one a terrorism widow, and the other a soon-to-be terrorism widow. Both women were with the president in the East Room of the White House to mark the bittersweet end to their quests for justice— though State made sure that their struggles did not end that day.

Edwina's husband, Charles, was on a hijacked plane in 1984, becoming the first American to die in a terrorist hijacking. The accountant was one of three employees of the U.S. Agency for International Development on Kuwaiti Airlines flight 221 on December 4, 1984. When the hijackers came looking for Americans on Charles' flight, he stood—proudly.[29]

Charles Hegna was marched to the front of the plane, and forced to his knees. He began praying. The Hezbollah hijackers then shot him in the stomach and pushed him out the side of the plane. He landed on the tarmac below—still alive. As he lay on the ground, his legs crumpled underneath him, the terrorists shot him again from the plane. Charles died at an Iranian hospital a few days later.[30]

Although she did not lose a loved one suddenly, Deanna Frazier has watched her husband die slowly, a gradual and steady decline that has stretched out over a decade. Her once-hulking steelworker husband, Jack, lies nearly incapacitated in an Arizona nursing home, too frail to do much of anything. The former avid basketball and racquetball player, known to friends as the "Mountain Man" is now unable to walk and is blind in one eye; he is only sixty-five.[31] Jack and Deanna both know his time is short.

Jack Frazier was working on an oil project in Iraq for the Bechtel Corporation in 1990 when he had to take refuge at ambassador April Glaspie's private residence. But as a diabetic, he needed medication, something Saddam Hussein would not allow U.S. officials to deliver to the "Mountain Man" and others. Jack and other men were eventually lured out of the diplomatic property with the promise of exit visas, but they were captured instead. They were used by Hussein as a "human shield" around locations the despot wanted to protect in the months before the first Gulf War.[32]

Jack lost sight in his right eye before leaving Iraq—but still helped put out oil fires after the war—and has been slowly robbed of his physical health as the years pass. Jack and Deanna found each other late in life, despite growing up in the same small town. But because of what Saddam Hussein did to Jack, they won't have the time together they dreamed about.

Edwina Hegna won a $42 million judgment against the Iranian mullahs, and the Fraziers a $1.75 million decision against Hussein. But State doggedly fought their efforts to collect from the frozen assets of the respective tyrants—obfuscation that continued even after the 2002 bill and the president's unmistakable signal that he wanted them compensated.

Lawyers for Jack and Deanna Frazier and some two hundred other victims of Iraqi terrorism finally collected $58 million in early 2003 from the Federal Reserve Bank of New York—a move that infuriated officials at Foggy Bottom.[33] Then, President Bush, before handing more than $1.5 billion in frozen assets over to post-Saddam Iraq in April 2003, ordered that those victims with final judgments be paid, resulting in payment of the remainder of the roughly $95 million in judgments against Iraq.[34] But approximately two hundred families who had cases pending—but without final judgments in hand—were not able to collect before the assets left United States control. Two months after he finally achieved justice, Jack Frazier died—moments after asking his wife to fluff his pillow.

AFTERMATH

Although the victims of Iraqi terrorism had received compensation by April 2003, Edwina Hegna and other victims of Iranian terrorism had not. Even with final judgments in hand, they are still being battled by State at every turn. Lawyers for the victims have actually identified over $50 million in Iranian assets around the United States, but State won't budge. Despite telling Congress in 2002 that that year's bill would make Iranian assets in the U.S. subject to collection by the victims with judgments, State started playing semantic games in 2003.[35] Claiming that the Iranian assets are "regulated" and not "blocked"—a distinction not spelled out anywhere in law—State is fighting efforts by victims to collect from those assets.[36]

The terrible irony of the whole situation is that collecting damages from a non-terrorist state, like Britain or Switzerland, would not be nearly as hard. If a judge rules that, say, Germany, is liable for $2 million in damages if one of its government officials accidentally runs over someone, then the German government would have no choice but to pay up. In short, notes international law scholar John Norton Moore, "blocked assets receive more protection than regular assets in the United States belonging to foreign governments."[37]

SUING THE SAUDIS

After families of September 11 victims filed a $1 trillion lawsuit against the Saudi royal family in summer 2002 for its financial support of al Qaeda, State badly wanted to intervene—on behalf of the Saudis. But Foggy Bottom officials were not sure how they could get involved. Even State Department lawyers realized that sitting on the other side of the courtroom would not be "good PR," yet they were still horrified about the "precedent" such a lawsuit could set.

Some State officials hatched a sort of "hibernation" plan, waiting for the court to ask for State's "opinion," something that almost always happens any time a case involves a foreign party or an international issue. Top State press flack Richard Boucher hinted at this approach when he said, "Sometimes courts ask us for things, and obviously we would respond to the wishes of the court [to give our opinion]."[38]

After much consternation and internal squabbling that lasted through the fall, State decided that opposing the September 11 victims' families—directly or in an "opinion"—would be too "hot" even for Foggy Bottom. It was not a decision made on principle or after reviewing the merits of the case. And it was certainly not for the reason given by State spokesman Gregory Sullivan immediately after the case had been filed: "It would be an obstruction of justice for us to get involved."[39]

10

Wrong Hands: The Arming of the Middle East

 "THERE IS NO CLEAR AUTHORITY TO SEIZE THE SHIPMENT OF SCUD MISSILES."[1]

When the United States allowed a shipment of Scud missiles from North Korea to continue to its final destination of Yemen in December 2002, White House spokesman Ari Fleischer defended the move by noting the lack of "clear authority" under international law. In fact, the call to allow the shipment to proceed to a nominal ally was made not by the White House, but by State. But because the White House deferred to State, it was forced to defend the decision.

Days before the U.S. allowed the vessel carrying the Scud missiles to proceed to Yemen on December 11, 2002, Spanish forces had boarded the pirate ship (meaning it had been flying no flag during the trip).[2] Spain, acting on a tip from U.S. intelligence, found the missiles hidden within a shipment of concrete.[3] This was the first test of the White House's new plans to get tough on illicit weapons transfers, a policy that was soon to be announced. (Of all days, the White House issued its six-page policy pronouncement, "National Strategy to Combat Weapons of Mass Destruction," the same day Yemen was allowed to acquire the Scud missiles.) The opportunity to follow rhetoric with action was squandered.

From that weekend until the Wednesday morning when the shipment was allowed to proceed to Yemen, a fierce internal battle raged within State. Two different recommendations had been drafted for Powell—one for seizing the Scuds, one against—by Tuesday night. But according to an administration official, Powell only reviewed the document that misstated the nature of the shipment and contained a questionable interpretation of international law.[4] A different administration official claims that Powell came to "regret" the speed with which he made the decision.[5]

The hasty decision ironically allowed Yemen to skirt stringent disclosure requirements that normally accompany such purchases. Yemen didn't have to prove, for instance, the final destination and true purpose for the missiles. The fair-weather ally also didn't have to offer evidence to support its claim that the shipment was the last installment in an old contract. According to an administration official, Yemen had actually negotiated the missile purchase from North Korea only months earlier.[6]

It is entirely possible that some interpretations of international law might not permit the United States to halt the shipment permanently. News stories of the event quoted various legal experts who echoed the view expressed by Fleischer. But "no clear authority" is not the same thing as saying that international law "prohibits" the seizure of contraband on board a pirate ship. In other words, the supposed gray area under international law cited as the justification for allowing the shipment to proceed is exactly the reason for halting it. It's a question of predisposition. State seems inclined to take the interpretation most favorable to a foreign government, even when trying to stop the spread of weapons and high technology in a post-September 11 world. And since the White House deferred to State in this situation, the Scud missiles completed their journey from North Korea to Yemen.

It wouldn't be the last time Pyongyang would receive a helping hand from State.

"THAT'S NONSENSE"

On March 31, 2003, two State Department officials—Jack Pritchard, the special envoy to Korea, and David Straub, the Korea desk officer—went to New York to meet with North Korean representatives to the United Nations, a line of communication known as the "New York channel."[7] The agents of Pyongyang made a stunning declaration: North Korea had begun reprocessing plutonium, a key step in developing nuclear weapons—and a flagrant violation of the 1994 "Agreed Framework."

State could not have been pleased. Not only was North Korea misbehaving, but it was doing so right on the cusp of new talks slated to start on April 23 in Beijing. Foggy Bottom officials knew that once the Pentagon and the White House received word of this—it was the first time North Korea had ever made such an announcement[8]—the talks might be canceled. State faced a decision: inform the other branches and risk cancellation of a meeting which it had forcefully promoted, or "forget" to inform the White House and the Pentagon of Pyongyang's unprecedented admission.

For State, a lot was on the line. Getting a three-way meeting between American, Chinese, and North Korean officials was a Foggy Bottom initiative. Bilateral talks—or one-on-one sessions—with North Korea were not a possibility, since the White House recognized the obvious: Kim Jong Il was developing nukes for the primary purpose of dramatically enhancing his stature on the world stage, and getting the U.S. to treat North Korea as an equal in negotiations would be a huge step in that direction. Despite this, State had been pushing throughout the early months of 2003 for direct negotiations—exactly what Kim Jong Il wanted. In January, State's policy planning director, Richard Haass, who had told Israel to engage Iran one month after the "axis of evil" speech, sent out an internal cable blasting the president's position and advocating one-on-one talks, in what one administration official described as a "broadside" against Bush. With all that was at stake, State chose silence.

State's "forgetfulness" meant that the White House and the Pentagon did not learn of Pyongyang's announcement until North Korean officials told the world that they had informed "relevant" parties on March 31. Administration officials who had been kept in the dark were miffed by the statement. It wasn't until the talks began in Beijing five days later—when North Korea told U.S. officials right off the bat about the "New York channel" communication some three weeks earlier—that White House and Pentagon officials learned the extent of what had happened. They were livid.

News of the deception—perhaps a generous description of what State did—broke at the end of the Beijing conference, right before the weekend. After the story had had a few days to simmer, the grilling Powell received the following Monday, April 28, boiled down to a single question: "There are some allegations that the rest of the administration didn't find out about it (North Korea's March 31 declaration), or other agencies. Can you address that?" His response? "That's nonsense." But then Powell continued with a remarkably lawyer-like explanation: "What we were told [that day] was shared within the administration."[9] But "within the administration" could also mean that the information was only shared with people inside Foggy Bottom. Yet no reporter followed up on this with Powell or minutes later with spokesman Boucher at the daily press briefing.

When questioned about it, Powell had a carefully crafted answer. That may have been because he had been given "carefully crafted" information about the March 31 admission; Powell might not have been told the entire truth about the incident. Rather than offering a defense of "Yes, we told the White House," Powell instead tried to cast doubt on the validity of North Korea's March 31 statement: "North Koreans have made different statements about reprocessing and whether they are or are not reprocessing.... And our intelligence community still cannot give us any validation or confirmation of what North Korea has said at various times and in various places with respect to reprocessing."[10] That answer obscures the real issue: why didn't State tell the White House or the Pentagon? Even if further examination about the truthfulness of Pyongyang's reprocessing claims needed to be made, there is no reason the White House and the Pentagon should have been kept in the dark.

While it is not clear what Powell did or did not know in this instance, it is not in his character to hoodwink the White House or the Pentagon—he may be a contrarian who regularly dissents, but he is not underhanded. The operative question, according to an administration official, is: "To the extent Powell knew, you have to ask, 'What was he told?'"[11] It is quite possible that information was misrepresented to him, and he may have been briefed that the declaration was not, in fact, "new" in the sense of it being different from past statements. But it was different—and something that both the White House and Pentagon doubtless would have liked to know before North Korea announced it publicly.

SOFT TOUCH ON PYONGYANG

Concerned about North Korea's increasing role in weapons proliferation, the White House decided to take a tough line on the Asian member of the "axis of evil." In summer 2002, the White House was presented with two competing blueprints for how to handle Pyongyang. The respective plans fell on different points on a 1 through 4 sliding scale, commonly used by administration officials to determine appropriate responses: "1" is the toughest response, and though different in each situation, it generally means something in the nature of preparing for war; "2" typically represents tough action—more than talk, less than conflict—that at the least lays down markers to make the foreign government aware of potentially harsh consequences; "3" is more or less a carrot-and-stick approach; and "4" is "pressure" through diplomacy.

Following the advice of many inside the White House and the Pentagon, the White House decided on the "2" approach to North Korea. State, however, charted its own course. When implementing the decision, Foggy Bottom officials put into practice a policy that closely resembled a hybrid of "3" and "4," notes an administration official.[12] Preoccupied by the run-up to war in Iraq, neither the Pentagon nor the White House effectively challenged State's insubordination. State undermined the president, and essentially got away with it.

If the White House had been more involved in the Yemen Scud missile incident, maybe Powell's rushed decision might have at least been second-guessed. Yet even after the war, State's shenanigans continued unpunished. White House officials were furious about State's refusal to inform them of Pyongyang's March 31 declaration. But after a few days passed, "everything was back to normal," says a frustrated White House official.[13] The controversy over that situation took place in late April, after the end of the war in Iraq, yet the White House did nothing to punish anyone for the transgression.

The net result of the White House's toleration of State's actions is that bad nations will continue to get their hands on weapons of mass destruction (WMD). North Korea garners 20 to 40 percent of its hard currency from weapons sales, most of which are to the Middle East.[14] North Korea is pushing full-steam ahead with proliferation and it is not alone. Many countries continue to acquire weapons of mass destruction, and a whole host of other nations are ready to supply them.

Chief among the suppliers is the United States.

FOR SPACE OR MISSILES?

Many nations, over the years, have bought military-enhancing items directly from the United States. But purchases by most foreign governments of items that fall under certain categories must be licensed by the U.S. government. There are generally two camps in battles over whether to license. Those who favor selling almost any item believe that if the U.S. does not sell something, some other nation will. So it makes no sense, the argument goes, to harm U.S. companies for no reason. Those who are uneasy with foreign governments obtaining WMD, however, believe that the U.S. has a better chance to stop allies from supplying dual-use technologies if it does not allow American companies to sell them.

The export control debate that plays itself out time and again typically revolves around a nation attempting to acquire "civilian" technology that also could be used to enhance military capabilities. One classic example is an attempt by Brazil in the mid-1980s to purchase materials for its space launch vehicle (SLV) program. Following is a firsthand account of a conversation with a high-ranking Pentagon official, written by Reagan administration Defense Department official Richard Speier:

> Brazil was the largest and most populous country in Latin America, he claimed. It was essential to keep Brazil friendly with the U.S. It was essential to have good military relations with Brazil. Brazil wanted to develop an SLV. No one could stop Brazil once it had committed itself. If the U.S. would not help Brazil, other major Western nations would. This would reduce U.S. influence with Brazil. And so, it was essential for the U.S. to cooperate with Brazil's ambitions to develop an SLV.
>
> I answered all these arguments for the third time. It was U.S. policy to prevent missile proliferation. SLV programs were interchangeable with ballistic missile programs, and there was

abundant evidence that Brazil wanted to use its rocket technology to produce ballistic missiles. We were working with the other major Western nations to jointly restrain the kind of rocket technology transfers that Brazil wanted. The partners would not restrain themselves unless the U.S. restrained itself as well.

The debate over Brazil's space launch vehicle program—which ended with Brazil not getting the equipment it needed—exemplifies the complexities of questions of dual-use items. As noted in the above passage, the same equipment that launches civilian rockets into space also can be used to launch ballistic missiles. Part of the issue comes down to trust: can the foreign government be trusted to use the dual-use technology for purely civilian purposes? The issue stretches back decades. Former Bush administration official Henry Sokolski, who handled arms control issues in the Defense Department, provides some historical perspective: "JFK, when he was asked the difference between the Atlas booster used to launch Glenn into orbit and the Atlas booster used for pointing nukes at the Soviet Union, said simply, 'Attitude.' But," Sokolski warns, "attitudes can change overnight."[15]

DUAL USES

The State Department position is to err on the side of trust when dealing with dual-use items. When "trust" becomes difficult to justify, the fallback position is that if the U.S. does not authorize the sale by an American company, corporations from France or Germany or wherever will. State, though, is often not alone. State's mindset has found allies in other quarters; notice the advocate of selling dual-use equipment to Brazil was a senior Pentagon official.

To appreciate more fully the complexities of dual-use debates, consider the following examples. Tops on the chemical list of the Chemical Weapons Convention is a substance known as thiodyglycol, which enjoys that distinction because it is a precursor to Sarin gas.[16] But aside from being a base ingredient for one of the deadliest poisons on earth, it is sometimes used in making certain types of ink.[17] Some of the most advanced microprocessor and electronic equipment that requires export licenses to ship—if a license is issued at all—can be found in such state-of-the-art products as the Playstation 2 machine and any of its successors. Notes arms control and proliferation expert James Swanson, "Micro-electronics is the biggest problem, because it is state-of-the-art and it changes every six months."[18]

And when one goes looking for items that would have dual uses, the search leads to a seemingly unlikely location. "When you have a modern hospital, you have a major biological warfare program," says Swanson.[19]

STOPPING PROLIFERATION

Efforts to stop the spread of arms and dual-use items started as part of an overall Cold War scheme to prevent, or at least hinder, the development of ballistic missiles and other WMD by the Soviet Union and Soviet-allied states. To achieve this, the United States and various allies formed the Coordinating Committee, or COCOM.[20] COCOM members drew up lists of suspect and prohibited items, meaning that COCOM nations would discuss potential purchases with each other before the Soviet Union or one of its allies could receive the weaponry or dual-use equipment. And for those items that required an export control license from the U.S. (meaning a U.S. company was the potential seller), the State Department had primary responsibility. Even though State often made excuses to allow purchases to happen,[21] dual-use items were at least scrutinized by U.S. officials before heading off to the Soviet Union or one of its allies. Thus, at the height of the Cold War in the mid-1980s, over 100,000 dual-use items were reviewed for export control licenses in the U.S. alone.[22]

Various countries with WMD capabilities began to realize—beginning in the late-1970s and early 1980s—that stopping the spread of WMD capabilities to other nations was a good idea. To that end, various treaties were drafted and signed, and different voluntary groups—whose membership is generally constituted of WMD-capable supplying nations—were formed.

Trying to master the tapestry of interwoven treaties and voluntary groups can be a mind-numbingly complex task. Three international treaties cover WMD: the Nuclear non-Proliferation Treaty (NPT), the Chemical Weapons Convention (CWC), and the Biological Weapons Convention (BWC). But that's not all. There are also a number of so-called suppliers groups: the Nuclear Suppliers Group (NSG), the Missile Technology Control Regime (MTR), the Australia Group (which covers chemical and biological agents), and the Wassenaar Arrangement (the successor to COCOM after the fall of the Soviet Union).[23] Members of these groups voluntarily agree not to license for export a whole array of goods to non-member nations. What does that panoply of treaties and voluntary groups produce? Mostly, a mixed bag.

After the fall of the Soviet Union, the primary focus of the various treaties and groups became to expand the number of nations that would sign the treaties or join the groups. And the 1980s emphasis on stopping the spread of dual-use items morphed almost entirely into preventing only dual-use items that were *intended* for "military" or "offensive" purposes.[24] Therein lies the trust factor. As State showed with its courting of Saddam Hussein from late 1988 through 1990, trust can turn deadly if it is misplaced. Foggy Bottom officials, of course, were not the only ones pushing for relaxed restrictions on the export of dual-use equipment. The European Union nations, for example, did their part to increase exports of such items, starting in the early 1990s.[25] Even some inside the administration, including the Pentagon, were embracing the enhanced exports that came with relaxed trade restrictions.

ONE STEP FORWARD, TWO STEPS BACK

While the treaties and groups often achieve some success in advancing their stated purposes, much of that is undone in the name of getting more nations to sign on the dotted line. One of the biggest problems, an administration officials notes, is that State often "sweetens the pot" for countries to sign treaties or join the groups.[26] How exactly do they "sweeten the pot?" In the early- to mid-1990s, for example, State allowed greater access to strategic technology for China, Russia, and Brazil—all in a bid to buy their better behavior.[27]

Sometimes, though, the incentives are built into the agreements themselves. Signing the Chemical Weapons Convention, for example, grants a nation not only greater access to chemical agents, but also allows "technical cooperation" on "civilian uses" of chemicals. But since chemical weapons can be developed using the same methods as those employed for "civilian" uses, the nations in effect receive skilled advice on enhancing military capabilities for chemical weapons of mass destruction. As a signee of the CWC, Iran is allowed to purchase items controlled by the treaty because— notwithstanding its well-documented history of state sponsorship of terrorism—it is considered a member in "good standing."[28] One item it could purchase is glass-lined vessels, which are critical for those seeking to move from prototype or pilot development to serial production of chemical agents.[29] Perhaps most amazing of all, in the nuclear context, Iran receives help (from the United Nations' International Atomic Energy Agency) on "technical cooperation" for "civilian uses" of nuclear technology.[30]

Signing up for treaties is not the only way nations can receive benefits to which they would otherwise not have access. Joining the voluntary groups in many ways can be advantageous for a nation trying to develop chemical or biological weapons of mass destruction. In 1992, at the end of the Bush administration, the State Department started allowing U.S. companies to ship chemical precursors (agents that help develop toxins and poisons used in weapons) to Australia Group member nations without an export license.[31] This was done partly out of trust, but partly as a way to reward nations for joining the group.[32]

Even non-member nations can get a helping hand in spreading deadly toxins. In 1993, the group—partly at State's request—began briefing non-members on what size shipments of chemical agents would raise suspicion with the group's members. Not surprisingly, China modified the size of its sales of chemical precursors to just below the threshold that it was told would draw the attention of the Australia Group. And if China were able to join the Australia Group, it would be able to purchase assorted poisons license-free—and then sell them to any number of tyrants.[33]

When looking at the tremendous failings of the various treaties and voluntary groups, it is important to note that State is not entirely to blame—though it is largely so, as State provided the greatest direction and input for most of these accords. And after problems had become apparent, State did little to correct them. But even when State has the power—either under the pacts or through laws passed by Congress—it often shuns the use of any tough measures to combat the spread of weapons of mass destruction.

SANCTION-FREE ZONE

When "controlled" items—meaning chemical or biological agents or goods that would help in the development of WMD—are transferred in violation of a treaty or international law, State usually has the power to act. More often than not, it chooses not to. State typically abhors applying sanctions because doing so might "damage" relations with the foreign government in question. Even though sanctions mostly apply to companies and not countries, Foggy Bottom officials believe that sanctioning a foreign company would in turn limit State's ability to influence that country's proliferation policies.

Congress has passed many laws (from the 1970s on) that require sanctions to be applied under certain conditions. Generally speaking, the proof required is that the combined evidence makes it more likely than not that a particular company has acted nefariously. But as with almost all laws, there is discretion in how the sanctions laws are enforced. That's where State is able to subvert the intent of Congress. Explains an administration official, "The legal department [at State] believes that you have to follow U.S. criminal standards before imposing sanctions."[34] Congress does not require the high threshold found in criminal standards before imposing sanctions, but State does so anyway.

When it would be politically impossible to drop sanctions, sometimes State's solution is to ease them using a catchy name. Before joining State from the left-leaning Brookings Institution in spring 2001, policy planning director Richard Haass (and his protégé, Meghan O'Sullivan) developed the idea for so-called "smart sanctions" for Saddam Hussein's Iraq. The sales pitch was that more attention could be paid to the really bad items, while allowing a greater number of "acceptable" goods to go to Iraq. With the Pentagon completely outmanned by State — Haass' counterpart, Doug Feith, didn't get confirmed until June 2001 — Haass won the fight. Sanctions on Saddam were eased in the name of "smart sanctions." An administration official complains, "Smart sanctions achieved two things. First, it convinced people we were losing steam on keeping Iraq in a box, and second, it allowed Saddam to get dual-use technologies that could have been used against us in a war."[35]

Oftentimes State manages to keep sanctions from being imposed in the first place. Early in the second Bush administration, the four committees at State that investigate sanctions issues reported to the same individual, Vann Van Diepen. According to an informed source, Van Diepen "buried tough recommendations, particularly those recommending sanctions."[36] But as is often the case when the will of Congress or the White House is flouted by a Foggy Bottom official, Van Diepen was not a lone rebel. His actions were tolerated by his superior, John Wolf, the assistant secretary of state, and actually encouraged by Richard Armitage, who was at the center of the Yemen Scud missile incident and the concealment of North Korea's March 31, 2003 declaration that it was reprocessing plutonium.

RUSSIAN PROTECTION RACKET

In summer 1998, Russia was caught red-handed selling missile technology to Iran, as well as helping the Iranian mullahs by sending them Russian missile engineers. Congress was furious. State was not. By overwhelming margins, Congress passed the Iran Missile Proliferation Sanctions Act. One of the bill's primary purposes was to punish those Russian companies that had been selling technology to Iran or otherwise helping Tehran's missile programs. Following heavy lobbying by State,[37] Clinton vetoed the bill exactly two weeks later, on June 23, 1998.[38] Since the bill passed with a clear two-thirds majority in both chambers—two-thirds vote is required to override a veto—it looked as if the bill would become law over Clinton's veto. But then State's lobbying kicked into overdrive.

Fortunately for Foggy Bottom officials, they were able to enlist support for their cause. National Security advisor Sandy Berger lobbied Congress. According to a former congressional official who participated in the fight over the bill, Berger told lawmakers, "The Russian financial system is on the verge of collapse."[39] State even got the pro-Israel lobby AIPAC (American-Israeli Political Action Committee) to try to convince lawmakers to hold off overriding President Clinton's veto.[40] With the battlelines drawn heading into the override vote, something unexpected happened.

Just days before Congress's planned vote to override Clinton's veto, the Russian government announced that "certain Russian firms" had proliferated missile technology to Iran. Coincidentally— in the most generous sense of the word—the White House announced sanctions would be imposed on those very companies on the *exact same day*. The imposition of the sanctions held Congress at bay, and the mandatory sanctions in the Iran Missile Proliferation Sanctions Act were not enacted. But the sanctions that were actually put in place did not fully address the original problem of Russian companies aiding Iran's missile program.[41]

The Russian Space Agency (RSA) played a key role in recruiting and sending missile engineers to Iran, yet it was mysteriously left off the list of sanctioned companies. Interestingly, of those companies sanctioned, none actually had any business with U.S. companies— meaning U.S.-imposed sanctions would have minimal, if any, impact.[42] RSA, though, had received by that point some $1 billion from the U.S. government for joint work on the space station[43]— meaning sanctions on RSA could have had significant impact. The only consequence RSA suffered was a temporary halt in direct U.S. subsidies.[44]

STATE OF INACTION

One of Saddam Hussein's more impressive military complexes before the first Gulf War was Saad-16, located in the Mosul area. To improve missile testing capabilities, Saddam's regime placed an order—through a German intermediary—for advanced hybrid computers from a U.S. company. Because the hybrid computer also had military capabilities, the company needed a dual-use export license, which has to be approved by State, Commerce, and the Department of Defense. State and Commerce wanted to approve the sale, but Defense did not.[45] Pentagon officials provided evidence to State and Commerce that the high-technology hybrid computer was going to be used for missile testing. But given that State wanted to please Saddam in the interest of forging closer ties (and Commerce wanted to please the American company), Defense officials were in for an uphill fight.

The most compelling proof that Defense offered on the hybrid computer's military capabilities was a U.S. army brochure showing the machine being used for missile testing.[46] Pentagon officials were led to believe that the export control license would be denied, but it was not.[47] Saddam Hussein was able to acquire the hybrid computer in 1990, shortly before he invaded Kuwait.

Not all dual-use fights involve underhanded deception and shipment of high technology to despots like Saddam Hussein. In far too many instances, State actively opposes taking tough measures to combat proliferation. The debate often comes down to the question of the extent of an item's military capabilities. In 1988 and 1989, for example, India was attempting to purchase equipment from a U.S. company that was supposedly for satellite testing.[48] State wanted to issue the export control license, but Defense didn't believe that the product was going to be used for testing satellites.

Nicknamed "Shake 'n Bake" by Pentagon officials, the unit had four main components:

1) a centrifuge to simulate acceleration/deceleration
2) a vibrating table to simulate take-off/exit and re-entry
3) a decompression chamber to simulate high altitudes
4) a heater/cooler to simulate the effect of either sun-in-space or re-entry

Defense ordered intelligence reports from four different agencies—CIA, DIA, MISIC, and Livermore Labs—and all four agreed that the device was only good for testing re-entry of intercontinental ballistic missiles (ICBMs). The export control license was denied.[49]

But just because an export control license is denied doesn't necessarily mean that the foreign entities won't try again. Just ask Brazil. After failing to obtain assistance from U.S. companies in the 1980s for its space launch vehicle (SLV) program, Brazil tried again in 1990. Though the U.S. had been asking other nations not to provide any assistance to Brazil's SLV program, Brazil found a helping hand in the U.S. In what Reagan administration Defense Department official Richard Speier dubs a "mix-up," State allowed an SLV into the U.S. in late 1990 for heat treatment, a process which strengthens rocket casings.[50]

The space launch vehicle that entered the U.S. was interchangeable with an ICBM, and it made no economic sense for Brazil to use it for aerospace purposes, since it could have paid other countries to use their programs for far less than it took to build its own.[51] The U.S. had intelligence that the real purpose for the device was for Brazil's burgeoning nuclear program—a view also held by the Brazilian press.[52] Defense believed that U.S. credibility would be damaged if Brazil successfully moved its SLV unit in and out of the United States. But in the end, State won, in the interest of avoiding an "international incident."[53]

GETTING TOUGH—ONCE

State does not always block efforts to fight proliferation. Just as State can be very bad when it moves to allow a dual-use transfer, it can (at times) be very good in combating proliferation. Although it happened back during the Reagan administration, the Toshiba Quieting case (as it's known) demonstrates that State can be effective.

In the 1970s and 1980s, the Soviet Union had a serious problem with its nuclear subs: they made both high and low noises, because of the shape and vibration of the propeller blade and because all propellers make "cavitation noises," which happen when water fills bubbles.[54] Noisy subs were bad news for the Soviets, making stealth travel nearly impossible; their subs almost always showed up on radar. Consequently, the Soviets wanted to make quieter propellers. In 1977,

State, Commerce, and Defense had all approved the transfer to the Soviet Union of the necessary equipment to make quiet propellers. The transfer was only stopped, for reasons that are not known, because of someone from the National Security Council.

Since the Soviets couldn't get what they wanted from the United States, they turned to Japan, which had functioning quiet subs. The Soviet Union tried to buy the Toshiba profiling machine, which cuts metal for propellers in the right way to make a quiet sub. Japan said no. Undeterred, the Soviets then went to France—and Forest Ligne sold them two profiling machines. The Forest Ligne devices, however, didn't work. But, since France had allowed its company to sell the machines, the Soviets had leverage with which to go back to Toshiba. After the Soviet Union informed Toshiba that it was going to get what it wanted with or without the company's help, Toshiba pressured the Japanese government to issue an export control license. The government complied, issuing an export control license for machines but without the computers needed to make them fully operational.[55]

To complete its objective, the Soviet Union finally went to a Norwegian company called Kongsberg Vapenfabric, which provided the needed computers.

Making matters worse, all three companies sent engineers to Leningrad to help the Soviets build the quiet subs. Clearly, corporate ignorance was not a legitimate excuse in this instance. The U.S. government's ignorance lasted, however, until 1985, when a Japanese businessman who had traveled to Leningrad called COCOM to inform the U.S. of what was going on. The head of COCOM immediately informed the CIA, but for whatever reason, the CIA sat on the information for a year. Because of an unrelated investigation involving Norway and the Soviet Union, the information was rediscovered. State and Defense jointly confronted Norway.

After substantial pressure was applied, Norway acted, prosecuting and convicting one person. In response to a threat to cut off U.S. government business with Kongsberg, which at the time supplied Penguin missiles to the U.S. government, Norway agreed to halt licenses for all such transactions in the future.[56] Which is at least more than what the French did; France did not prosecute anyone or agree to stop future transactions. (Then again, their non-working machines probably would have been of minimal value.)

Showing uncommon resolve, State "came down hard on Japan," notes Steve Bryen, who was a firsthand participant as events unfolded.[57] State actually threatened Japan with the end of military "cooperation," which would have the same effect as leaving Japan without a modern military, since the country has almost no national defense-oriented armed forces to speak of. The pressure tactic worked. The president of Toshiba resigned, and in the U.S., Congress sanctioned Toshiba, prohibiting the company from selling machine tools and heavy equipment in the U.S. for one year[58]—a sizeable sanction, given how lucrative those markets were to Toshiba.

Even though the Toshiba Quieting case can be counted as a success in the sense that State showed it could stiffen its backbone when it wanted to, it was a failure in the most important element of all: the Soviet Union acquired the technology it had sought.

AXIS OF PROLIFERATION

Arms control experts have come to notice eerie patterns in how various countries are acquiring the goods necessary to develop WMD. Pakistan, for example, receives help on its nuclear and ballistic missile programs from China, Russia, and North Korea. Egypt, another country of increasing concern because of its growing war machine, receives most of its Scuds and other ballistic missiles from China, Russia, and North Korea. And Iran, a country near the top of every "bad guys" list, is developing its ballistic missile and nuclear, chemical, and biological WMD programs primarily with assistance from China, Russia, and North Korea.[59] China, Russia, and North Korea, in other words, constitute the "axis of proliferation"—and their actions are helping to create a secondary axis of suppliers in Pakistan, Egypt, and Iran.

China has assumed the role of the world's top weapons supplier to questionable countries, but it did not get there without help. China has received weapons for its fighter aircraft from Russia; high technology to enhance its development capabilities primarily from Israel, France, and Britain; and dual-use technology from the U.S., Japan, and various European Union nations.[60] So how to stop it?

With China, unlike with many other countries, the U.S. has substantial leverage. For its economy to continue to grow, China desperately needs access to the $10 trillion U.S. economy. But State has never threatened Chinese access to U.S. markets in response to proliferation of WMD capabilities to Iran, among others. With Russia, there is less leverage—in part because transactions could shift to former Soviet states—although the U.S. could threaten either the loans and various subsidy packages or the technical assistance programs upon which the Russians have come to rely. With North Korea, the answers are even more elusive, since there is little beyond food and medicine that the U.S. provides Pyongyang.

FINGER IN THE DIKE

The one thing every arms control expert agrees on is that if a country wants to acquire a particular weapons program, it will get it, sooner or later. The job of State, of course, should be to make the answer "later"—much later. But it's not that easy. Notes proliferation expert James Swanson, "We can't prevent proliferation. Most of these countries we worry about already have chemical, biological, and/or nuclear capabilities."[61] For starters, State has to be willing to apply greater scrutiny to dual-use items bound for almost any country.

Aside from tighter export controls on U.S.-produced goods, the spread of weapons and high technology can only be slowed in one of two ways: more agreements or tough action.

Although agreements are appealing on paper, they often have little impact—and sometimes actually help bad guys develop their programs. Think of Iran as a signee on the Chemical Weapons Convention, now receiving assistance for "civilian" uses of chemical agents. Inherent to the effectiveness of any agreement is the trustworthiness of the other party. Which demands the question: how can you negotiate with dictators or governments who have shown no propensity for honesty or integrity? Former Pentagon official Henry Sokolski, for one, doesn't buy it, noting that the likes of Kim Jong Il and the Iranian mullahs "are not people who are a little different that you can somehow work with."[62] Consider the infamous 1994 agreement, brokered by former president Jimmy Carter, in which North Korea pledged to halt its nuclear weapons program. Less than a decade later, Pyongyang was openly defying the terms of the deal. An administration official commented, "Jimmy Carter did not defuse the crisis; he did not solve the crisis. He merely postponed the crisis."[63]

This is not to say that pursuit of any treaty or pact is meaningless. As an administration official points out, "Treaties can lull you into a false sense of security, but it's still better to have them, because cheaters have to cheat in secret, which makes it more difficult." But the effectiveness of agreements becomes eviscerated unless State is willing, at least on occasion, to take a tough line with a foreign government or company that has done something in violation of an accord. If achieving a deal becomes the ultimate goal, however, then what happens afterward is of lesser concern. Sokolski notes that it comes down to the purpose of accords: "The question is, do we want agreements from bad people that they won't do bad things, or do we want to deprive bad people of the ability to do bad things?"[64]

U.S. credibility on taking tough action is likely near bottom, and one vivid example is the Yemen Scud missile incident. On the same day the White House released a tough new policy on fighting proliferation, the North Korean-made Scud missiles carried on a pirate ship were allowed to proceed to Yemen, and the Yemeni government didn't even have to disclose the basic information normally required when making such a purchase. It would probably take several high-profile examples of the U.S. cracking down on bad actors for U.S. threats to carry any weight.

ONLY TRUE SOLUTION

With the never-ending advance of technology and the seemingly endless number of countries willing to sell illicit items to bad regimes, there is no way actually to stop the spread of arms and military technology—except one. Free and open societies—not just "democracies," because voting alone does not a free society make— do not develop weapons of mass destruction for offensive purposes. South Africa, Brazil, Argentina, and Chile all scrapped their WMD and/or nuclear programs upon becoming democracies in the 1980s. Taiwan and South Korea also abandoned their biological weapons programs when making the transition to free societies.

As freedom spreads, weapons of mass destruction do not. But a doctrine committed to promoting "stability" is inherently inimical to the spread of freedom—and thus inherently conducive to the spread of weapons of mass destruction.

11

Fixing State — To the Extent It's Possible

★ *"I'M SORRY."*[1]

Then-U.S. ambassador to Jordan, William Burns, had heard some disturbing news, and he rushed to make an apology. A Jordanian citizen, Ishaq Farhan, had received a visa from the State Department, only to be turned back by U.S. customs officials as he tried to enter the country to give a speech at a conference for the American Muslims for Jerusalem in Santa Clara, California. Burns personally assured Farhan that he was sorry for any inconvenience the incident caused.[2]

Farhan was head of the fundamentalist group Islamic Action Front (IAF) and had possible ties to terrorism. Not sketchy, far-fetched ties, either. A fax threatening possible terrorist action against the United States came from his office fax machine, which is why he was added to the terrorism watch list in 1999 and his visa (issued in 1998) was revoked.[3]

On November 10, 1996, the American embassy in Amman, Jordan, received the following fax from IAF demanding the release of a Hamas leader, Dr. Musa Abu Marzook.

> We demand that you immediately release Dr. Musa Abu Marzook and urge you not to hand him over to the Zionist enemy. We warn you that if you do not release Dr. Musa Abu Marzook, and if you hand him over to the Jews, we will turn the ground upside down over your heads in Amman, Jerusalem, and the rest of the Arab countries and you will lament your dead just as we did to you in Lebanon in 1982 when we destroyed the Marine House with a booby-trapped car, and there are plenty of cars in our country. You also still remember the oil tanker with which we blew up your soldiers in Saudi Arabia.[4]

Granted, this might not constitute sufficient evidence for a criminal conviction in a court of law—but then the question of whether someone qualifies for a visa is not one for which the U.S. has to prove guilt beyond a reasonable doubt.

Since the incident happened in May 2000—more than a year before September 11—State still had the power to "correct" matters. The suspected terrorist, who had told the *Jordan Times* in 1998, "The resistance of the enemy Israel is a right and legitimate jihad holy war," had his visa reinstated, giving him an open door to come to the United States.[5]

Less than a year later, Burns was named assistant secretary of state for Near Eastern Affairs (NEA), one of the most coveted positions at Foggy Bottom. The next step is usually a lucrative private sector or foreign policy institute job (often funded with Saudi petro-dollars). There are few positions with more power at State. During his first two years as head of NEA, Burns' bureau opposed reauthorization of the Iran-

Libya Sanctions Act; actively undermined the pro-democracy Iraqi National Congress, and ignored the massive student protests against the ruling mullahs in Iran in summer 2002, only to later "engage" those same mullahs so despised by the people they oppress. Over the course of 2001 and 2002, Burns personally guided efforts to re-legitimize Libyan tyrant Moammar Gadhafi.

As disturbing as Burns' tenure as head of NEA is, however, it is roughly similar to the track records compiled by previous NEA chiefs. Burns, in other words, is not the problem at State; he is merely the latest symptom of the problem: Foggy Bottom's corrosive culture.

MISPLACED PRIORITIES

A look at how State handles itself in a wide range of areas—abandoning abducted children trapped overseas, intentionally making it easier for even suspected terrorists to get visas, coddling the House of Saud, courting Saddam Hussein after the end of the Iran-Iraq war and after the gassing of the Kurds, ignoring pro-democracy groups in the name of "stability"— shows that the causes for those actions are few in number but broad in scope. It's not that Foggy Bottom officials are anti-American, although far too many seem to have forgotten the country they should be representing. It's not that officials at State think they are doing anything other than advancing America's interests. It's a question of priorities, and the necessary means for achieving them.

Regardless of the issue at hand, State's primary goal is "stability," a thoroughly value- and moral-neutral word. Within the United States, "stability" would mean continued freedom of religion and speech, regular elections for government positions from the local town council to the president of the United States, and the ability to say and write things highly critical of the government without any fear of punishment or retribution. In countries like Saudi Arabia, Iran, Syria, or North Korea, "stability" means something far different: constant fear of the government, no freedom to speak or pray as you please, and a life side by side with thugs and terrorists who roam freely.

It is simply unconscionable that the country that is the embodiment of freedom would be complicit in the denial of God-given rights. It is against U.S. interests to tolerate such regimes. Regimes that have no respect for their own people are not likely to have any for the United States. U.S. strategic interests will surely at times require partnerships with disreputable leaders and even brutal regimes, but in working with such entities, the U.S. should push them down the path of freedom.

Freedom does not magically appear; it happens in stages—a process that can be measured not in months, but years or even decades. And it's not about holding elections or casting ballots, it's about building institutions of freedom—such as a free press, free enterprise, and free and independent churches, synagogues, and mosques—and pushing governments to implement internal reforms and place the highest priority on human rights.

To say that Foggy Bottom officials hate freedom or cheerfully support the tactics of tyrants would be grossly unfair. But the State Department mindset generally does not focus on questions of values and morals. State truly believes that "stability" is sacrificed if the spread of freedom becomes a top objective.

PROCESS OVER SUBSTANCE

State's actions in the realm of arms control and child abductions are remarkably similar in one key respect: State does not want to "anger" foreign governments. If State believed there would be no consequence from asking for the return of U.S. children, it would almost assuredly push for them to be reunited with their American parents. But because the foreign governments—whether Saudi Arabia or Sweden—will not hand over the American children without a fight, State does not want to "risk" a good relationship over a "few" U.S.

citizens. State typically sets its sights on less volatile goals, such as so-called "welfare visits" by U.S. embassy staff or even extremely limited, brief visits by the American parents. What State doesn't seem to understand is that such subservience breeds nothing but a lack of respect for the U.S. and a feeling of invincibility on the part of the foreign government.

In arms control, State doesn't come down hard on mass-proliferators like China and North Korea, because Foggy Bottom officials sincerely believe that such actions might close the channels of communication, resulting in diminished American influence over the actions of those governments. Look at what former State Department official Flynt Leverett (a ten-year Foggy Bottom veteran who stepped down in April 2003) told the *Washington Post* in May 2003, criticizing those who believe that "engaging" the Iranian mullahs only serves to bolster a corrupt and illegitimate regime: "What it means is we will end up with an Iran that has nuclear weapons and no dialogue with the United States with regard to our terrorist concerns."[6]

Success at State is measured by the level of communication and the number of deals signed. After North Korea flagrantly violated its 1994 pledge to stop developing nuclear weapons, what State wanted was further "talks" and another deal. With Iran topping the State Department's own annual global terror reports as the "most active state sponsor of terrorism" year after year, State's answer was to "engage" the mullahs, while steadfastly refusing to "engage" the millions of Iranians who desperately want the freedom Americans sometimes take for granted. After Saddam gassed thousands of his own people, State turned around and praised Iraq for agreeing to abide by international law and no longer use chemical weapons. The "substance"—Saddam gassing his own people—didn't matter as much to State as the "process"—his subsequent pledge not to use chemical weapons again.

MAKING FRIENDS

With smooth relations considered essential to maintaining American influence and thus "stability," State often goes to great lengths to make despots happy. It could be something as simple as Madeline Albright dancing with Kim Jong Il or William Burns apologizing to the suspected terrorist. It could be a bureaucratic favor, such as removing Saudi Arabia from the list of "countries of particular concern" in the religious freedom report or making it incredibly easy for Saudi nationals to obtain visas—even after fifteen of their fellow countrymen helped kill three thousand Americans on September 11, 2001. It could be helping in an area of significant concern for the dictatorship, such as lobbying Congress to lift sanctions on ruthless regimes in Iran and Libya. Or it could be fighting behind the scenes for $1 billion in loans for Saddam Hussein in the year before Iraq invaded Kuwait.

What State seems unable to understand is that groveling before foreign governments does not increase the likelihood of favorable action down the road. If anything, it encourages them to ask for— or demand—more favors. Regimes realize that they can get State to do what they want without having to open up their societies and reform their governments. State's "favors" only serve to perpetuate tyranny.

GRAY ZONE

Foggy Bottom officials face a dilemma: How can you work in good faith with some of the worst people alive, people with the blood of millions on their hands? Worse yet, how can you do favors for those very same people? Either as an occupational hazard, or because they joined State with these beliefs, Foggy Bottom officials are typically infected with extreme moral relativism. How else to explain looking the other way as Saudi Arabia persecutes its own people and threatens America's security by funding radical Islamic organizations? How else to explain viewing Saddam Hussein as a "moderating force" even after he had killed some 100,000 of his own people? Some people at State even see America as morally no better than many of the despotic regimes, says former Reagan administration State Department official Charles Hill. "There's a mentality that anything bad that happens in the world, America is responsible. You have perfectly bright college graduates who believe they are living in a semi-tyranny."[7]

Former Defense Department official Henry Sokolski's comment bears repeating: "There are two kinds of people in Washington: those who see gray because they know the difference between black and white, and those who see gray because they don't believe in black and white."[8] Some degree of realpolitik is understandable, even necessary. FDR had to work with Stalin in order to defeat Hitler. After that, communism was defeated, in part, with the help of regimes that were far from free. But communism eventually fell not because of realpolitik, but because of Reagan's impeccable moral clarity. Aside from referring to the Soviet Union as the "evil empire," the real value of what his administration did was to place human rights as the foremost priority in all dealings with the Soviets.

The first agreement that the U.S. reached with the Soviet Union under Reagan, notes former Reagan administration secretary of state George Shultz, was to free a group of Pentecostals who had taken refuge in the U.S. embassy in Moscow at the end of the Carter administration.[9] They had not been free to practice their religion and were not free to leave the country. He explains, "If they had been ejected from the embassy, they probably would have been murdered."[10] After the Pentacostals had lived in the basement there for several years, President Reagan personally told Soviet ambassador Anatoliy F. Dobrynin in early 1983 that the U.S. wanted them to be allowed to leave the Soviet Union. In time, they were allowed to leave the Soviet Union.

Ensuring freedom for several dozen people was not just another "agreement;" it established credibility with the Soviet Union. It showed the Soviets, says Shultz, that Reagan "really cares about human rights. What he's really after is to get these people out, not to get *credit* for getting them out."[11] Reagan made no political hay of what he had accomplished, as part of his pledge to Dobrynin.

The Reagan administration continued its emphasis on human rights, according to a former State Department official who notes, "We always started every meeting with our human rights concerns, and the Soviets knew they weren't going to get anywhere with us until they showed us that some real progress had been made."[12] Far from making negotiations more difficult, standing firm and promoting U.S. principles makes it possible for the U.S. to maintain respect as it pushes to exert its influence. If the U.S. is seen fighting for purely strategic benefits without much regard for American values or morals, exerting influence becomes much more difficult. Notes Sokolski: "If you're not fighting for something worthwhile, people get tired of you fighting."[13]

REWARDING FAILURE

Within a month of Yael Lempert being exposed in the *Wall Street Journal* for having asked auditors to help "shut down the INC [Iraqi National Congress]," State acted. It promoted her. She was given the lucrative perch of special assistant to undersecretary of state Mark Grossman, and was appointed in May 2003 to a special unit designated to help implement a democratic government in Iraq.[14]

Already in Iraq, as one of the first non-military U.S. officials inside the country after the fall of Saddam's regime, was the former assistant secretary of state for South Asia, Robin Rafael, the woman who loved the Taliban's "wonderful senses of humor." One of her first key moves in Iraq was in keeping with her past fondness for loathsome creatures: she reinstated as president of Baghdad University Saddam Hussein's personal physician.[15] And the person initially leading the U.S. effort to bring about democracy was Zalmay Khalilzad, the former Unocal consultant who early on supported the Taliban and promoted the building of an oil and gas pipeline through Afghanistan.

These curious promotions are part of a larger State Department predilection of rewarding failure. Look at Charles Parish, the official in the U.S. embassy in China whose alleged corruption was so notorious that it was written about in a local newspaper. Rather than getting fired, he was transferred to Washington—and later promoted. Look at Maura Harty, the woman who was in charge of helping recover abducted American children, yet who did nothing to help bring them back to the United States, and who was a part of the top management at State's Consular Affairs (CA) bureau when many of the terrorists got their visas through lax policies she strongly supported. She was tapped to replace Mary Ryan as head of CA in summer 2002. Sadly, this was merely in keeping with State's awarding of bonuses of $10,000—$15,000 each to four of the top five CA officials for "outstanding performance" in a twelve-month period that included September 11.

REVOLVING DOORS

But the greatest rewards for acting in ways that benefit foreign governments come not from State but from post-retirement employment. Vast sums of cash await those who were friendly to—or at least tolerated—despots and tyrants, particularly those in the Middle East. Places like the Middle East Institute and Meridian International Center, both of which feed from the Saudi trough, are filled with former State Department officials who were cozy with the House of Saud while at Foggy Bottom. Then there are others who work directly for the foreign governments as consultants and lobbyists, or for private companies that have joint interests with foreign governments (such as Khalilzad consulting Unocal, which wanted the Afghanistan pipeline built). This is not to say that Foggy Bottom officials consciously act with a mind toward future rewards, but the lure is there.

But a possibly more ominous revolving door—more dangerous because it is less obvious—is the one through which congressional staff head off to the State Department, or vice versa. Committees that handle State Department issues—International Relations in the House and Foreign Relations in the Senate—are brimming with former State Department officials, leading to warm relations with State and an abandonment of any real oversight. Even more worrisome, though, are congressional staffers angling for lucrative State Department positions. One Senate Foreign Relations Committee staffer, for example, pushed through Maura Harty's nomination in fall 2002, just as the staffer's tenure on the committee was about to end. It was well-known to others at the committee and to many at State that the staffer wanted a Foggy Bottom job. Sure enough, the person was given a job at State shortly after leaving Capitol Hill.

Congressmen who should be providing meaningful oversight of State Department activities are either unaware of or actively support State's agenda. Because congressmen typically look at the policy arena on an issue-by-issue basis, even those who would be appalled at much of what State does do not view State as the source of various problems. In other words, if a congressman does not like a particular State Department position, he or she will complain about State's posture on *that issue*, but fail to see it as part of a larger pattern. That being the case, there has been little movement on Capitol Hill to reform State, although that has changed in the wake of State's actions before and after the war in Iraq.

Standing in the way of any reforms is the bipartisan trifecta of congressional enablers: Senators Richard Lugar, Joseph Biden, and Chuck Hagel. These three are State's strongest allies, advancing its priorities and blocking bills it doesn't like. Lugar and Hagel, in particular, agree so strongly with State's worldview and are so willing to fight for it that they were the only two senators who voted against reauthorizing the Iran-Libya Sanctions Act in 2001.

STOCKHOLM SYNDROME

If you watched any Pentagon press briefings in the months before or after Operation Iraqi Freedom, you saw a press corps that was relentless in bombarding Defense secretary Donald Rumsfeld with tough questions. Which is exactly what they should be doing. Various media outlets ran stories challenging the Pentagon's positions and actions. In sharp contrast are the daily press briefings at State, where the questions are comparatively mild and rather benign. State spokesman Richard Boucher does field some tough questions, yet it is mostly a decidedly low-key affair. But it's not what questions are asked and how, but what questions are not asked.

In the eight months after the Visa Express program in the country that was home to fifteen September 11 terrorists was revealed—by Boucher himself, no less, as a throwaway line in a press briefing on October 31, 2001—exactly two questions were asked by people other than this author at the daily press briefings: one by a Fox News reporter, and the other by someone from the Saudi Press Agency. That was it. And after Congress held hearings on Visa Express in late June 2002, exactly two print stories could be found in Lexis-Nexis. (There were a handful of stories in late 2001 and early 2002 that mentioned Visa Express.) If the Pentagon, the White House, or Congress had kept open a program that had let in a number of the September 11 terrorists, the entire press corps would surely have mustered more than two questions and two stories—or at least so one would hope.

As another example, consider the reaction of State Department reporters after the *Washington Post* revealed that State kept secret North Korea's March 31, 2003 declaration to Foggy Bottom officials that it was reprocessing plutonium. The story broke over a weekend, and the following Monday, a single journalist asked Powell about it.

His response? "That's nonsense."

The secretary of state, though, refused to specify exactly who in the administration learned of North Korea's admission, only answering that the "appropriate" people knew. No one followed up by asking what "appropriate" meant, though in fairness, Powell was holding one of those brief "walk and talks" outside the building. But no one asked at the daily press briefings for a clarification. Nearly a month later, this author asked if anyone at the White House or Pentagon was informed of the March 31 declaration, but Boucher declined to answer, stating, "We have discussed all of that at many junctures here."[16] Boucher was incorrect; it hadn't been discussed in any fashion in a press briefing. Yet no other journalist challenged him on the point.

Several quality journalists cover the State Department, but they are outnumbered by pliant reporters who typically take what State says at face value. It is impossible to know for sure why they don't challenge Boucher more at press briefings or dig for dirt the way their Pentagon- and White House-based colleagues do. One possibility is that State's press corps believes that "access" is premised on favorable coverage. One journalist, several days before I was detained, told me, "You really need to go easy on Boucher. He's not such a bad guy— he gives me great access." After I was detained, the State Department press corps held a meeting (which I attended) to discuss whether they should write a letter expressing concern that a journalist was detained in the U.S. They opted not to.

It is probably true that criticizing State would cause a loss of "access." One journalist stopped me after a press briefing one day to tell me that several State Department officials would not talk to him because they thought he might "pull a Joel Mowbray." The journalist said that he assured them, "I'm not out to criticize you like that." Nevertheless, the reporter begged me, "Please just stay away from me. Don't sit next to me [at the press briefings.]" I thought he was kidding. He was not. As if to drive home his point, he moaned, "Dude, you're f—ing my sh— up."

"GUT IT"

When Ronald Reagan took over the White House in 1981, many conservatives focused on the need to reform State. Former Reagan administration official Morton Blackwell says that at a meeting in early 1981 of the "kitchen cabinet"—Reagan supporters who had yet to be placed in administration jobs—the new secretary of state asked the attendees for advice on reforming State. "When Al Haig went around the table," Blackwell explains, "every person gave the same basic answer: 'Gut it.'"[17] Haig told them that though he appreciated their concerns, he was going to attempt incremental reform. Although he brought on a number of capable and qualified political appointments, he was gone from his post before he had a chance to accomplish much.

Haig's successor, George Shultz, made concerted efforts to reform State, achieving mixed results. He placed a strong emphasis on human rights, and he tried to protect and promote people who didn't share State's worldview. To the extent he was successful beyond that, it was largely because he had an unusually large amount of contact with people outside his inner circle. Each morning, Shultz had three to four meetings, including one with officials below the assistant secretary level, which had the effect of minimizing direct undermining of President Reagan's agenda.[18] But it was during Shultz's tenure, for example, that Saddam acquired the massive amounts of chemical and biological agents and would have received—if State officials had had their way—1.5 million militarized atropine injectors, which would have allowed Saddam to immunize his troops with the injectors before unleashing a nerve gas attack. And while State successfully promoted freedom and human rights in Asia and Latin America, precious little on that front was done in the Middle East.

ULTIMATE JOB SECURITY

Even if a secretary of state were to devote himself full-time to the daunting task of reforming Foggy Bottom, it is not a sure thing that he would succeed. Once the normal day-to-day duties—such as talking to and meeting with world leaders—are completed, there is not a lot of time left over for implementing relatively sweeping changes. Aside from internal revolt—not to be discounted, since a secretary of state needs his "troops" in order to get almost anything done—the rules are stacked against reform. The secretary of state does not have the power to fire any member of the Foreign Service, even if someone is convicted of a felony. Only the independent Foreign Service Grievance Board has the power to fire members of the Foreign Service.

The ten thousand members of the Foreign Service—who constitute roughly sixty percent of State's U.S. citizen employees—will probably never lose their jobs. Although they can be sent to the grievance board for serious violations, Foreign Service officers (FSOs) rarely, if ever, are referred there. The system is rigged to minimize the number of people who could ever be forced out of the Foreign Service. Only if someone has been found to be among the lowest five percent in terms of performance twice in any five-year period does that person even face the review board. In 2002, only forty-four were sent before the board; just twelve were "asked to leave" the Foreign Service. That year, *not one* person out of ten thousand was fired for incompetence.[19] The figure for the number fired for insubordination would be interesting—likely the same number as those canned for incompetence—but State *doesn't even list* "insubordination" as a category of grounds for termination.

PERSONNEL IS CULTURE

Any reform of State must be premised on changing the institutional culture of Foggy Bottom—a herculean undertaking when ten thousand FSOs are essentially beyond reproach and the other careerists, the civil servants, also have incredibly strong, union-negotiated work-place protection rules. Changing the culture without changing almost any of the people within it is remarkably difficult; the old adage that "personnel is policy" applies just as easily to culture. But there are some changes that can—and should—be made.

Out of the roughly seventeen thousand U.S. citizen employees in the second Bush administration's State Department, fewer than two percent are political appointments from outside State. This is Colin Powell's greatest shortcoming as secretary of state. While it makes sense for a general to trust his troops—one of Powell's earliest pledges was to promote and enhance the role of State's careerists—Foggy Bottom is not the military. It would be hard to imagine that he does not know the level of insubordination against the president that occurs underneath him, but to be fair, most of the information he receives is from those around him—people who don't want reform.

What Powell needs to do is bring in fresh blood from the outside, people who are willing to challenge State's beliefs and actions. But of the thirty-nine undersecretary and assistant secretary positions, forty percent of them are held by career State officials, and half of the remaining are filled by people who are part of Washington's foreign policy establishment, which was created and is populated largely by former State Department officials. The foreign policy establishment is incredibly in-synch with State, and serious dissent within the community is both frowned-upon and rare. When asked what percent of deputy assistant secretary (DAS) positions were filled by career State Department employees, State's press office refused to answer. But according to estimates from several State officials, fewer than twenty percent of DAS-level positions are filled by people who are not part of the foreign policy establishment.

Having political appointments alone is not a measure of success-ful reform. Haig brought in many good people, including Francis Fukuyama and Michael Ledeen, but he changed little. It also depends on the type of people hired. Richard Armitage, for example, has become the greatest defender of State's careerists. He was intimately involved in State's efforts to "shut down the INC [Iraqi National Congress]," he was the one who removed Saudi Arabia from the list of "countries of particular concern" on the religious freedom report, called Iran a "democracy" in February 2003, shielded Powell from the true nature of the Scud missile shipment from North Korea to Yemen in late 2002, and has led numerous witch hunts to intimidate his political enemies—the ones who want reform—inside State. This should not have been entirely unexpected; he was, after all, the biggest advocate for selling Saddam Hussein 1.5 million militarized atropine injectors in 1988. He is the embodiment of everything that is wrong at State—but the only upside of getting rid of him would be making the potential for reform greater.

FIXING STATE

In the short term, reforming State would take enormous effort to achieve modest results. The maximum number of positions should go to reform-minded political appointments, though there should always be room for those outstanding FSOs who have served their country well. If the secretary of state refuses to fill positions with people from the outside, then the White House should insert itself into the hiring process and insist that people committed to reform must be hired. But even with good personnel, reform is not a given. Managing thousands of employees who are potentially hostile to an administration's policies is enormously challenging but crucial. According to several veterans of the Shultz era, Reagan's second secretary of state made great strides with his strong emphasis on open lines of communication with careerists below the top levels. It is worth noting that the Foreign Service loved Shultz, whose policies it largely despised, much more than Madeline Albright, whose policies it generally supported. The key difference is that, unlike Shultz, Albright used her top advisers as a virtual cocoon to shield herself from contact with most of State's careerists.

For the longer term, the rules inhibiting reform must be changed or scrapped. The president and the secretary of state need to be given a free hand to fire all felons and anyone who attempts to undermine the president's foreign policy. This does not mean abandoning all employment protections, but flagrant insubordination should never be protected. The number of potential political appointments must be increased, and those positions filled by people willing to challenge State's traditional worldview.

The most important reform of all is deceptively simple—and one that has been used before. All new hires at the State Department should be brought up to the secretary of state's office, walked over to a globe, and asked, "Point to your country."

Appendix: Documents

Cable No. 7: Drop Box and Personal Appearance Waiver (PAW) Programs

State 211672

November 1997

Ref: State 185823

Go to Cable 8

Introduction

1. As a follow-up to REFTEL, which laid the groundwork for best practices in the NIV area, this cable provides further guidance on drop box and personal appearance waiver (PAW) programs-both effective ways to free up limited consular resources. Even posts that have a relatively high refusal rate can find segments of the applicant pool that are likely issuances. Consular officers should step back and analyze their workload to identify those applicants for whom a personal interview only slows down the issuance process. Interview time should be devoted to the difficult and problematic cases.

Personal Appearance Waivers: the Legal Basis

2. Section 222(e) of the INA and 9 FAM 41.102(a) cover the general requirement that all aliens applying for a nonimmigrant visa appear before a consular officer unless the consular officer waives personal appearance. The FAM reference specifically authorizes such a waiver for children under 14, officials and diplomats, airline crew, certain USG-financed exchange visitors, and applicants for B, C-1, H-1, or I visas. All other NIV applicants can also benefit from a waiver of personal appearance if the consular officer determines that a waiver is warranted "in the national interest or because of unusual circumstances, including hardship to the visa applicant."

3. Although the regulations have not been amended to incorporate several new visa categories (M through S), it is clear that the intent of the regulation was to encourage interviews in E, F, H-2/3, and L cases. Given the complexity of many E, H-2/3, and L cases, interviews are often warranted, particularly in countries where these categories are prone to fraud. Interviews in these cases may be necessary to establish that the applicant's knowledgeability regarding his/her planned activities, reflect his/her claimed position, or role in the US venture. In the case of students, consular officers are encouraged to make an assessment of English language skills when relevant, although secondary evidence such as TOEFL scores can provide a useful basis for judging proficiency as well, if there is little evidence to raise fraud concerns. Despite the

This document (which continues on the next two pages) comes from the "best practices" handbook, which lays out the policies that must be followed by consular officers in issuing visas. The highlighted sentence, which was still current policy in summer 2002, shows how courtesy was a higher concern than security. Because of the "courtesy culture," consular officers were strongly encouraged to minimize the number of visa applicants interviewed, so as not to "slow down the issuance process."

The actual range of criteria selected by a post is virtually unlimited, but common criteria include age, prior visas, evidence of prior overseas travel, employment by certain companies or in certain sectors, salary levels, and type of visa requested. If posts find that they are requesting additional information or requiring interviews for more than ten percent of drop box applicants, they should reevaluate their drop box criteria, since such extra handling negates any savings in resources achieved by reducing the number of interviews.

Mail-in Applications

11. Posts that allow mail-in applications generally establish procedures not unlike those employed with an unmanned drop box system. The main difference is the manner in which the MRV fee is paid. Since neither the applicant nor the applicant's agent will be dropping off the application at the post, payment of the MRV fee to the consular cashier may not be convenient and any advantage to the public which a mail-in procedure would have over use of a drop box is lost. At posts where MRV fees can be paid to third parties (such as local post offices or banks), the mail-in option will be an attractive alternative to the drop box system. If fees must be paid to the consular cashier, however, posts will generally want to encourage applicants to use the drop box, although posts can mail back visa and passports and accompanying documents if a franked, self-addressed envelope is included with the application (as stated above).

12. Needless to say, implementation of a mail-in application system should only be considered in areas where the local postal service is reasonably reliable. Posts will also need to make application forms and instructions easily available to the public by mailing forms on request and/or disseminating forms to travel agencies or other third-party entities throughout the consular district.

Third-Party Screening

13. There are several procedures commonly used by consular sections, which would qualify as "third-party screening." The most common systems are: 1) embassy referrals (the subject of other cables and described in the Consular Management Handbook), 2) corporate referrals, and 3) travel agency cases. In all three systems, the referring party is responsible for preparing and presenting the application and any supporting evidence and, in the case of embassy and corporate referrals, certifying that there are no apparent factors that would disqualify the applicant for the NIV category sought. Consular officers cannot, of course, delegate visa adjudication authority to any outside entity, but the ability of a third party to pre-screen ostensibly qualified applicants is important. All three systems work best when it is understood that improperly submitted cases can terminate PAW privileges. For this reason, posts should establish some type of validation system whereby referred applicants can be tracked, at least on a random basis, to ensure that they return within the timeframe indicated in the application. This

Although Saudi Arabia was the only country to have a nationwide program where all residents were expected to apply for visas at travel agencies, partial versions of Visa Express exist throughout the world. State claims that travel agencies do nothing more than pass on the visa applications to the consulates or embassies, but it is clear that the travel agents are expected to help in "preparing and presenting the application," as well as taking the time to "pre-screen ostensibly qualified applicants."

tracking can be accomplished by having the referring party submit evidence of return (such as a stamped passport) or contacting the applicant directly. The subject of validation studies will be dealt with more fully SEPTEL.

14. In the case of corporate referrals, the relationship between the company and the applicant must be substantive, i.e., the applicant must be an employee, contractor, consultant or be otherwise involved substantially in the company's business. In some instances, posts may broaden this category to include major clients or suppliers of the company whose travel to the US directly supports the company's business. The selection of companies given visa referral privileges and the criteria for referred applicants is varied and depends upon post's assessment of local conditions as well as the integrity and capability of the company. Many posts give preference to US-based or US-owned companies, often consolidating the referral process through the local American Chamber of Commerce. Posts must also devise procedures, which are not overly onerous to the company but preserve the integrity of the process. It is advisable to restrict referral privileges to only a small number of designated company officers. Other factors to consider are a company's size, the volume of travel it sponsors to the US, and its reputation. It is inappropriate for companies to refer individuals who have no relationship to the company or whose only relationship is payment of a fee for visa referral privileges.

15. In the case of travel agency cases, there is generally no substantive relationship between the travel agency and the applicant whose case is being submitted. The applicant simply purchases tickets and/or makes other travel arrangements through the agency. The integrity and judgment of the travel agency is important, since the consular officer is relying on the travel agency to a degree to screen out obviously unqualified applicants. In many, if not most cases, this screening process will be largely based on financial factors, i.e., if the travel agency is reasonably satisfied that the traveler has the means to buy a tour "package," there will be little further evaluation of the applicant's qualifications for an NIV. Posts will want to work with experienced, reputable, and knowledgeable agencies and encourage them to refer dubious clients to the consular section for a personal interview. In many countries, local conditions and fraud concerns will lead posts to reject any use of travel agencies for pre-screening of visa applicants. But in those countries where posts are able to use travel agencies as third-party screeners, the system can greatly expand the volume of applicants who can benefit from a personal appearance waiver.

16. Posts have the flexibility to hold third-party screeners to whatever standard of performance is felt appropriate. SEPTEL will address the remote data entry system (RDS). RDS is a system used in a number of posts which require travel agencies and, in some cases other third-party screeners, to prepare electronic media with applicant information which can be downloaded into the post's own automated systems to reduce data input by consular staff. As noted above, posts can encourage good performance by following up with randomly selected applicants to ensure that they complied with the

As of June 2002—some nine months after September 11—State refused visas for Saudi nationals only if their names were on a "watch list" or if they didn't have much money. And financial determinations apparently were not made by U.S. citizens, but by travel agents, who were expected to help "screen out obviously unqualified applicants." Most disturbing of all, though, is that "if the travel agency is reasonably satisfied that the traveler has the means to buy a tour 'package,' there will be little further evaluation of the applicant's qualifications for an NIV (non-immigrant visa.)"

O 061329Z AUG 02
FM AMEMBASSY RIYADH
TO SECSTATE WASHDC IMMEDIATE 3364
INFO GULF COOPERATION COUNCIL COLLECTIVE

UNCLAS RIYADH 005308

CA FOR LANNON, NEA FOR CROCKER, NEA/ARP FOR CORBIN

E.O. 12958: N/A
TAGS: CVIS, CMGT, AMGT, PREL, SA
SUBJECT: UPDATE ON NONIMMIGRANT VISA PROCESSING IN SAUDI
ARABIA

REF: Riyadh 04784

1.   Summary: Since we started interviewing all nonimmigrant
     (NIV) applicants 12 to 70 years of age on July 20, the NIV
     Units in both Riyadh and Jeddah have been forced to make
     major adjustments in processing procedures. Interviewing is
     labor-intensive and we have requested additional staffing,
     both temporary and permanent, to deal with the new realities
     of visa processing in Saudi Arabia. We also are negotiating
     with a local call center company to set an NIV
     appointment/information system for NIV applicants
     countrywide and expect to have a system in place in
     September. We have approximately 1,850 approved NIV
     applicants in queue for clearances, many of whom are
     students on scholarships or family members of individuals
     requiring emergency medical treatment. End Summary.

2.   Since July 20, both Riyadh and Jeddah consular sections
     have required applicants between the ages of 12 and 70 to
     apply personally for their nonimmigrant visas. The only
     exceptions to this rule are applicants for A and G visas,
     Class A referrals and the bedridden travelling to the U.S.
     for emergency medical treatment. In Riyadh, we are
     interviewing between 80 and 120 applicants a day and in
     Jeddah between 40 and 60 a day. Although these numbers may
     not seem high, interviews are extremely labor-intensive due
     to poorly completed applications, language barriers, and the
     need to gather a wide range of information on the applicant
     to initiate clearance procedures. Mandatory clearance
     requirements for the majority of our applicants have
     resulted in the introduction of whole new layers of NIV
     processing procedures. Applications are now further

UNCLASSIFIED
1

After a month of public outcry over Visa Express, State finally requires
applicants in Saudi Arabia to apply for a visa in person at the embassy
in Riyadh or consulate in Jeddah.

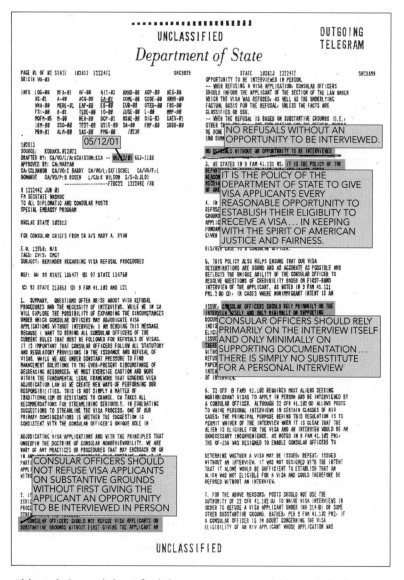

Although State did not feel that interviews would be helpful for what they considered "obviously qualified applicants," it did believe in interviews—for people who might otherwise be refused a visa. Part of the "courtesy culture" was the concept of "fundamental fairness"— for foreign visa applicants. As shown above, State wanted "to give visa applicants every reasonable opportunity to establish their eligibility to receive a visa."

UNCLASSIFIED   OUTGOING
TELEGRAM

Department of State

SHCS899

PAGE 02 OF 02 STATE   102813 122247Z
SUBMITTED BY MAIL OR MESSENGER, THE OFFICER SHALL REQUEST
THE ALIEN TO APPEAR IN PERSON.

8. WE RECOGNIZE THAT THIS POLICY HAS WORKLOAD IMPLICATIONS
AND ALSO MAY ENGENDER COMPLAINTS FROM SOME ALIENS WHO MAY
TRAVEL GREAT DISTANCES FOR INTERVIEWS, ONLY TO BE REFUSED.
NONETHELESS, WE BELIEVE THAT FUNDAMENTAL FAIRNESS REQUIRES
US TO FOLLOW THIS POLICY. WE ARE HOWEVER EXPLORING
MODIFICATION OF THIS POLICY WHICH, WHILE REMAINING TRUE TO
THE UNDERLYING PRINCIPLE OF FAIRNESS, MAY PROVIDE FOR
AVENUES TO REDUCE SOME WORKLOAD IN THIS AREA. SUCH
MODIFICATIONS WILL REQUIRE REGULATORY CHANGES. POSTS WILL
BE INFORMED AS SOON AS ANY SUCH AMENDMENTS ARE IMPLEMENTED.

PERSONALLY INFORM THE APPLICANT OF THE GROUND OF REFUSAL

9. INA 212(B) AND 22 CFR 41.121 AND 42.81 REQUIRE
CONSULAR OFFICERS TO INFORM THE APPLICANT OF THE PROVISION
OF THE LAW UPON WHICH A REFUSAL IS BASED. IN ADDITION, AS

NOTED IN REFS B AND C, IT HAS BEEN THE LONG-STANDING POLICY
THAT CONSULAR OFFICERS GENERALLY SHOULD ALSO INFORM THE
APPLICANT OF THE FACTUAL BASIS UNDERLYING THE REFUSAL.
HOWEVER, THE UNDERLYING FACTUAL INFORMATION SHOULD NOT BE
DIVULGED TO THE APPLICANT IF THE INFORMATION IS CLASSIFIED
OR SBU, OR IF IT WAS OBTAINED FROM ANOTHER AGENCY AND THE
AGENCY HAS NOT AUTHORIZED RELEASE OF THE INFORMATION.

10. AS WITH THE NO-REFUSAL-WITHOUT-AN-INTERVIEW POLICY,
THE POLICY OF INFORMING THE APPLICANT OF THE FACTS
UNDERLYING THE DENIAL IS ROOTED IN NOTIONS OF FUNDAMENTAL
FAIRNESS AND ALSO SERVES TO ENSURE THAT OUR VISA DECISIONS
ARE BASED ON A THOROUGH AND ACCURATE UNDERSTANDING OF THE
FACTS. FROM A FAIRNESS PERSPECTIVE, THE APPLICANT, WHERE
POSSIBLE, OUGHT TO BE TOLD THE FACTUAL BASIS FOR THE
FINDING SO THAT HE UNDERSTANDS THE DECISION AND HAS A
REASONABLE OPPORTUNITY TO REBUT IT. IN ADDITION, IF THE
CONSULAR OFFICER'S DECISION IS BASED ON AN ERRONEOUS
UNDERSTANDING OF THE FACTS, THERE IS A SIGNIFICANT
LIKELIHOOD THAT THE FACTUAL ERROR WILL BE CORRECTED BY THE
ALIEN WHEN THE CONSULAR OFFICER INFORMS THE APPLICANT OF
THE OFFICER'S FACTUAL FINDINGS, THUS INCREASING THE
LIKELIHOOD THAT A PROPER DECISION WILL BE MADE.

11. 9 FAM 41.121 PN1.2 STATES THAT WHEN AN ALIEN IS FOUND
INELIGIBLE TO RECEIVE A VISA, THE CONSULAR OFFICER SHOULD
INFORM THE ALIEN ORALLY OF THE BASIS FOR THE REFUSAL. IN
ADDITION TO THE REQUIRED WRITTEN NOTICE, PER REF A, WHILE
WE ARE WILLING TO PERMIT CONSULAR OFFICERS TO FOREGO AN
ORAL EXPLANATION IN CASES INVOLVING NON-SUBSTANTIVE
REFUSALS UNDER 221(G), WE DO NOT BELIEVE IT IS APPROPRIATE

TO SUBSTITUTE A WRITTEN EXPLANATION FOR AN IN-PERSON ORAL
EXPLANATION IN CASES WHERE THE REFUSAL IS BASED ON 214(B)
OR SOME OTHER SUBSTANTIVE GROUND. AS NOTED ABOVE, SUCH
REFUSALS REQUIRE A PERSONAL INTERVIEW, AND THE REQUIRED
ORAL EXPLANATION OF THE BASIS FOR THE REFUSAL CAN BE MADE
AT THE END OF THE PERSONAL INTERVIEW.

12. WHILE PROVIDING A THOROUGH ORAL EXPLANATION FOR THE
BASIS OF THE REFUSAL MAY TAKE A LITTLE MORE TIME, IN THE
LONG RUN IT SAVES WORK FOR EVERYONE. INADEQUATE (OR NO)

EXPLANATIONS FOR REFUSALS MERELY PROMPT SUBSEQUENT WRITTEN
AND PHONE INQUIRIES FROM THE APPLICANT, HIS/HER FAMILY,
MEMBERS OF CONGRESS, AND OTHERS. MANY SUCH INQUIRIES ARE
DIRECTED TO VO, WHICH MUST THEN CONTACT POST TO FIND OUT
THE BASIS FOR THE REFUSAL. REGARDLESS OF WHETHER POST IS
CONTACTED BY VO OR BY THE INQUIRER DIRECTLY, POST ENDS UP
HAVING TO PROVIDE A REPORT ON THE BASIS FOR THE REFUSAL.

STATE   102813 122247Z   SHCS899

AND IN MOST INSTANCES THE TIME SPENT ON SUCH FOLLOW-UP
QUERIES, AT POST AND IN THE DEPARTMENT, FAR EXCEEDS THE
TIME IT WOULD HAVE TAKEN TO PROVIDE A SUFFICIENT
EXPLANATION AT THE TIME OF INTERVIEW.

13. WE KNOW THAT MANY OF YOU WOULD LIKE TO BE ABLE TO
FURTHER STREAMLINE THE NIV APPLICATION PROCESS AND RELY TO
A GREATER EXTENT ON MAIL, DROP BOX, AND OTHER PROCEDURES
THAT DO NOT REQUIRE PERSONAL APPEARANCE. WE AGREE THAT
THIS IS A VERY WORTHY GOAL, AND WE FULLY SUPPORT YOU IN
YOUR EFFORTS TO STREAMLINE THE PROCESS FOR VISA ISSUANCES.
VISA REFUSALS, HOWEVER, REQUIRE EXTRA PROTECTIONS, AND
THERE ARE LIMITS TO HOW FAR WE CAN GO IN THAT AREA. WHILE

WE UNDERSTAND THAT PROHIBITING SUBSTANTIVE REFUSALS BY MAIL
WILL HAVE WORKLOAD IMPLICATIONS, WE WANT TO BE AS FAIR AS
WE CAN TO THOSE APPLICANTS WE REFUSE, AND WE DO NOT WANT TO
RISK CONSULAR NONREVIEWABILITY FOR THE SAKE OF EFFICIENCIES
IN PROCESSING. IT IS IN LIGHT OF THESE CONSTRAINTS THAT WE
ARE REMINDING POSTS TO CONTINUE FOLLOWING CURRENT REFUSAL
PROCEDURES, AS WE EXAMINE POSSIBLE REGULATORY CHANGES THAT
MIGHT ADDRESS SOME OF THE WORKLOAD CONCERNS. WHILE STILL
ENSURING THAT REFUSED APPLICANTS ARE GIVEN FULL AND FAIR
CONSIDERATION OF THEIR CASES. WARM REGARDS.
POWELL

> RELY TO A GREATER EXTENT ON MAIL...
> PROCEDURES THAT DO NOT REQUIRE
> PERSONAL APPEARANCE. WE AGREE
> THAT THIS IS A VERY WORTHY GOAL.

UNCLASSIFIED

In the second page of this cable, which was dated June 12, 2001, State says it wants to work with consulates and embassies to further advance the "courtesy culture." Notice that State believes it is a "very worthy goal" to "rely to a greater extent on...procedures that do not require [a] personal appearance [of visa applicants]."

```
Ipppdts

                    CONFIDENTIAL    PTP8636

PAGE 01        RIYADH 04340  00 OF 02 0914052

ACTION: CA(01)

INFO: CMS(01) D(01)  NEA(01) P(01)  S(01)
      SWO(01)
------------------ 091015L JUL 02 MEW [TOTAL COPIES:007]


INFO: CWG(00) CWG(00) DSCC(00) D(00)
      M(00)   M(00)   R(00)    SCT(00)
      SSEX(00) SSO(00) SSWO(00)
      SSO(00) SS(00)  SS(00)
      USNW(00) USNW(00) WO(00)
------------------ 091407Z JUL 02 STePS [TOTAL COPIES:000]

ACTION SSO-00

INFO  LOG-00  CA-01  ANHR-00  DS-00  TEDE-00  M-00   NEA-00
      MSCE-00  SCT-00  SS-00   DSCC-00  EAS-00   /001W
      ------------------CSBP96  0914062 /38

O 091403Z JUL 02
FM AMEMBASSY RIYADH
TO SECSTATE WASHDC IMMEDIATE 2351
NSC WASHDC IMMEDIATE
INFO GULF COOPERATION COUNCIL COLLECTIVE
AMCONSUL JEDDAH

C O N F I D E N T I A L   RIYADH 004340

FOR U/S GREEN, CA A/S RYAN AND NEA A/S BURNS
NSC FOR JOHN CRAIG
S/CT FOR MARK WONG
CA ALSO FOR WAYNE GRIFF[...]
FROM THE AMBASSADOR       07/09

E.O. 12958: DECL: 07/[..]/2012
TAGS: CVIS, ASEC, PTER, SA
SUBJECT: REQUEST FOR GUIDANCE ON TERMINATION OF VISA EXPRESS
```

REQUEST FOR GUIDANCE ON TERMINATION OF VISA EXPRESS

```
                              ONS 1.5 (D).
                                     ting on
June 24 as part of on-going review of NIV policies and
practices post 9/11. Posts in Saudi Arabia have continually
sought to enhance and improve NIV processing following 9/11
and will continue to do so. A key to effective screening
remains better and constantly updated intel available online
for visa issuing officers. Although the group believes that
our policies are consistent with Department guidelines, best
practices, and security procedures, Mission efforts have been
undermined by uninformed media reports. The Ambassador
consider[..] that the confidence of the American public in our
eff[..]                                   thus recommends
that                                      gthen
cons[..]                                  fforts by
ass[..]                                   [..]t is needed.
Pla[..]                                   summary.
```

Mission efforts have been undermined by uninformed media reports.

```
2. (C) On June 24, the Ambassador chaired a meeting of senior
Mission officers, including the Consul General in Riyadh and
head of consular office in Jeddah (our two visa issuing
posts) to review the Mission's NIV policies and practices in
the post-9/11 environment.

Current NIV procedures
----------------------

3. (C) The Consul General provided an overview of how the
Mission's NIV practices have changed since 9/11. Immediately
following the terrorist attack, both Riyadh and Jeddah began
```

```
requiring that most young men and students appear personally
for interviews before visa issuance. Both posts complied
immediately with every new guidance received from the
Department as to new clearance requirements for certain types
of travelers.

4. (C) Currently, it is Mission practice that, with very few
exceptions, all men from countries of concern, between the
ages of 16-48, present themselves for a personal interview.
Approximately 45 % of all visa applicants are getting a
personal interview or are dependents of an applicant who
requires an interview. Consular officers continue to waive
personal appearance for most women, minors, and the elderly.
```

Approximately 45% of all visa applicants are getting a personal interview or are dependents of an applicant who requires an interview.

```
5. (C) Consul General made clear that a cleared, qualified
American consular officer remains in charge of the entire
process and that all adjudications are made by a consular
officer who affirms that the appropriate security clearances
have been obtained.

Waiver authority
----------------

6. (C) The ambassador then asked that the group discuss the
visa referral policy and current waiver authority for the
visas condor clearance process and how we are using it. He
stressed his insistence that we use this authority sparingly
and with very careful consideration of each and every case.
The Consul General is the overall reviewing officer for visa
referrals that sometimes also include a recommendation to
waive the Visas Condor process for those well and favorably
known to Mission officers. He stressed the importance of
making sure that each such recommendation convey a clear,
definite explanation of how such a waiver would be in the
interest of the US government and that some urgent
circumstances should be present in order to consider the
recommendation.

7. (C) The group also agreed that domestic servants would
never be the subject of a visa referral, with the possible
exception of long-term servants of very senior government
officials on official business.

A visas
-------

8. (C) The consuls briefed that they are also scrutinizing
notes requesting official (A) visas and at times calling in
the applicants to assure that their intended travel is, in

fact, official.

9. (C) USMTM representatives and consuls explained that Saudi
military trainees routinely receive A-2 visas and that they
are not interviewed. USMTM believed that going to formal
individual interviews could derail the training programs,
which have just restarted. USMTM has approved a suggestion
to institute an "orientation program," which will take place
before the travel and visa application for trainees going to
the United States. The Embassy and USMTM are consulting to
develop the detailed requirements for this program. It will
be conducted by a USMTM officer, who would meet each proposed
trainee, to gain some sense of his background, interests, and
service specialty. Should the USMTM officer believe that any
trainee exhibited any questionable attitudes or behavior, he
would further consult with his command and the Consul General
and possibly other concerned embassy offices before
proceeding with the visa application, which might also
include a request for a personal interview with the consular
officer. Consul General also urged section and agencies to
```

This is the infamous cable that the author of this book asked State spokesman Richard Boucher about at a daily press briefing. Boucher said "no" when asked if the U.S. Ambassador to Saudi Arabia had asked that Visa Express be shut down. But read the subject line: "Request for guidance of termination of Visa Express." Also, if you look at the highlighted sentence in paragraph 4, you'll see that even after State beefed up the number of interviews conducted, more than half of all visa applicants were not being interviewed.

...ke clearance checks through the consular section and interested agencies of all potential USG-sponsored visitors part of the selection process.

Other vulnerabilities?
----

10. (C) The Ambassador asked that the group consider other possible vulnerabilities in the current process. The DCM asked about moving to a full, 100% interview policy and to scrapping the use of travel agencies. The Consul General stated that he would certainly institute such a process if the Department believed it appropriate and provided additional resources. The current process of limiting interviews to defined groups, with some random interviewing, allowed consular officers to focus more time and attention on applicants from a higher-risk pool. Using the travel agents to assure that documentation is complete and in compliance with guidelines saved the consular officers from spending valuable time pre-interviewing applicants whose paperwork was not in order. In addition, the current system prevented large crowds from forming outside the Embassy and Consulate which posed additional security concerns.

Ambassador's Comment
----

11. (C) I am satisfied that we are taking reasonable precautions to assure the integrity of my Mission's non-immigrant visa issuing process. I have explained to my staff that this Mission has no higher priority than to assure that we do our utmost to prevent terrorists from entering the United States. We will continue to evaluate this process on an on-going basis.

12. (C) However, I am deeply troubled about the prevailing perception in the media and within Congress and possibly among the American public at large that our current practices represent a shameful and inadequate effort on our part. It is extremely demoralizing to my officers to see these stories and to realize that the truth of the matter is of no interest. Not only must I be concerned with the processes at work here, but also with the perception of what we are doing. If the public and the Congress have no faith in us, then I must recommend further changes.

3. (C) Accordingly, I have asked the Consul General to develop within the next week, a proposal to the Department that will outline further measures: a move toward interviewing all adult applicants and toward eliminating the role of travel agencies in forwarding visa applications to the Embassy and Consulate. This will certainly require additional resources. I would urge that the Department immediately send its best consular operational expert to Saudi Arabia to work with us to develop a system in which all Americans may have confidence. I want to move on these proposals immediately.

ordan
ordan

CONFIDENTIAL

The second page of the cable spells out in no uncertain terms that travel agencies under Visa Express were helping ensure "compliance" and were "pre-interviewing applicants."

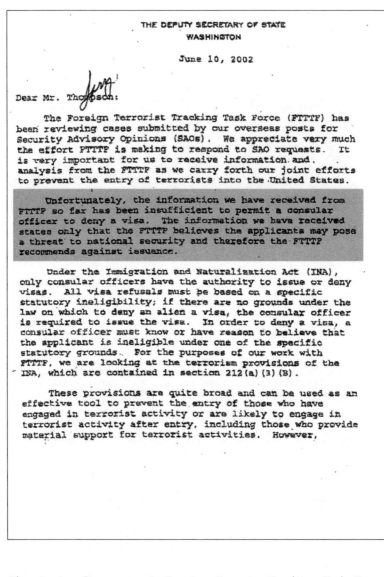

THE DEPUTY SECRETARY OF STATE
WASHINGTON

June 10, 2002

Dear Mr. Thompson:

The Foreign Terrorist Tracking Task Force (FTTTF) has been reviewing cases submitted by our overseas posts for Security Advisory Opinions (SAOs). We appreciate very much the effort FTTTF is making to respond to SAO requests. It is very important for us to receive information and analysis from the FTTTF as we carry forth our joint efforts to prevent the entry of terrorists into the United States.

Unfortunately, the information we have received from FTTTF so far has been insufficient to permit a consular officer to deny a visa. The information we have received states only that the FTTTF believes the applicants may pose a threat to national security and therefore the FTTTF recommends against issuance.

Under the Immigration and Naturalization Act (INA), only consular officers have the authority to issue or deny visas. All visa refusals must be based on a specific statutory ineligibility; if there are no grounds under the law on which to deny an alien a visa, the consular officer is required to issue the visa. In order to deny a visa, a consular officer must know or have reason to believe that the applicant is ineligible under one of the specific statutory grounds. For the purposes of our work with FTTTF, we are looking at the terrorism provisions of the INA, which are contained in section 212(a)(3)(B).

These provisions are quite broad and can be used as an effective tool to prevent the entry of those who have engaged in terrorist activity or are likely to engage in terrorist activity after entry, including those who provide material support for terrorist activities. However,

The Justice Department's Foreign Terrorist Tracking Task Force (FTTTF) had made a reasonable recommendation to the State Department: deny visas to all suspected terrorists. State didn't agree. It wanted Justice's information so that it could make its own determination. As State's number-two official, Richard Armitage writes, it is not enough to deny a visa based on FTTTF's belief that "the applicants may pose a threat to national security."

DECLASSIFIED

SECRET   RELEASED

GUIDELINES FOR U.S.-IRAQ POLICY

The U.S. transition comes as we must choose a new direction in our policy towards Iraq. The war with Iran is over, and much of the basis for our previous dialogue is gone with it. It is up to the new Administration to decide whether to treat Iraq as a distasteful dictatorship to be shunned where possible, or to recognize Iraq's present and potential power in the region and accord it relatively high priority. We strongly urge the latter view. Because of the narrow focus of past dialogue, our relations have tended to swing from over-enthusiasm to over-hostility, depending on events. We believe steady relations concentrating on trade can avoid both extremes and further U.S. interests in the region.

I.   **Why Bother**

Iraq has come through its war with Iran with great military and political power, and is aiming higher. President Saddam Hussein has the wherewithal to be a major player in regional affairs, as a prominent member in a loose alignment of conservative Arab states featuring Egypt, Jordan, Saudi Arabia and Kuwait. Iraq's prestige among these nations, its vast oil reserves promising a lucrative market for U.S. goods, and its status as a wavering Soviet quasi-client all give our bilateral political relationship importance and room for opportunity.

The lessons of war may have changed Iraq from a radical state challenging the system to a more responsible, status-quo state working within the system, and promoting stability in the region. We use "may have changed" because Iraq's postwar intentions are still evolving, and it is this evolution which lends importance to U.S. efforts. Even aligned with our regional friends, however, dealing with Iraq will remain difficult. Iraq has never lost its heavy touch in foreign affairs -- as we can see by its big stick approach to the Kuwait border issue and in Lebanon -- and its heavy-handedness will probably come to the fore in dealing with the GCC when it comes to terms with Iran. S.-Iraqi ties.

II.   **Factors in the Relationship**

The U.S. and Iraq began to draw closer in 1984, when traditional hostility and suspicion were outweighed by the shared goal of containing Iran and seeking peace in the Gulf War. Diplomatic relations, severed in 1967, were resumed in November, 1984. Iraq offered a counterweight to our ruptured ties with the more strategically placed Iran, and a bulwark against expansion of the Islamic Revolution. Iraq also sought

SECRET
DECL: OADR

DECLASSIFIED

As President George Bush was taking office in January 1989, the Iran-Iraq war had ended and Saddam Hussein had already killed some 100,000 of his own people just five months earlier. It was in this context that State Department careerists from the Near Eastern Affairs (NEA) bureau recommended (in this then-classified memo which continues on the next three pages) to the incoming secretary of state, James Baker, that the U.S. "recognize Iraq's present and potential power in the region and accord it relatively high priority."

DECLASSIFIED

these ties in its desire for evidence of international respectability. We cooperated with Iraq politically and, increasingly, militarily in an effort to end the Gulf War and the threat to important friends such as Saudi Arabia and Kuwait.

When war ended, much of the impetus to draw closer to Iraq was lost -- we have much less to talk about, and several factors have emerged to pull us apart:

-- The tendency to view our relations with Iran and Iraq as a "zero-sum" game may lead us to offer our relations with Iraq as a hostage to improved relations with Iran.

-- Iraq's unlawful use of chemical weapons has aroused great emotions in the U.S.; any Iraqi resumption of CW use will probably destroy the entire relationship.

-- Iraq's new military capabilities and aspirations, coupled with its 1970's reputation as a radical, rejectionist, terrorist "outlaw" state, make it an alarming prospect to Israel -- and to many in the U.S.

-- Iraq's abominable human rights record, especially with regard to use of chemical weapons to suppress Kurdish rebels, provides a convenient hook for efforts to scuttle the U.S.-Iraq relationship.

-- Iraq tends to react to our differences by swinging a big stick, exacerbating bilateral tensions.

-- Iraq's failure to settle the first set of claims for the attack on the USS Stark presents a major obstacle to development of relations. We presented the first and most politically sensitive set of claims, for wrongful death, on April 4, 1988.

These factors give rise to disunity in the USG approach to Iraq. The Department of Agriculture finds Iraq one of its best customers for commodities; parts of Commerce, the Pentagon, and State have an interest in continuing political dialogue and fostering broader trade; parts of Congress and the Department would scuttle even the most benign and beneficial areas of the relationship, such as agricultural exports.

The Iraqi Government may be similarly divided on the value of the relationship. The strongest pressure for improved U.S.-Iraqi relations comes from the trade and business sector. Saddam's key economic ministers, notably Finance and Trade, actively promote these ties. Minister of Industry and head of military-industrial production Husayn Kamil al-Majid, President

DECLASSIFIED

Notice the way State's NEA bureau referenced Saddam's use of chemical weapons against Iran and his own people: "Iraq's unlawful use of chemical weapons has aroused great emotions in the U.S." Not that the slaughter of 100,000 innocent people was morally wrong or a good reason to punish Saddam or at least distance the U.S. from the madman. A few lines down, in fact, the argument that the U.S. should not embrace Saddam because of the tyrant's use of chemical weapons is dismissed as a "convenient hook."

DECLASSIFIED

SECRET
- 3 -

Saddam Hussein's son-in-law, appears to be pushing ties, often through military channels. Kamil wants U.S. exporters to help in the economic development Saddam believes will give Iraq commercial punch to match its military might and thus gain the regional political clout he wants. Iraq seeks to gain a stronger hand with the U.S. through oil and trade. In May Iraq began to offer U.S. oil companies large price incentives, and U.S. oil imports from Iraq have skyrocketed. Iraq's military attache has been active in trying to buy dual-use and high tech items Iraq needs. By focusing efforts on agricultural exporters, oil companies and large U.S. corporations, Iraq hopes to counter negative attitudes in Congress.

These Iraqi approaches complement areas in which the U.S. wants to develop relations, but our response has lagged. Non-agricultural exports are small, and we have not matched competitors in extending credits to make U.S. participation in reconstruction more attractive. Although there is some scope for U.S. firms, easy credit terms are of overriding importance to Iraq, which owes $35-$40 billion to Western creditors and cannot service all its current debt, let alone new loans for Saddam's ambitious development schemes.

III.   Policy Guidelines

We should be clear-headed in our expectations. It has been just four years since we re-established diplomatic relations: our political dialogue is still in its infancy. We may not want a cozy political relationship, but Iraq's political, economic and military strength -- and especially its growing leadership role among Arab friends of ours -- will make it impossible to isolate it as we have tried with Libya or Syria. All this argues that we should encourage Iraq's professed desire to play a responsible role in the region. It is therefore in our interest to have businesslike, profitable, and above all stable relations with Iraq that can withstand the inevitable buffets to the relationship, edging us closer to Iraq in trade and political dialogue while stressing our military and human rights concerns. After concentrating on settling the Stark claims, which may give us more room to maneuver, the following are some areas we can work on.

o   Redirecting the Political Dialogue

Our political dialogue with Iraq has focused on the shared goal of ending the Iran-Iraq war. With the turn in military fortunes and the ceasefire, Iraq's interest has been to see us back out of the peace process, because we can only blunt some of Iraq's more excessive demands (this may change as it becomes more difficult to threaten a renewal of hostilities)

SECRET

DECLASSIFIED

The key word in the highlighted sentence is "stable." As one former State Department official noted, State viewed Saddam as a "moderating force" in the Middle East. As this document makes clear, State wanted a much closer relationship with Saddam after the end of the Iran-Iraq war and after the gassing of the Kurds.

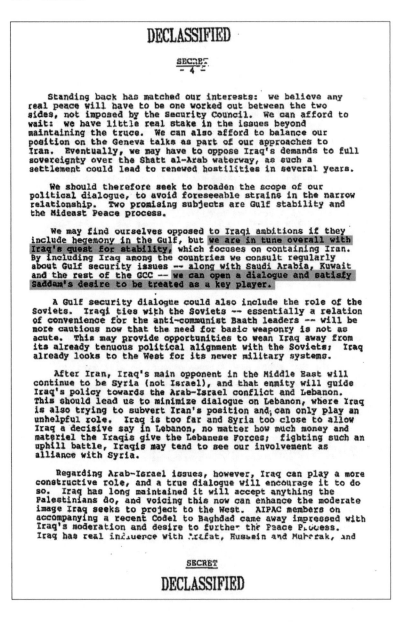

DECLASSIFIED

SECRET
- 4 -

Standing back has matched our interests: we believe any
real peace will have to be one worked out between the two
sides, not imposed by the Security Council. We can afford to
wait: we have little real stake in the issues beyond
maintaining the truce. We can also afford to balance our
position on the Geneva talks as part of our approaches to
Iran. Eventually, we may have to oppose Iraq's demands to full
sovereignty over the Shatt al-Arab waterway, as such a
settlement could lead to renewed hostilities in several years.

We should therefore seek to broaden the scope of our
political dialogue, to avoid foreseeable strains in the narrow
relationship. Two promising subjects are Gulf stability and
the Mideast Peace process.

We may find ourselves opposed to Iraqi ambitions if they
include hegemony in the Gulf, but we are in tune overall with
Iraq's quest for stability, which focuses on containing Iran.
By including Iraq among the countries we consult regularly
about Gulf security issues -- along with Saudi Arabia, Kuwait
and the rest of the GCC -- we can open a dialogue and satisfy
Saddam's desire to be treated as a key player.

A Gulf security dialogue could also include the role of the
Soviets. Iraqi ties with the Soviets -- essentially a relation
of convenience for the anti-communist Baath leaders -- will be
more cautious now that the need for basic weaponry is not as
acute. This may provide opportunities to wean Iraq away from
its already tenuous political alignment with the Soviets; Iraq
already looks to the West for its newer military systems.

After Iran, Iraq's main opponent in the Middle East will
continue to be Syria (not Israel), and that enmity will guide
Iraq's policy towards the Arab-Israel conflict and Lebanon.
This should lead us to minimize dialogue on Lebanon, where Iraq
is also trying to subvert Iran's position and, can only play an
unhelpful role. Iraq is too far and Syria too close to allow
Iraq a decisive say in Lebanon, no matter how much money and
materiel the Iraqis give the Lebanese Forces; fighting such an
uphill battle, Iraqis may tend to see our involvement as
alliance with Syria.

Regarding Arab-Israel issues, however, Iraq can play a more
constructive role, and a true dialogue will encourage it to do
so. Iraq has long maintained it will accept anything the
Palestinians do, and voicing this now can enhance the moderate
image Iraq seeks to project to the West. AIPAC members on
accompanying a recent Codel to Baghdad came away impressed with
Iraq's moderation and desire to further the Peace Process.
Iraq has real influence with Arafat, Hussein and Mubarak, and

SECRET

DECLASSIFIED

Again, "stability" rears its ugly head. State wanted to help "Iraq's
quest for stability"—which one has to wonder what "stability" means
considering the slaughter of the Kurds just five months earlier—by
"satisfy[ing] Saddam's desire to be treated as a key player."

State showed that it is absolutely incapable of critical self-appraisal when, instead of punishing those responsible for giving visas to the September 11 terrorists for which they did not qualify under the law, it gave $10,000–$15,000 bonuses to some 200 senior members of the foreign service. The bonuses were given for "outstanding performance" for the twelve month period from April 16, 2001–April 15, 2002, a period during which five of the terrorists got their visas and all nineteen of them killed 3,000 Americans on September 11.

Some notable award recipients listed in the cable:
(The first page of the cable appears on page 260.)

Dianne Andruch—A top deputy at Consular Affairs who succeeded Harty as Mary Ryan's right-hand woman. Andruch misled Congress when she implied at a June 12, 2002, congressional hearing that Visa Express has ended. It had not.

Richard Boucher—State's teflon spokesman thought his bonus was being challenged by this book's author during a press briefing. It wasn't.

Thomas Furey—Furey was the consular general at the U.S. embassy in Saudi Arabia from summer 2000 to fall 2001, and he helped set up Visa Express. He is known by his colleagues for his catchphrase "People gotta have their visas." Not surprisingly, fourteen of the Saudi terrorists got their visas during his tenure.

Maura Harty—Harty was Ryan's go-to woman at Consular Affairs, until she left there to head Secretary of State Colin Powell's executive office. In 2002 in that post, she lobbied Congress hard to keep open gaping holes in our border security, and she masterminded the lobbying campaign to hold onto the visa-issuance function. Worst of all, in the ten weeks between the time when she was tapped to replace Ryan and her Senate confirmation hearing, Harty didn't even bother to review the terrorists' visa-application forms.

George Lannon—Number-two official at Consular Affairs during at least part of the time in question when the September 11 terrorists got visas for which they did not qualify under the law.

Mary Ryan—Ryan was the architect of the "courtesy culture," and she was a Clinton holdover who wanted to eliminate the interview requirement for visa applicants wherever possible. She knowingly deceived Congress by telling lawmakers—while she was under oath—that there was nothing State could have done to prevent the terrorists from obtaining visas. She knew that State could have followed the law and denied the visas—but she kept that from Congress.

Cable Text:

```
UNCLAS    INFORM CONSULS       SECSTATE 206262
CXOSCE:
    ACTION: IPC_OS ADM_OS
    INFO:   JCS_OS OSD_OS PAA_OS ACDA_OS AMB_OS ASG_OS
            DCM_OS POLEC_OS RSO_OS

DISSEMINATION: ALLOFF
CHARGE: OSCE

VZCZCVEO634
RR RUEHVEN
DE RUEHC #6262/01 2912236
ZNR UUUUU ZZH
R 182229Z OCT 02 *** DISTRO WIDENED ***
FM SECSTATE WASHDC
TO ALL DIPLOMATIC AND CONSULAR POSTS
SPECIAL EMBASSY PROGRAM
RUEHDBU/AMEMBASSY DUSHANBE 1300
RUESKT/AMEMBASSY KHARTOUM 2018
RUEHBUL/AMEMBASSY KABUL 6057
RUEHAB/AMEMBASSY ABIDJAN 3718
BT
UNCLAS SECTION 01 OF 03 STATE 206262

INFORM CONSULS, USEU, ICAO, JAKARTA FOR DILI

E.O. 12958: N/A
TAGS: APER
SUBJECT: SENIOR FOREIGN SERVICE PERFORMANCE PAY AWARDS -
FY-2002 RECIPIENTS

1.   The members of the Senior Foreign Service of the
Department of State listed below have been named to
receive Department Performance Pay Awards for outstanding
performance during the period April 16, 2001 through April
15, 2002.  Payment of these awards, which range from
$15,000 to $10,000 each, will be made as soon as possible.
We will send a telegram in the near future with payment
details.

2.   Performance pay is being awarded in accordance with
the recommendations of the 2002 Senior Foreign Service
Selection Boards, which met this summer.

3.   The FY-2002 Senior Foreign Service Performance Pay
recipients are:

AMSELEM, W. Lewis
ANDRUCH, Dianne M.
ARNETT, David L.
AUSTIN-FERGUSON, Kathleen T.
BACA, John R.
BACH, William
BADER, Jeffrey A.
BAER, Lawrence Rea
```

UNCLASSIFIED

1

Expert analyses of the September 11 hijackers' visa application forms concluded that at least fifteen of the nineteen hijackers should have been denied visas under then-existing law. Even to the untrained eye it is easy to see why many of the visas should have been denied. Consider, for example, the U.S. destinations most of them listed. Only one of the fifteen provided an actual address—and that was only because his first application was refused—and the rest listed only general locations—including "California," "New York," "Hotel D.C.," and "Hotel." One terrorist amazingly listed his U.S. destination as simply "No." Even more amazingly, he got a visa.

On the following pages are four of the fifteen that should have been denied.

Wail and Waleed al-Shehri

Brothers Wail and Waleed al-Shehri applied together for travel visas on October 24, 2000. Wail claimed his occupation was "teater," while his brother wrote "student." Both listed the name and address of his respective employer or school as simply "South City." Each also declared a U.S. destination of "Wasantwn." If they were referring to "Washington," then it is not apparent whether they meant the state or the District of Columbia. Either way, that is hardly an address. But what should have further raised a consular officer's eyebrows is the fact that a student and his nominally employed brother were going to go on a four-to-six-month vacation, paid for by Wail's "teater" salary, which he presumably would be foregoing while in the United States. Even assuming very frugal accommodations, such a trip for two people would run north of $15,000, yet there is no indication that the consular officer even attempted to determine if Wail had the financial means to fund the planned excursion. They appear to have received their visas the same day they applied.

Abdulaziz Alomari

On June 18, 2001, Abdulaziz Alomari filled out a simple, two-page application for a visa to come to the United States. Alomari was not exactly the ideal candidate for a visa. He claimed to be a student, though he left blank the space for the name and address of his school. He checked the box claiming he was married, yet he left blank the area where he should have put the name of his spouse. Although he claimed to be a student, he marked on his form that he would self-finance a two-month stay at the "JKK Whyndham Hotel"—and provided no proof, as required under law, that he could actually do so.

Despite the legal requirement that a visa applicant show strong roots in his home country (to give him or her a reason to come back from America), Alomari listed his home address as the "ALQUDOS HTL JED" (a hotel in Jeddah, Saudi Arabia). Alomari didn't even bother filling in the fields asking for his nationality and gender, apparently realizing that he didn't need to list much more than his name to get a visa to the United States. As it turns out, he didn't. He got his visa.

Hani Hanjour

The most troubling of the applications is Hanjour's. It appears that Hanjour was the only applicant of the fifteen who was initially refused. Hanjour had received a student visa in 1997 in order to study English. On his first of two attempts to obtain a second visa in 2000, Hanjour requested a travel visa for the purpose of a "visit"—for "three years." A consulate employee, likely a Foreign Service national (a Saudi resident), highlighted the obvious problem with an applicant stating a desire to overstay his visa (the maximum length for a travel visa is twenty-four months) with an extra-long "visit." The unknown employee wrote in the comment box: "like to stay three years or more!" and circled the remark. That employee or a different one also scribbled something underneath about Hanjour's wish to find a flight school during the trip. This application was refused—but only temporarily.

On the subsequent application filed two weeks later, Hanjour was armed with all the right answers. Rather than stating "AZ, Rent home" as his U.S. location, he gave a specific address, complete with a house number and street name—the only one of the fifteen applicants to have done so. On the second go-round, Hanjour applied for a twelve-month student visa, and changed the purpose of the visit to "study" and the desired length of stay to a more appropriate "one year." But so many changes, all of which smoothed out rough spots on the original application, should have troubled the consular officer. "It's never a good sign if someone cleans up his paperwork too well," comments the current consular officer stationed in Latin America.

J28

PLEASE TYPE OR PRINT YOUR ANSWERS IN THE SPACE PROVIDED BELOW EACH ITEM.

1. SURNAMES OR FAMILY NAMES *(Exactly as in Passport)*

AL _ Shehri

2. FIRST NAME AND MIDDLE NAME *(Exactly as in Passport)*

Wail Mohammad

3. OTHER NAMES *(Maiden, Religious, Professional, Aliases)*

24 OCT 2000

4. DATE OF BIRTH *(Day, Month, Year)*

31 - 7 - 1973

8. PASSPORT NUMBER

C 348870

5. PLACE OF BIRTH

City Province — AL. Khamis

Country — k.s.A

DATE PASSPORT ISSUED *(Day, Month, Year)*

3 - 10 - 2000

6. NATIONALITY

Saudi

7. SEX

☑ MALE
☐ FEMALE

DATE PASSPORT EXPIRES *(Day, Month, Year)*

18 - 10 - 2005

9. HOME ADDRESS *(Include apartment no., street, city, province, and postal zone)*

Jeddah   6213358

10. NAME AND STREET ADDRESS OF PRESENT EMPLOYER OR SCHOOL *(Postal box number unacceptable)*

south City

11. HOME TELEPHONE NO.

6213358

12. BUSINESS TELEPHONE NO.

13. COLOR OF HAIR

Blak

14. COLOR OF EYES

Brown

15. COMPLEXION

Arab

16. HEIGHT

160

17. MARKS OF IDENTIFICATION

Nicl

18. MARITAL STATUS

☐ Married ☑ Single ☐ Widowed ☐ Divorced ☐ Separated

If married, give name and nationality of spouse.

19. NAMES AND RELATIONSHIPS OF PERSONS TRAVELING WITH YOU *(NOTE: A separate application must be made for a visa for each traveler, regardless of age.)*

my brather. Waleed

20. HAVE YOU EVER APPLIED FOR A U.S. VISA BEFORE, WHETHER IMMIGRANT OR NONIMMIGRANT?

☑ No
☐ Yes   Where? _____

When? _____ Type of visa? _____

☐ Visa was issued   ☐ Visa was refused

21. HAS YOUR U.S. VISA EVER BEEN CANCELED?

☑ No
☐ Yes   Where? _____

When? _____   By whom? _____

22. Bearers of visitors visas may generally not work or study in the U.S.
DO YOU INTEND TO WORK IN THE U.S.? ☑ No ☐ Yes
If YES, explain.

23. DO YOU INTEND TO STUDY IN THE U.S.? ☑ No ☐ Yes
If YES, write name and address of school as it appears on form I-20.

24. PRESENT OCCUPATION *(If retired, state past occupation)*

teater

25. WHO WILL FURNISH FINANCIAL SUPPORT, INCLUDING TICKETS?

my self

26. AT WHAT ADDRESS WILL YOU STAY IN THE U.S.A.?

wasantwn

27. WHAT IS THE PURPOSE OF YOUR TRIP?

toutest

28. WHEN DO YOU INTEND TO ARRIVE IN THE U.S.A.?

After two weeks

29. HOW LONG DO YOU PLAN TO STAY IN THE U.S.A.?

4 - 6 month

30. HAVE YOU EVER BEEN IN THE U.S.A.?

☑ No
☐ Yes When? _____

For how long? _____

DO NOT WRITE IN THIS SPACE

B-1/B-2 MAX   B-1 MAX   B-2 MAX

OTHER _____ MAX
Visa Classification

MULT OR _____
Number Applications

MONTHS _____
Validity

L.O. CHECKED _____

ISSUED/REFUS.

ON _____

UNDER SEC. _____ INA

REFUSAL REVIEWED BY _____

251/4

C

NONIMMIGRANT VISA APPLICATION

COMPLETE ALL QUESTIONS ON REVERSE OF FORM

OPTIONAL FORM 156 (Rev. 6-93) PAGE 1
Department of State

50156-108
PREVIOUS EDITIONS OBSOLETE

NSN 7540-00-139-0053

31. (a) HAVE YOU OR ANYONE ACTING FOR YOU EVER INDICATED TO A U.S. CONSULAR OR IMMIGRATION EMPLOYEE DESIRE TO IMMIGRATE TO THE U.S.? (b) HAS ANYONE EVER FILED AN IMMIGRANT VISA PETITION ON YOUR BEHALF? HAS LABOR CERTIFICATION FOR EMPLOYMENT IN THE U.S. EVER BEEN REQUESTED BY YOU OR ON YOUR BEHALF?

(a) ☒ No ☐ Yes   (b) ☒ No ☐ Yes   (c) ☒ No ☐ Yes

32. ARE ANY OF THE FOLLOWING IN THE U.S.? (If YES, circle appropriate relationship and indicate that person's status in the U.S., i.e., studying, working, U.S. permanent resident, U.S. citizen, etc.) No

HUSBAND/WIFE _____   FIANCE/FIANCEE _____   BROTHER/SISTER _____
FATHER/MOTHER _____   SON/DAUGHTER _____

33. PLEASE LIST THE COUNTRIES WHERE YOU HAVE LIVED FOR MORE THAN 6 MONTHS DURING THE PAST 5 YEARS. BEGIN WITH YOUR PRESENT RESIDENCE. NON

Countries	Cities	Approximate Dates

34. IMPORTANT: ALL APPLICANTS MUST READ AND CHECK THE APPROPRIATE BOX FOR EACH ITEM:

A visa may not be issued to persons who are within specific categories defined by law as inadmissible to the United States (except when a waiver is obtained in advance). Are any of the following applicable to you?

- Have you ever been afflicted with a communicable disease of public health significance, a dangerous physical or mental disorder, or been a drug abuser or addict? . . . . ☐ Yes ☒ No

- Have you ever been arrested or convicted for any offense or crime, even though subject of a pardon, amnesty, or other such legal action? . . . . ☐ Yes ☒ No

- Have you ever been a controlled substance (drug) trafficker, or a prostitute or procurer? . . . . . ☐ Yes ☒ No

- Have you ever sought to obtain or assist others to obtain a visa, entry into the U.S., or any U.S. immigration benefit by fraud or willful misrepresentation? . . . . ☐ Yes ☒ No

- Were you deported from the U.S.A. within the last 5 years? . . . . ☐ Yes ☒ No

- Do you seek to enter the United States to engage in export control violations, subversive or terrorist activities, or any unlawful purpose? . . . . ☐ Yes ☒ No

- Have you ever ordered, incited, assisted, or otherwise participated in the persecution of any person because of race, religion, national origin, or political opinion under the control, direct or indirect, of the Nazi Government of Germany, or of the government of any area occupied by, or allied with, the Nazi Government of Germany; or have you ever participated in genocide? . . . . . . ☐ Yes ☒ No

A YES answer does not automatically signify ineligibility for a visa, but if you answered YES to any of the above, or if you have any question in this regard, personal appearance at this office is recommended. If appearance is not possible at this time, attach a statement of facts in your case to this application.

35. I certify that I have read and understood all the questions set forth in this application and the answers I have furnished on this form are true and correct to the best of my knowledge and belief. I understand that any false or misleading statement may result in the permanent refusal of a visa or denial of entry into the United States. I understand that possession of a visa does not entitle the bearer to enter the United States of America upon arrival at port of entry if he or she is found inadmissible.

DATE OF APPLICATION 24 . 10 . 2000

APPLICANT'S SIGNATURE _____

If this application has been prepared by a travel agency or another person on your behalf, the agent should indicate name and address of agency or person with appropriate signature of individual preparing form.

SIGNATURE OF PERSON PREPARING FORM
(If other than applicant) _____

DO NOT WRITE IN THIS SPACE

OPTIONAL FORM 156 (Rev 6-93) PAGE 2
Department of State

J33

PLEASE TYPE OR PRINT YOUR ANSWERS IN THE SPACE PROVIDED BELOW EACH ITEM.

1. SURNAMES OR FAMILY NAMES *(Exactly as in Passport)* AL-Shehri	DO NOT WRITE IN THIS SPACE B-1/B-2 MAX B-1 MAX B-2 MAX
2. FIRST NAME AND MIDDLE NAME *(Exactly as in Passport)* Waleed Mohammad	OTHER _____ MAX Visa Classification
3. OTHER NAMES *(Maiden, Religious, Professional, Aliases)* 24 OCT 2000	MULT OR _____ Number Applications

4. DATE OF BIRTH *(Day, Month, Year)* 20-12-1978	8. PASSPORT NUMBER C348871	MONTHS _____ Validity
5. PLACE OF BIRTH City, Province Country Namas K.SA	DATE PASSPORT ISSUED *(Day, Month, Year)* 3.10-2000	I.O. CHECKED _____ ISSUED/REFUSED ON _____
6. NATIONALITY Saudi	7. SEX ☐ MALE ☐ FEMALE	DATE PASSPORT EXPIRES *(Day, Month, Year)* 11.8-2005	UNDER SEC. _____ INA REFUSAL REVIEWED BY _____ 25?/3

9. HOME ADDRESS *(Include apartment no., street, city, province, and postal zone)*
Jeeddah

10. NAME AND STREET ADDRESS OF PRESENT EMPLOYER OR SCHOOL *(Postal box number unacceptable)*
Southcity

11. HOME TELEPHONE NO. 6213358	12. BUSINESS TELEPHONE NO

13. COLOR OF HAIR black	14. COLOR OF EYES brawn	15. COMPLEXION Arab

16. HEIGHT 175	17. MARKS OF IDENTIFICATION Nil

18. MARITAL STATUS
☐ Married ☑ Single ☐ Widowed ☐ Divorced ☐ Separated
If married, give name and nationality of spouse.

19. NAMES AND RELATIONSHIPS OF PERSONS TRAVELING WITH YOU *(NOTE: A separate application must be made for a visa for each traveler, regardless of age.)*
My brother Wail

20. HAVE YOU EVER APPLIED FOR A U.S. VISA BEFORE. WHETHER IMMIGRANT OR NONIMMIGRANT?
☑ No
☐ Yes   Where? _____
When? _____   Type of visa? _____
☐ Visa was issued   ☐ Visa was refused

21. HAS YOUR U.S. VISA EVER BEEN CANCELED?
☑ No
☐ Yes   Where? _____
When? _____   By whom? _____

22. Bearers of visitors visas may generally not work or study in the U.S.
DO YOU INTEND TO WORK IN THE U.S.?   ☑ No   ☐ Yes
If YES, explain.

23. DO YOU INTEND TO STUDY IN THE U.S.?   ☑ No   ☐ Yes
If YES, write name and address of school as it appears on form I-20.

24. PRESENT OCCUPATION *(if retired, state past occupation)*
student

25. WHO WILL FURNISH FINANCIAL SUPPORT, INCLUDING TICKETS?
My brother

26. AT WHAT ADDRESS WILL YOU STAY IN THE U.S.A?
Wasantwn

27. WHAT IS THE PURPOSE OF YOUR TRIP?
tourd?

28. WHEN DO YOU INTEND TO ARRIVE IN THE U.S.A?
After two weeks

29. HOW LONG DO YOU PLAN TO STAY IN THE U.S.A?
4.6 month

30. HAVE YOU EVER BEEN IN THE U S A?
☑ No
☐ Yes. When? _____
For how long? _____

NONIMMIGRANT VISA APPLICATION

COMPLETE ALL QUESTIONS ON REVERSE OF FORM

OPTIONAL FORM 156 (Rev 6-93) PAGE 1
Department of State
50156-108
PREVIOUS EDITIONS OBSOLETE
NSN 7540-00-139-0053

31. (a) HAVE YOU OR ANYONE ACTING FOR YOU EVER INDICATED TO A U.S. CONSULAR OR IMMIGRATION EMPLO DESIRE TO IMMIGRATE TO THE U.S ? (b) HAS ANYONE EVER FILED AN IMMIGRANT VISA PETITION ON YOUR BEHAL HAS LABOR CERTIFICATION FOR EMPLOYMENT IN THE U.S. EVER BEEN REQUESTED BY YOU OR ON YOUR BE

(a) ☑ No ☐ Yes (b) ☑ No ☐ Yes (c) ☑ No ☐ Yes

32 ARE ANY OF THE FOLLOWING IN THE U.S.? (If YES, circle appropriate relationship and indicate that person's status i U.S., i.e., studying, working, U.S. permanent resident, U.S. citizen, etc.)

HUSBAND/WIFE _____ FIANCE/FIANCEE _____ BROTHER/SISTER _____

FATHER/MOTHER _____ SON/DAUGHTER _____

33 PLEASE LIST THE COUNTRIES WHERE YOU HAVE LIVED FOR MORE THAN 6 MONTHS DURING THE PAST 5 YEAR! BEGIN WITH YOUR PRESENT RESIDENCE ᑎ ᒪᑎ

Countries _____ Cities _____ Approximate Dates

34 IMPORTANT: ALL APPLICANTS MUST READ AND CHECK THE APPROPRIATE BOX FOR EACH ITEM:

A visa may not be issued to persons who are within specific categories defined by law as inadmissible to the United Stat (except when a waiver is obtained in advance). Are any of the following applicable to you?

- Have you ever been afflicted with a communicable disease of public health significance, a dangerous physical or mental disorder, or been a drug abuser or addict? . . . . ☐ Yes ☑ No

- Have you ever been arrested or convicted for any offense or crime, even though subject of a pardon, amnesty, or other such legal action? . . . . ☐ Yes ☑ No

- Have you ever been a controlled substance (drug) trafficker, or a prostitute or procurer? . . . . . ☐ Yes ☑ No

- Have you ever sought to obtain or assist others to obtain a visa, entry into the U.S., or any U.S. Immigration benefit by fraud or willful misrepresentation? . . . . ☐ Yes ☑ No

- Were you deported from the U.S.A. within the last 5 years? . . . . ☐ Yes ☑ No

- Do you seek to enter the United States to engage in export control violations, subversive or terrorist activities, or any unlawful purpose? . . . . ☐ Yes ☑ No

- Have you ever ordered, incited, assisted, or otherwise participated in the persecution of any per- son because of race, religion, national origin, or political opinion under the control, direct or indi- rect, of the Nazi Government of Germany, or of the government of any area occupied by, or allied with, the Nazi Government of Germany; or have you ever participated in genocide? . . . . ☐ Yes ☑ No

A YES answer does not automatically signify ineligibility for a visa, but if you answered YES to any of the above, or if you have any question in this regard, personal appearance at this office is recommended. If appearance is not possible at this time, attach a statement of facts in your case to this application.

35. I certify that I have read and understood all the questions set forth in this application and the answers I have furnished o: this form are true and correct to the best of my knowledge and belief. I understand that any false or misleading statement ma: result in the permanent refusal of a visa or denial of entry into the United States. I understand that possession of a visa does no entitle the bearer to enter the United States of America upon arrival at port of entry if he or she is found inadmissible

DATE OF APPLICATION 24 / 0 / 2000

APPLICANT'S SIGNATURE _____

If this application has been prepared by a travel agency or another person on your behalf, the agent should indicate name and address of agency or person with appropriate signature of individual preparing form.

SIGNATURE OF PERSON PREPARING FORM _____
(If other than applicant)

DO NOT WRITE IN THIS SPACE

OPTIONAL FORM 156 (Rev. 6-93) PAGE 2
Department of State

J6

PLEASE TYPE OR PRINT YOUR ANSWERS IN THE SPACE PROVIDED BELOW EACH ITEM.

1. SURNAMES OR FAMILY NAMES *(Exactly as in Passport)*

ALOMaRI · 18 JUN 2001

2. FIRST NAME AND MIDDLE NAME *(Exactly as in Passport)*

ABDUL AZIZ

3. OTHER NAMES *(Maiden, Religious, Professional, Aliases)*

DO NOT WRITE IN THIS SPACE

B-1/B-2 MAX   B-1 MAX   B-2 MAX

OTHER _____ MAX

Visa Classification

MULT OR _____

Number Applications

4. DATE OF BIRTH *(mm-dd-yyyy)*

28-5-1979

8. PASSPORT NUMBER

C165015

MONTHS _____

Validity

L.O. CHECKED

5. PLACE OF BIRTH
City, Province   Country

HOWRAN   K.S.A

DATE PASSPORT ISSUED *(mm-dd-yyyy)*

5-6-2000

ON _____ BY _____

ISSUED/REFUSED

6. NATIONALITY

7. SEX
☐ MALE
☐ FEMALE

DATE PASSPORT EXPIRES *(mm-dd-yyyy)*

11-4-2005

ON _____ BY _____

UNDER SEC.   214(b)   221(g)

9. HOME ADDRESS *include apartment no., street, city, province, and postal zone)*

ALQUDOS HTL JC

OTHER: 059/10 INA

REFUSAL REVIEWED BY _____

10. NAME AND STREET ADDRESS OF PRESENT EMPLOYER OR SCHOOL *(Postal box number unacceptable)*

11. HOME TELEPHONE NO.

6473994

12. BUSINESS TELEPHONE NO.

6491463

13. MARITAL STATUS
☑ Married ☐ Single ☐ Widowed ☐ Divorced ☐ Separated
If married, give name and nationality of spouse

14. NAMES AND RELATIONSHIPS OF PERSONS TRAVELING WITH YOU
(NOTE: A separate application must be made for a visa for each traveler, regardless of age.)

ALON

15. HAVE YOU EVER APPLIED FOR A U.S. NONIMMIGRANT VISA?
☑ NO ☐ YES

HAVE YOU EVER APPLIED FOR A U.S. IMMIGRANT VISA?
☑ NO ☐ YES

WHERE? _____
WHEN? _____
VISA WAS ISSUED ☐   VISA WAS REFUSED ☐

16. HAS YOUR U.S. VISA EVER BEEN CANCELED?
☑ NO ☐ YES

WHERE? _____
WHEN? _____
BY WHOM? _____

17. Bearers of visitors may generally not work or study in the U.S.
DO YOU INTEND TO WORK IN THE U.S.?   ☑ NO ☐ YES
If YES, explain.

18. DO YOU INTEND TO STUDY IN THE U.S.?   ☑ NO ☐ YES
If YES, write name an address of school as it appears on form I-20.

19. PRESENT OCCUPATION *(If retired, state past occupation)*

STUDENT

20. WHO WILL FURNISH FINANCIAL SUPPORT, INCLUDING TICKETS?

MYSELF

21. AT WHAT ADDRESS WILL YOU STAY IN THE U.S.A.?

JKK
WHYNDHAM HTL

22. WHAT IS THE PURPOSE OF YOUR TRIP?

TOURISSM

23. WHEN DO YOU INTEND TO ARRIVE IN THE U.S.A.?

25 JUN 01

24. HOW LONG DO YOU PLAN TO STAY IN THE U.S.A.?

2 MONTHS

25. HAVE YOU EVER BEEN IN THE U.S.A.?

☑ NO ☐ YES

WHEN? _____
FOR HOW LONG? _____

NONIMMIGRANT VISA APPLICATION

COMPLETE ALL QUESTIONS ON REVERSE OF FORM

NSN 7540-00-139-0053

OPTIONAL FORM 156   PAGE 1
REV. 10-1999
Department of State

50156-109
PREVIOUS EDITIONS OBSOLETE

26. HAVE YOU OR ANYONE ACTING FOR YOU EVER INDICATED TO A U.S. CONSULAR OR IMMIGRATION EMPLOYEE A DESIRE TO IMMIGRATE TO THE U.S., OR HAVE YOU EVER ENTERED A U.S. VISA LOTTERY?

☑ NO ☐ YES

HAS ANYONE EVER FILED AN IMMIGRANT VISA PETITION ON YOUR BEHALF?

☑ NO ☐ YES

HAS A LABOR CERTIFICATION FOR EMPLOYMENT IN THE U.S. EVER BEEN REQUESTED BY YOU OR ON YOUR BEHALF?

☑ NO ☐ YES

27. ARE ANY OF THE FOLLOWING IN THE U.S., RESIDE IN THE U.S., OR HAVE U.S. LEGAL PERMANENT RESIDENCE? (Circle YES or NO and indicate that person's status in the U.S., i.e., studying, working, permanent resident, U.S. citizen, etc.)

YES NO Husband/Wife ___NO___ YES NO Fiance/Fiancee ___NO___ YES NO Brother/Sister ___NO___

YES NO Father/Mother ___NO___ YES NO Son/Daughter ___NO___

28. WHERE HAVE YOU LIVED FOR THE PAST FIVE YEARS? DO NOT INCLUDE PLACES YOU HAVE VISITED FOR PERIODS OF SIX MONTHS OR LESS.

Countries	Cities	Approximate Dates
SAUDI ARABIA	JEDDAH	

29. IMPORTANT: ALL APPLICANTS MUST READ AND CHECK THE APPROPRIATE BOX FOR EACH ITEM.

A visa may not be issued to persons who are within specific categories defined by law as inadmissible to the United States (except when a waiver is obtained in advance). Are any of the following applicable to you?

- Have you ever been afflicted with a communicable disease of public health significance, a dangerous physical or mental disorder, or been a drug abuser or addict? [212(a)(1)] ☐ YES ☑ NO

- Have you ever been arrested or convicted for any offense or crime, even though subject of a pardon, amnesty or other similar legal action? Have you ever lawfully distributed or sold a controlled substance (drug), or been a prostitute or procurer for prostitutes? [212(a)(2)] ☐ YES ☑ NO

- Do you seek to enter the United States to engage in export control violations, subversive or terrorist activities, or any other unlawful purpose? Are you a member or representative of a terrorist organization as currently designated by the U.S. Secretary of State? Have you ever participated in persecutions directed by the Nazi government of Germany; or have you ever participated in genocide? [212(a)(3)] ☐ YES ☑ NO

- Have you ever been refused admission to the U.S., or the subject of a deportation hearing, or sought to obtain or assist others to obtain a visa, entry into the U.S., or sought to obtain a visa or any U.S. immigration benefit by fraud or willful misrepresentation? Have you attended a U.S. public elementary school on student (F) status, or a public secondary school without reimbursing the school after November 30, 1996? [212(a)(6)] ☐ YES ☑ NO

- Have you ever departed or remained outside the United States to avoid military service? [212(a)(8)] ☐ YES ☑ NO

- Have you ever violated the terms of a U.S. visa, or been unlawfully present in, or deported from, the United States? [212(a)(9)] ☐ YES ☑ NO

- Have you ever withheld custody of a U.S. citizen child outside the United States from a person granted legal custody by a U.S. court, voted in the United States in violation of any law or regulation, or renounced U.S. citizenship for the purpose of avoiding taxation? [212(a)(10)] ☐ YES ☑ NO

A YES answer does not automatically signify ineligibility for a visa, but if you answered YES to any of the above, or if you have any question in this regard, a personal appearance at this office is recommended. If an appearance is not possible at this time, attach a statement of facts in your case to this application.

30. I certify that I have read and understood all the questions set forth in this application and the answers I have furnished on this form are true and correct to the best of my knowledge and belief. I understand that any false or misleading statement may result in the permanent refusal of a visa or denial of entry into the United States. I understand that possession of a visa does not entitle the bearer to enter the United States of America upon arrival at port of entry if he or she is found inadmissible.

DATE OF APPLICATION (mm-dd-yyyy)   18/6/2001

APPLICANT'S SIGNATURE _____

If this application has been prepared by a travel agency or another person on your behalf, the agent should indicate name and address of agency or person with appropriate signature of individual preparing form.

SIGNATURE OF PERSON PREPARING FORM _____
(if other than applicant)

DO NOT WRITE IN THIS SPACE

OPTIONAL FORM 156 PAGE 2
REV. 10-1999
Department of State

J2

1. SURNAMES OR FAMILY NAMES *(Exactly as in Passport)*
· Hanjour · 25 SEP 2000

2. FIRST NAME AND MIDDLE NAME *(Exactly as in Passport)* ;
Hani S.H

3. OTHER NAMES *(Maiden, Religious, Professional, Aliases)*

4. DATE OF BIRTH *(Day, Month, Year)*
30. 8. 1972

5. PLACE OF BIRTH
City Province — Taif
Country — Saudi Arabia

6. PASSPORT NUMBER
C24 1922

DATE PASSPORT ISSUED *(Day, Month, Year)*
24. 7. 2000

6. NATIONALITY
Saudy

7. SEX
☑ MALE ☐ FEMALE

DATE PASSPORT EXPIRES *(Day, Month, Year)*
30. 5. 2005

9. HOME ADDRESS *(Include apartment no., street, city, province, and postal zone)*
Taif. AL-fesaleh
P.O Box 1717

10. NAME AND STREET ADDRESS OF PRESENT EMPLOYER OR SCHOOL
(Postal box number unacceptable)
Taif. AL.jaish st

11. HOME TELEPHONE NO.
73-42751

12. BUSINESS TELEPHONE NO.

13. COLOR OF HAIR
Black

14. COLOR OF EYES
Brown

15. COMPLEXION

16. HEIGHT
5.8

17. MARKS OF IDENTIFICATION

18. MARITAL STATUS
☐ Married ☑ Single ☐ Widowed ☐ Divorced ☐ Separated
If married, give name and nationality of spouse.

19. NAMES AND RELATIONSHIPS OF PERSONS TRAVELING WITH YOU (NOTE: A separate application must be made for a visa for each traveler, regardless of age.)

20. HAVE YOU EVER APPLIED FOR A U.S. VISA BEFORE, WHETHER IMMIGRANT OR NONIMMIGRANT?
☐ No ☑ Yes Where? Jeddah
When? 10 sep 2000 Type of visa? Visitor
☐ Visa was issued ☐ Visa was refused

21. HAS YOUR U.S. VISA EVER BEEN CANCELED?
☐ No
☐ Yes Where?
When? By whom?

22. Bearers of visitors visas may generally not work or study in the U.S.
DO YOU INTEND TO WORK IN THE U.S ? ☐ No ☐ Yes
If YES, explain.

23. DO YOU INTEND TO STUDY IN THE U.S ? ☐ No ☑ Yes
If YES, write name and address of school as it appears on form I-20.
ELS Language Centers cn 9464
3510 Mountain Boulevard. okland.

NONIMMIGRANT VISA APPLICATION

OPTIONAL FORM 156 (REV. 6-93) PAGE 1
Department of State
50156-108
PREVIOUS EDITIONS OBSOLETE
NSN 7540-00-139-0053

DO NOT WRITE IN THIS SPACE

B-1/B-2 MAX   B-1 MAX   B-2 MAX
OTHER F-1 MAX
Visa Classification
C

MULT OR
MONTHS 12
Number Applications
Validity

L.O. CHECKED
ISSUED/REFUSED
ON B'
UNDER SEC. INA

REFUSAL REVIEWED BY
22(8) 10 Sept

Saip Paid MRV.

24. PRESENT OCCUPATION *(If retired, state past occupation)*
Student

25. WHO WILL FURNISH FINANCIAL SUPPORT, INCLUDING TICKETS?
My father and my

26. AT WHAT ADDRESS WILL YOU STAY IN THE U.S.A?
3510 mountain Boulev-
okland, CA 94619

27. WHAT IS THE PURPOSE OF YOUR TRIP?
Study.

28. WHEN DO YOU INTEND TO ARRIVE IN THE U.S.A?
10/09/2000

29. HOW LONG DO YOU PLAN TO STAY IN THE U.S.A?
one Years

30. HAVE YOU EVER BEEN IN THE U.S.A?
☐ No ☑ Yes When? 1998
For how long? for one Year

COMPLETE ALL QUESTIONS ON REVERSE OF FORM

31. (a) HAVE YOU OR ANYONE ACTING FOR YOU EVER INDICATED TO A U.S. CONSULAR OR IMMIGRATION EMPLOYEE A DESIRE TO IMMIGRATE TO THE U.S.? (b) HAS ANYONE EVER FILED AN IMMIGRANT VISA PETITION ON YOUR BEHALF? (c) HAS LABOR CERTIFICATION FOR EMPLOYMENT IN THE U.S. EVER BEEN REQUESTED BY YOU OR ON YOUR BEHALF?

(a) ☑ No ☐ Yes   (b) ☑ No ☐ Yes   (c) ☑ No ☐ Yes

32. ARE ANY OF THE FOLLOWING IN THE U.S.? (If YES, circle appropriate relationship and indicate that person's status in the U.S., i.e., studying, working, U.S. permanent resident, U.S. citizen, etc.)

HUSBAND/WIFE __no__   FIANCE/FIANCEE _____   BROTHER/SISTER __no__

FATHER/MOTHER __no__   SON/DAUGHTER _____ __no__

33. PLEASE LIST THE COUNTRIES WHERE YOU HAVE LIVED FOR MORE THAN 6 MONTHS DURING THE PAST 5 YEARS. BEGIN WITH YOUR PRESENT RESIDENCE.

Countries	Cities	Approximate Dates
Phoniex	AR zow	1947 - 1998

34 IMPORTANT: ALL APPLICANTS MUST READ AND CHECK THE APPROPRIATE BOX FOR EACH ITEM:

A visa may not be issued to persons who are within specific categories defined by law as inadmissible to the United States (except when a waiver is obtained in advance). Are any of the following applicable to you?

- Have you ever been afflicted with a communicable disease of public health significance, a dangerous physical or mental disorder, or been a drug abuser or addict? . . . . ☐ Yes ☑ No

- Have you ever been arrested or convicted for any offense or crime, even though subject of a pardon, amnesty, or other such legal action? . . . . ☐ Yes ☑ No

- Have you ever been a controlled substance (drug) trafficker, or a prostitute or procurer? . . . . ☐ Yes ☑ No

- Have you ever sought to obtain or assist others to obtain a visa, entry into the U.S., or any U.S. immigration benefit by fraud or willful misrepresentation? . . . . ☐ Yes ☑ No

- Were you deported from the U.S.A. within the last 5 years? . . . . ☐ Yes ☑ No

- Do you seek to enter the United States to engage in export control violations, subversive or terrorist activities, or any unlawful purpose? . . . . ☐ Yes ☑ No

- Have you ever ordered, incited, assisted, or otherwise participated in the persecution of any person because of race, religion, national origin, or political opinion under the control, direct or indirect, of the Nazi Government of Germany, or of the government of any area occupied by, or allied with, the Nazi Government of Germany; or have you ever participated in genocide? . . . . . . ☐ Yes ☑ No

A YES answer does not automatically signify ineligibility for a visa, but if you answered YES to any of the above, or if you have any question in this regard, personal appearance at this office is recommended. If appearance is not possible at this time, attach a statement of facts in your case to this application.

35. I certify that I have read and understood all the questions set forth in this application and the answers I have furnished on this form are true and correct to the best of my knowledge and belief. I understand that any false or misleading statement may result in the permanent refusal of a visa or denial of entry into the United States. I understand that possession of a visa does not entitle the bearer to enter the United States of America upon arrival at port of entry if he or she is found inadmissible.

DATE OF APPLICATION   25   9   2000

APPLICANT'S SIGNATURE _____

If this application has been prepared by a travel agency or another person on your behalf, the agent should indicate name and address of agency or person with appropriate signature of individual preparing form.

SIGNATURE OF PERSON PREPARING FORM _____
(if other than applicant)

DO NOT WRITE IN THIS SPACE

OPTIONAL FORM 156 (Rev 6-93) PAGE 2
Department of State

Notes

1 ★ DETAINED: MY OWN ROAD TO DAMASCUS

1. Interview, State Department official, August 1, 2002.
2. State Department Daily Press Briefing, July 12, 2002.
3. The website text has since been changed, but I reproduced the old text in my article "Visa Express No More? Consular Affairs offers a belated response," *National Review Online*, July 21, 2002.
4. Ibid.
5. Fox News Channel, "The Big Story with John Gibson," June 20, 2002.
6. Ibid.
7. "Visa Process Should Be Strengthened as an Antiterrorism Tool," General Accounting Office Report, October 2002, 19.
8. Interview, Consular Affairs official, May 7, 2003.
9. "Best Practices" handbook, U.S. Department of State.

2 ★ UNBREAKABLE: THE STATE-SAUDI ALLIANCE

1. Interview, March 30, 2003.
2. Interview, George Schultz, April 2, 2003.
3. Robert G. Kaiser and David Ottaway, "Oil for Security Fueled Close Ties; But Major Differences Led to Tensions," *Washington Post*, February 11, 2002.
4. Ibid.
5. Interview, Hume Horan, April 14, 2003.
6. For a far more comprehensive discussion on Arabists, Lawrence Kaplan's *The Arabists* is required reading.
7. Hermann F. Eilts, "Uncle Sam Supreme Guardian of the Saudi Crown," *American Diplomacy*, vol. v, no. 2, 2000.
8. Ibid.
9. Interview, Fr. Keith Roderick, April 12, 2003.
10. Kaiser and Ottaway, "Oil for Security Fueled Close Ties."
11. Ibid.
12. Foreign Agent Registration Act filing, signed and dated July 21, 1995.
13. Foreign Agent Registration Act filing, signed and dated September 15, 1977.
14. Foreign Agent Registration Act filing, signed and dated December 1, 1996.
15. Kaiser and Ottaway, "Oil for Security Fueled Close Ties."
16. Interview, Laurent Murawiec, March 18, 2003.
17. Michael R. Gordon, "U.S. Action in Iraq Slowed by Rift Over Whom to Support," *New York Times*, May 10, 2002.
18. Ibid.
19. Department of Justice statement, Attorney General John Ashcroft, June 21, 2001.
20. Interview, former consular officer Jessica Vaughan, June 1, 2002.
21. I reproduce the text of this statement in my article "Catching the Visa Express," *National Review*, July 1, 2002.
22. Interview, State Department official, August 15, 2002.
23. Interview, informed source, April 15, 2003.
24. Ibid.

25. Douglas Farah and John Mintz, "Muslim Money, Ties; Clues Raise Questions About Terror Funding," *Washington Post*, October 7, 2002.

26. Fox TV, *Fox News Sunday*, June 30, 2002.

27. Details can be found in my article "The Saudi Pipeline: Petro-dollars, Palestinian terror—and a U.S. blind eye," *National Review*, July 15, 2002.

28. Interview, administration official, June 28, 2002.

29. Documents described in Mowbray, "The Saudi Pipeline."

30. Interview, administration official, April 9, 2003.

31. Michael Isikoff, "Blacklist Battles," *Newsweek*, March 10, 2003.

32. Interview, administration official, April 9, 2003.

33. Interview, administration official, April 7, 2003.

34. Interview, administration official, April 9, 2003.

35. Interview, January 11, 2003.

36. Interview, Diplomatic Security official, December 15, 2002.

37. Interview, Jean Bruggeman, January 30, 2003.

38. Interview, Keith Roderick, January 28, 2003.

39. Gregory Jaynes, "Royal Saudi Family in Miami Shows it has a Gift for Giving," *New York Times*, May 27, 1982.

40. Steven Emerson, *The American House of Saud*, New York: Franklin Watts, 1985, 372.

41. Jaynes, "Royal Saudi Family in Miami."

42. Ibid.

43. Emerson, 373.

44. Interview, Diplomatic Security officer, April 1, 2003.

45. Interview, State Department official, April 8, 2003.

3 ★ COLD SHOULDER: STATE'S SMALLEST VICTIMS

1. Monica Stowers, Written testimony submitted to House Government Reform Committee, June 11, 2002.

2. Ibid.

3. Ibid.

4. Ibid.

5. Interview, Dan Burton, August 30, 2002.

6. Ibid.

7. Ibid.

8. Ibid.

9. This information appears in a response by the editor of the *Washington Times* to a letter from the State Department: "State Department Defends Harty Nomination," Letter to Editor, *Washington Times*, October 19, 2002.

10. Interview, Danielle Pletka, April 23, 2003.

11. On this point, Muslim scholars disagree. Some believe Mohammed's last wife, 'Aisha, was actually as old as fourteen when they married, and some also believe it may have been several years before they consummated the relationship.

12. House Government Reform Committee, "Summary of witness cases," October 2, 2002.

13. Interview, Michael Rives, April 16, 2003.

14. Ibid.

15. Ibid.

16. Ibid.

17. Interview, Larry Synclair, April 17, 2003.

18. Ibid.

19. ABC, *Nightline*, May 11, 2000.

20. Interview, administration official, February 23, 2003.

21. Interview, Consular Affairs official, February 23, 2003.

22. Interview, Bill Cowan, April 5, 2003.

23. Interview, Sam Seramur, April 17, 2003.

24. Ibid.

25. Ibid.

26. Ibid.

27. Her book *At Any Price* (WND Books, 2003) is a necessary read to appreciate the child abduction issue fully.

28. Interview, Patricia Roush, April 14, 2003.

29. Ibid.

30. Interview, Consular Affairs official, April 3, 2003.

31. Interview, Patricia Roush, April 17, 2003.

4 ★ TOLERATING TYRANTS

1. Interview, informed source, April 21, 2003.

2. Ibid.

3. Daily press briefing, U.S. Department of State, September 27, 1996.

4. Ibid.

5. "The Road to Koranistan," *The Economist*, October 5, 1996, 21.

6. Interview, Julie Sirrs, April 27, 2003.

7. Interview, Julie Sirrs, April 29, 2003.

8. Interview, former Congressional staffer, April 25, 2003.

9. "Afghanistan," *Current Digest of the Post-Soviet Press*, November 6, 1996.

10. Interview, informed source, April 25, 2003.

11. Michael Dobbs, "Analysts Feel Militia Could End Anarchy; Little Known in U.S. About Movement, Which Backs Strict Adherence to Islamic Law," *Washington Post*, September 28, 1996.

12. Ibid.

13. "The Road to Koranistan."

14. Rod Nordland, et al., "The Islamic Nightmare," *Newsweek*, October 14, 1996, 51.

15. John F. Burns, "A New 'Great Game?'; Afghanistan reels back into view," *New York Times*, October 6, 1996.

16. Interview, John Jennings, May 29, 2003.

17. John Jennings, "The Taleban and Foggy Bottom," *Washington Times*, October 25, 1996.

18. Daily Press Briefing, U.S. Department of State, September 27, 1996.

19. Daily Press Briefing, U.S. Department of State, October 7, 1996.

20. Kenneth Freed, "Odd Partners in UNO's Afghan Project War and Turmoil in Afghanistan," *Omaha World-Herald*, October 26, 1997.

21. Ibid.

22. Interview, Julie Sirrs, April 29, 2003.

23. Barbara Crossette, "Taliban's Ban On Poppy A Success, U.S. Aides Say," *New York Times*, May 20, 2001.

24. Ibid.

25. Jennings, "The Taleban and Foggy Bottom."

26. Freed, "Odd Partners."

27. Interview, Richard Schifter, March 22, 2003.

28. Ibid.

29. Joe Stephens and David B. Ottaway, "Afghan Roots Keep Adviser Firmly in the Inner Circle; Consultant's Policy Influence Goes Back to the Reagan Era," *Washington Post*, November 23, 2001.

30. Jean-Charles Brisard and Guillaume Dasquie, *Forbidden Truth: U.S.-Taliban, Secret Diplomacy, and the Failed Hunt for Bin Laden*, Thunder's Mouth Press/Nation Books, New York: 2002, 22.

31. Zalmay Khalilzad, "Afghanistan: Time to Reengage," *Washington Post*, October 7, 1996.

32. Ibid.

33. Stephen Buttry, "Book claims U.S. eased terrorism probe to advance oil-pipeline talks," *Omaha World Herald*, January 13, 2002.

34. Freed, "Odd Partners."

35. Ibid.

36. Ibid.

37. Stephen Buttry and Jake Thompson, "UNO's connection to Taliban centers on education UNO Program," *Omaha World Herald*, September 16, 2001.

38. Freed, "Odd Partners."

39. Ibid.

40. Michael J. Berens, "University helped U.S. reach out to Taliban; Afghanistan center hosted officials during '80s, 90s," *Chicago Tribune*, October 21, 2001.

41. Ibid.

42. Freed, "Odd Partners."

43. Freed, "Odd Partners."

44. Interview, John Jennings, April 28, 2003.

45. Stephens and Ottaway, "Afghan roots."

46. Kenneth Freed and Jena Janovy, "UNO Partner Pulls Out of Afghanistan Project," *Omaha World Herald*, June 6, 1998.

47. Brisard, 40-41.

48. "Bush Urged to Forge Special Ties With India," *Economic Times*, December 29, 2000.

49. Interviews, informed sources, April 24-5, 2003.

50. Eric Lekus, "The Afghan ambiguity in D.C.," *Baltimore Sun*, July 7, 1997.

51. Interview, former Congressional staffer, April 24, 2003.

52. Peter Slevin, "At State, Giving Dissent its Due," *Washington Post*, June 28, 2002.

53. Ibid.

54. Interview, administration official, December 15, 2002.

55. Interview, administration official, November 24, 2002.

56. "Profile: Elie Hobeika," *BBC News Online*, http://news.bbc.co.uk/2/hi/world/middle_east/1779321.stm, January 24, 2002.

57. Ibid.

58. Interview, informed source, April 7, 2003.

59. Interview, Danielle Pletka, April 22, 2003.

60. Interview, administration official, April 24, 2003.

61. Ibid.

62. Interview, former Congressional staffer, April 25, 2003.

63. William Safire, "Baltics to Baghdad," *New York Times*, March 30, 1990, A31, quoting a VOA broadcast of February 15, 1990.

64. Safire, "Baltics to Baghdad."

65. Interview, Congressional staffer, March 18, 2003.

66. "Patterns of Global Terrorism 2002," Office of the Coordinator for Counterterrorism, U.S. Department of State, April 30, 2003.

67. Newt Gingrich, speech, American Enterprise Institute, April 22, 2003.

68. Interview, Congressional staffer, March 18, 2003.

69. "Patterns of Global Terrorism 2002."

70. "Syria Accountability Act," S. 2215, introduced April 18, 2002.

71. Letter from assistant secretary of state for Legislative Affairs Paul Kelly to Congressman Nick Rahall, May 24, 2002.

72. Ibid.

73. Gingrich, AEI speech.

74. "Syria Accountability Act."

75. Ibid.

76. Interview, Congressional staffer, March 25, 2003.

77. Marc Lerner, "Philippine terrorists claim financial link to Iraq," *Washington Times*, March 4, 2003.

78. "Patterns of Global Terrorism, 2002."

79. Lerner, "Philippine terrorists."

80. "U.S. demands Philippine captive be freed on medical grounds," *New York Times*, September 1, 2000.

81. Interview, administration official, March 4, 2003.

82. Seth Mydans, "American's Philippine Captors Known for Torture," *New York Times*, August 31, 2000.

83. Ibid.

84. Ibid.

85. Ibid.

86. Ibid.

87. Interview, U.S. official, May 1, 2003.

88. Interview, administration official, March 4, 2003.

89. "UN 'assured Libya' over Lockerbie trial," *BBC News*, August 26, 2000, http://news.bbc.co.uk/1/hi/world/896708.stm.

90. Ibid.

91. Barbara Slavin, "Libya to compensate Pan Am 103 families," *USA Today*, May 28, 2002.

92. Interview, Danielle Pletka, April 22, 2003.

93. Interview, Dan Cohen (meeting participant), March 18, 2003.

94. Ibid.

5 ★ UNDERSTANDING STATE—TO THE EXTENT IT'S POSSIBLE

1. Interview, George Shultz, April 2, 2003.

2. Interview, senior administration official, February 10, 2003.

3. "Road Map for National Security: Imperative for Change, Phase III Report," United States Commission on National Security/21st Century, January 31, 2001.

4. Ibid.

5. "Some Causes of Organization Ineffectiveness Within the Department of State," Chris Argyris, p 25-26.

6. Ibid., 11.

7. Ibid.

8. Ibid., 27.

9. Ibid., 6.

10. Ibid., 7.

11. Ibid., 16.

12. Ibid., 10.

13. Ibid., 24.

14. Ibid., 31.

15. Ibid., 23.

16. Ibid., 36.

17. Interview, State Department official, April 6, 2003.

18. Interview, State Department official, July 16, 2002.

19. State Department daily press briefing, July 10, 2002.

20. Interview, senior State Department official, August 1, 2002.

21. "Axe Maura Harty's Nomination," *Washington Times*, unsigned editorial, October 10, 2002.

22. Interview, Charles Hill, March 16, 2003.

23. Details can be found in my article "Illegal But Paid?" *National Review*, January 27, 2003.

24. Interview, State Department official, March 27, 2003.

25. "Visa Process Should Be Strengthened as an Antiterrorism Tool," General Accounting Office Report, October 2002, Appendix II, 46.

26. Interview, State Department official, April 7, 2003.

27. Interview, administration official with significant desk officer experience, April 6, 2003.

28. Ibid.

29. Ibid.

30. Interview, Richard Schifter, March 22, 2003.

31. Ibid.

32. Foreign Agents Registration Act form completed and signed by Robert H. Pelletrau, signed November 23, 1998.

33. Ibid.

34. *Washington Representatives 2002*, 26th Annual Edition, Washington, DC: Columbia Books, Inc., 1322.

35. Interview, former State Department official, April 6, 2003.

36. Letter from Robert Oakley to Nabil Nasser outlining details of consulting contract, signed and dated March 12, 1993.

37. "Ex-official fined $5,000 for lobbying," *Chicago Tribune*, December 3, 1994.

38. Interview, former State Department official with direct knowledge of the case, April 6, 2003.

39. Ibid.

40. Interview, Henry Sokolski, March 30, 2003.

6 ★ COURTING SADDAM

1. Interview, Steve Bryen, March 28, 2003.

2. Ibid.

3. Mark Fazlollah, "N.J. firm's Iraq shipment halted," *Philadelphia Inquirer*, June 28, 1990.

4. R. Jeffrey Smith and Benjamin Weiser, "Commerce Dept. Urged Sale to Iraq; Furnaces Useful In Making A-Arms," *Washington Post*, September 13, 1990.

5. Ibid.

6. Fazlollah, "N.J. firm's Iraq shipment halted."

7. Smith and Weiser, "Commerce Dept. Urged Sale to Iraq."

8. Ibid.

9. Ibid.

10. Ibid.

11. Ibid.

12. Interview, former Pentagon official Henry Sokolski, May 8, 2003.

13. William B. Scott, "National labs fill gap in weapons' stewardship," *Aviation Week and Space Technology*, vol. 144, no. 4, January 22, 1996.

14. Smith and Weiser, "Commerce Dept. Urged Sale to Iraq."

15. Fazlollah, "N.J. firm's Iraq shipment halted."

16. Interview, Henry Sokolski, May 8, 2003.

17. Smith and Weiser, "Commerce Dept. Urged Sale to Iraq."

18. "'Chemical Ali' found dead, British officer says," *New York Times*.

19. Patrick Worsnip, "Gas bombing empties town of life," *Chicago Tribune*, March 24, 1988, 5.

20. *Facts on File*, "Iraqi Poison Gas Attack Kills Kurds in Iraqi Town; Town Bombed After Capture By Iran," April 1, 1988, 215, F2.

21. Ibid.

22. Ibid.

23. Interview, Richard Schifter, March 22, 2003.

24. Interview, Nathan Kingsley, April 24, 2003.

25. Interview, Richard Schifter, March 22, 2003.

26. *Federal News Service*, State Department, Regular Briefing, August 25, 1988.

27. *Federal News Service*, State Department, Regular Briefing, August 31, 1988.

28. *Federal News Service*, State Department, Regular Briefing, September 1, 1988.

29. *Federal News Service*, State Department, Regular Briefing, September 6, 1988.

30. Ibid.

31. *Federal News Service*, State Department, Regular Briefing, September 7, 1988.

32. Ibid.

33. *Federal News Service*, State Department, Regular Briefing, September 8, 1988.

34. *Federal News Service*, State Department, Regular Briefing, September 14, 1988.

35. THOMAS (Library of Congress web site), http://thomas.loc.gov/cgi-bin/bdquery/z?d100:HR05337:@@@X|/bss/d100query.html|.

36. *Federal News Service*, State Department, Regular Briefing, September 20, 1988.

37. Ibid.

38. Interview, Richard Schifter, March 22, 2003.

39. Ibid.

40. State Department Memorandum: "Export-Import Financing for Iraq," December 29, 1988.

41. Ibid.

42. Interview, Richard Schifter, May 13, 2003.

43. Briefing memo from Paul Hare to James Baker, March 23, 1989, Subject: "Meeting with Iraqi under secretary Nizar Hamdun. March 24, 1989 at 2:00 PM in your conference room."

44. Internal State Department memo from John Kelly to James Baker, October 26, 1989, Subject: "The Iraqi CCC program."

45. Congressman Henry Gonzalez, *Congressional Record*, "Oil Sales to Iraq, and more details on Matrix-Churchill Cor," September 1, 1992.

46. United States Congress House of Representatives Subcommittee on International Economic Policy and Trade of the Committee on Foreign Affairs. United States Exports of Sensitive Technology to Iraq, 8 April and 22 May 1991. (Washington: Government Printing Office, 1991).

47. Ibid.

48. Chairman of the Senate Committee on Banking, Housing and Urban Affairs, Donald W. Riegle, Jr., "Arming Iraq: The export of biological materials and the health of our gulf war veterans," *Congressional Record*, vol. 140 no. 12, February 9, 1994.

49. Ibid.

50. Ibid.

51. Ibid.

52. Ibid.

53. Ibid.

54. Patrick J. Sloyan, "Undisclosed connection/scientist on Gulf War syndrome linked to supplier of Iraqi anthrax," *Newsday*, November 27, 1996.

55. Congressman Henry Gonzalez, *Congressional Record*, "Oil Sales to Iraq, and more details on Matrix-Churchill Cor," September 21, 1992.

56. William Blum, "Anthrax for export: U.S. companies sold Iraq the ingredients for a witch's brew," *The Progressive*, April 1998.

57. "Hearing of the Senate Foreign Relations Committee, Subject: US-Iraq Relations," *Federal News Service*, June 15, 1990.

58. Internal State Department cable to U.S. Embassy Jakarta, "Subject: Talking points on Indonesian super-puma sale," November 7, 1989.

59. Christopher Dickey, et al., "How Saddam Happened," *Newsweek*, September 23, 2002.

60. Ibid.

61. Internal Defense Department memo, Richard Perle to Caspar Weinberger, "Subject: High Technology Dual-Use Export to Iraq."

62. Letter from George Shultz to Caspar Weinberger, April 30, 1985.

63. Ibid.

64. Ibid.

65. Interview, Charles Krauthammer, April 22, 2003.

66. "Senator Sees 'Horror' of Stark," *Chicago Tribune*, May 26, 1987.

67. Ibid.

68. John H. Cushman Jr., "Position of Stark Focus of Dispute," *New York Times*, June 4, 1987.

69. Ibid.

70. Jim Hoagland, "Turning a Blind Eye to Baghdad," *Washington Post*, July 5, 1990.

71. Flora Lewis, "Baghdad Rages On," *New York Times*, April 28, 1990.

72. "Hearing of the Senate Foreign Relations Committee, Subject: US-Iraq Relations."

73. Ibid.

74. Lewis, "Baghdad Rages On."

75. "Hearing of the Senate Foreign Relations Committee, Subject: US-Iraq Relations."

76. Ibid.

77. Ibid.

78. Interview, Joshua Gilder, May 4, 2003.

79. Ibid.

80. H. Con. Res. 298, Condemning the deliberate and systematic human rights violations by the Government of Iraq, 101st Cong., (1990). Introduced in the U.S. House of Representatives, April 3, 1990.

81. Interview, former Yatron staffer Mark Tavlarides, April 17, 2003.

82. Allen Friedman and Victor Mullet, "Iraq 'Used Unauthorised BNL Credits For Military Purchases'," *Financial Times*, September 20, 1989.

83. Ibid.

84. Ibid.

85. Ibid.

86. Ibid.

87. United States. Congress. House (1992) Representative Henry Gonzales of Texas speaking on oil sales to Iraq and more details on Matrix-Churchill Cor. 102nd Cong., 2nd sess., Congressional Record 138, no. 129 (September 21, 1992): H 8820.

88. Ibid.

89. Ibid.

90. Ibid.

91. Ibid.

92. Ibid.

93. Barnaby J. Feder, "Ohio Company Seized as Iraqi Front," *New York Times*, September 20, 1990.

94. State Department Memorandum, "The Iraqi CCC Program," October 26, 1989.

95. Ibid.

96. Ibid.

97. Ibid.

98. Ibid.

99. Ibid.

100. Minutes of National Council of Advisors Deputies Meeting, November 6, 1989.

101. State Department Memorandum, "CCC Program for Iraq," November 6, 1989.

102. "BNL Subpoena Renewal," Congressional Record, 102nd Cong. 1st Sess., April 25, 1991.

103. Minutes of National Council of Advisors Deputies Meeting.

104. Ibid.

105. Ibid.

106. State Department Memorandum, "The Iraqi CCC Program," October 26, 1989.

107. U.S. Attorney's Office: "Notice to USDA of Iraqi Complicity in Criminal Violations," May 4, 1990.

108. CIA Memorandum: "Iraq-Italy: Repercussions of the BNL-Atlanta Scandal," November 6, 1989.

109. Ibid.

110. Ibid.

111. State Department Memorandum, "Second Tranche of CCC Credits for Iraq," January 4, 1990.

112. Ibid.

113. State Department Memorandum, "NAC Meeting on Iraq CCC Program," March 5, 1990.

114. Ibid.

115. U.S. Attorney's Office: "Notice to USDA of Iraqi Complicity in Criminal Violations," May 4, 1990. Quoting from a February 23 memo.

116. State Department Memorandum, "Weekly Report," May 18, 1990.

117. U.S. Attorney's Office: "Notice to USDA of Iraqi Complicity in Criminal Violations," May 4, 1990.

118. State Department Memorandum, "Possible Indictment of Iraqi Officials," May 22, 1990.

119. "The Iraqi CCC Program."

120. Dean Baquet, "Investigators say U.S. Shielded Iraqis from Bank Inquiry," New York Times, March 20, 1992.

121. Ibid.

122. Ibid.

123. Ibid.

124. "Notice to USDA of Iraqi Complicity in Criminal Violations."

125. Ibid.

126. Agreement between BNL and Central Bank of Iraq, January 20, 1990.

127. R. Jeffrey Smith, "U.S. to Pay $400 Million to Cover Iraq's Bad Debt," Washington Post, February 17, 1995.

128. Ibid.

129. BNL Chronology: Relating to the Department of Agriculture (USDA) and the National Advisory Council on International Monetary and Financial Policy (NAC), National Security Archives, April 19, 1991, 13.

130. Saul Friedman, "Probes: Iraq Farm Aid Went to Arms," *New York Times*, June 7, 1992.

131. Dean Baquet, "Investigators say U.S. Shielded Iraqis from Bank Inquiry," *New York Times*, March 20, 1992.

132. Ibid.

133. Ibid.

134. Ibid.

135. Ibid.

7 ★ CRUSHING FREEDOM

1. "Smearing Mr. Chalabi: The State Department tries to corrupt its own audit process," *Wall Street Journal*, April 10, 2003.

2. Interview, administration official, April 23, 2003.

3. Vernon Loeb, "Saddam's Iraqi Foes Heartened by Clinton," *Washington Post*, November 16, 1998.

4. "Smearing Mr. Chalabi."

5. Eli J. Lake, "Anyone But Chalabi? Washington battles over how to organize the Iraqi opposition." *Weekly Standard*, June 24, 2002.

6. Ibid.

7. Interview, administration official, April 17, 2003.

8. Interview, administration official, March 11, 2003.

9. Daily Press Briefing, U.S. Department of State, January 31, 2002.

10. "Smearing Mr. Chalabi."

11. Ibid.

12. Daily Press Briefing, U.S. Department of State, May 1, 2002.

13. Interview, informed source, May 7, 2003.

14. Ibid.

15. Ibid.

16. Ibid.

17. Ibid.

18. Interview, administration official, May 15, 2003.

19. Ibid.

20. Daily Press Briefing, January 7, 2002.

21. Interview, informed source, May 7, 2003.

22. Interview, informed source, April 23, 2003.

23. Ibid.

24. Ibid.

25. Interview, informed source, May 7, 2003.

26. Interview, informed source, April 23, 2003.

27. Interview, informed source, May 7, 2003.

28. Letter to President Bush signed by Senators Jon Kyl, Sam Brownback, Rick Santorum, John McCain, and Norm Coleman, March 31, 2003.

29. "Subverting Iraqi Democracy," *Washington Times*, April 7, 2003.

30. A more complete discussion of Kubba and his group can be found in my article "Stifling Democracy: State stacks an important Iraq meeting against the INC," *National Review Online*, April 14, 2003.

31. This poll information is included in Mowbray, "Stifling Democracy."

32. Interview, administration official, April 13, 2003.

33. Ibid.

34. Judith Miller, "Driver in Embassy Bombing Identified as Pro-Iranian Iraqi," *New York Times*, December 17, 1983.

35. Interview, informed source, April 13, 2003.

36. Adam Daifallah, "Support for True Democracy in Iraq," *New York Sun*, December 23, 2002.

37. This and more on Kubba is in Mowbray, "Stifling Democracy."

38. Interview, informed source, April 13, 2003.

39. Interview, administration official, April 1, 2003.

40. Glenn Frankel, "Denmark charges Hussein foe with war crimes," *Washington Post*, November 20, 2002.

41. Ibid.

42. Interview, administration official, March 20, 2003.

43. Frankel, "Denmark charges Hussein foe."

44. Sebastian Rotella, "A Key Iraqi Defector Vanishes in Denmark," *Los Angeles Times*, March 19, 2003.

45. "U.S.-picked Iraqi health minister, a Ba'ath party member, quits after 10 days," *International Herald-Tribune*, May 14, 2003.

46. Ibid.

47. Ibid.

48. Patrick E. Tyler, "Hussein Loyalists Rise Again, Enraging Iraqis," *New York Times*, May 8, 2003.

49. Ibid.

50. Interviews, multiple administration officials, May 12–20, 2003.

51. Transcript, Foreign Relations Committee mark-up of Foreign Relations Authorization Act, April 9, 2003.

52. Ibid.

53. Interview, May 15, 2003.

54. Interview, May 16, 2003.

55. S.Res. 306, 107th Congress, Sen. Sam Brownback.

56. "Iran Students and Police Clash over Press Curbs," *New York Times*, July 10, 1999.

57. Douglas Jehl, "Despite Police Dismissals, Iran Protest Is the Angriest Yet," *New York Times*, July 12, 1999.

58. Daily Press Briefing, U.S. Department of State, July 8, 2002.

59. Interview, administration official, July 11, 2002.

60. Statement by the president, July 12, 2002.

61. Federal News Service, Daily Press Briefing, U.S. Department of State, July 8, 2002.

62. Robin Wright, "U.S. Now Views Iran in More Favorable Light; A top official makes a distinction between the regime in Tehran and those of fellow 'axis of evil' members North Korea and Iraq." *Los Angeles Times*, February 14, 2003.

63. Michael Rubin, "Khatami and the Myth of Reform in Iran," *The Politic*, Spring 2002.

64. Jacques Charmelot, "Ten more years needed to boost US image abroad, senior official says," Agence France Presse, February 19, 2002.

65. Hearing of the Senate Foreign Relations Committee, "International Campaign Against Terrorism," Federal News Service, October 25, 2001.

66. Joshua Muravchik, "Hearts, minds, and the war against terror," *Commentary*, May 2002.

8 ★ VISAS: EVERYWHERE TERRORISTS WANT THEM TO BE

1. "The State Department's handling of allegations of visa fraud and other irregularities at the United States embassy in Beijing," report by Committee on Government Reform, House of Representatives, July 29, 1999, 94.

2. Ibid., 107.

3. Ibid.

4. Ibid., 112.

5. Ibid.

6. Ibid., 131.

7. Ibid.

8. Ibid.

9. Ibid., 126.

10. Ibid., 93.

11. Ibid., 132.

12. Ibid., 133.

13. Ibid.

14. Ibid.

15. Ibid.

16. Ibid.

17. Ibid., 60.

18. Ibid., 135.

19. Ibid., 146.

20. Ibid., 112.

21. Ibid., 134.

22. Ibid., 107.

23. Ibid., 307.

24. Ibid., 134.

25. "Visa Officers Rarely Face Investigation Into Fraud," *Los Angeles Times*, May 9, 1999.

26. Report by Committee on Government Reform, 112.

27. Ibid., 298.

28. Ibid., 147.

29. Ibid.

30. Ibid., 257.

31. Ibid., 308.

32. Ibid.

33. Ibid., 311.

34. Ibid.

35. Ibid., 328.

36. Ibid., 313.

37. Ibid., 319.

38. Ibid.

39. Congressional hearing before Government Reform Committee, July 29, 1999.

40. Ibid., 320.

41. Interview, administration official, June 1, 2002.

42. "Visa Officers Rarely Face Investigation Into Fraud."

43. Interview, former Diplomatic Security official, April 17, 2003.

44. "Ex-diplomat gets 21 years for visa scheme," *Seattle Post-Intelligencer*, June 14, 2002.

45. Jeffrey Gold, "Consulate official admits offering false visas," Associated Press, May 22, 2002.

46. Abdullah Noman plea agreement, provided by U.S. Attorney's office in New Jersey.

47. Interview, former State Department official, April 13, 2003.

48. Interview, John Aalders, December 18, 2002.

49. Ibid., 4/20/03.

50. Interview, senior State Department official, May 28, 2002.

51. "Visa Process Should Be Strengthened as an Antiterrorism Tool," General Accounting Office Report, October 2002, 17.

52. Ibid., 19.

53. Ibid., 18.

54. Interview, U.S. government official, October 18, 2003.

55. "Courtesy and Communications Count," State Department Best Practices Handbook.

56. "Review of Nonimmigrant Visa Issuance Policy and Procedures," U.S. Department of State, Office of the Inspector General, December 2002, 18.

57. Interview, State Department official, April 2, 2003.

58. Letter from Richard Armitage to Larry D. Thompson, June 10, 2002.

59. GAO Report, 25.

60. Interview, congressional source, November 18, 2002.

61. Interview, congressional source, October 18, 2002.

9 ★ JUSTICE DENIED

1. State Department Daily Press Briefing, June 27, 2000.

2. Graham Rayman, "Zimbabwe Leader Sued—Mugabe served with papers at Harlem church," Newsday, September 9, 2000.

3. Interview, former State Department official, April 17, 2003.

4. Interview, State Department official, April 22, 2003.

5. "US sends $62 million Iran compensation," United Press International, July 2, 1996.

6. Ibid.

7. "Navy makes a deal over sub collision," Associated Press, November 14, 2002.

8. Ibid.

9. Ibid.

10. Interview, State Department official, April 22, 2003.

11. Interview, former State Department official, April 21, 2003.

12. Interview, former State Department official, April 17, 2003; interview, State Department official, April 22, 2003.

13. Interview, State Department official, June 20, 2003.

14. Interview, former State Department official, April 16, 2003.

15. Interview, informed source, April 15, 2003.

16. CNN.com, http://www.cnn.com/US/9602/cuba_shootdown/27/, February 27, 1996.

17. Ibid.

18. David Lyons, "Kin sue Cuba for Brothers to the Rescue shoot-down," *Miami Herald*, November 13, 1997.

19. Mireya Navarro, "U.S. Judge Assesses Cuba $187 Million in Deaths of 4 Pilots," *New York Times*, December 17, 1997.

20. Interview, informed source, April 15, 2003.

21. For a more complete discussion of this legislative history, see my article "So you wanna sue the Saudis?: Expect a Fight from Foggy Bottom," *National Review*, November 25, 2002.

22. Ibid.

23. "Patterns of Global Terrorism," 2001 report, U.S. Department of State, May 2002.

24. For a more complete discussion and analysis, see Mowbray, "So you wanna sue the Saudis?"

25. Ibid.

26. Letter from Richard Armitage to Sen. George Allen, December 2001.

27. 2000 Foreign Policy Report (table 1), Bureau of Export Administration, U.S. Department of Commerce.

28. Details in Mowbray, "So you wanna sue the Saudis?"

29. More details can be found in my article "Justice, Finally: Congress helps American victims of terror get past the State Department," *National Review Online*, November 26, 2002.

30. Ibid.

31. Ibid.

32. Ibid.

33. Interview, informed source, April 8, 2003.

34. Ibid.

35. Interview, informed source, April 25, 2003.

36. Ibid.

37. Interview, John Norton Moore, November 3, 2002.

38. Daily press briefing, U.S. Department of State, October 31, 2002.

39. Details can be found in my article "Who's the enemy?" *Pittsburgh Tribune-Review*, November 17, 2002.

10 ★ WRONG HANDS: THE ARMING OF THE MIDDLE EAST

1. Daily press briefing, December 11, 2002.

2. Kevin Drew, "Law allows search, but does not address seizure of cargo," *CNN.com*, December 11, 2002. (http://www.cnn.com/2002/LAW/12/11/missiles.legal/)

3. Interview, administration official, December 12, 2002.

4. Interview, administration official, December 13, 2002.

5. Interview, administration official, December 13, 2002.

6. Interview, administration official, December 12, 2002.

7. Interview, administration official, April 27, 2003.

8. Ibid.

9. Federal News Service, April 28, 2003.

10. Ibid.

11. Interview, administration official, April 27, 2003.

12. Interview, administration official, December 12, 2002.

13. Interview, administration official, May 6, 2003.

14. Interview, administration official, February 10, 2003.

15. Interview, Henry Sokolksi, March 30, 2003.

16. Interview, administration official, April 2, 2003.

17. Ibid.

18. Interview, James Swanson, April 27, 2003.

19. Ibid.

20. Henry D. Sokolski, "Best of Intentions: America's Campaign Against Strategic Weapons proliferation," Praeger Publishers: Westport, CT, 2001, 65.

21. Interview, Richard Perle, March 19, 2003.

22. Sokolski, 80.

23. Sokolski.

24. Ibid., 73.

25. Ibid., 71.

26. Interview, administration official, April 10, 2003.

27. Sokolski, 71.

28. Interview, James Swanson, April 27, 2003.

29. Ibid.

30. Interview, administration official, April 27, 2003.

31. Sokolski, 72.

32. Ibid.

33. Sokolski, 84.

34. Interview, administration official, April 3, 2003.

35. Interview, administration official, April 8, 2003.

36. Interview, informed source, April 15, 2003.

37. Interview, former Congressional official, April 18, 2003.

38. Sokolski, 78.

39. Interview, former Congressional official, April 18, 2003.

40. Ibid.

41. Ibid.

42. Sokolski, 78.

43. Ibid.

44. Ibid., 78-79.

45. Interview, Steve Bryen, March 28, 2003.

46. Ibid.

47. Ibid.

48. Interview, Richard Speier, March 31, 2003.

49. Ibid.

50. Ibid.

51. Ibid.

52. Ibid.

53. Ibid.

54. Interview, Steve Bryen, March 28, 2003.

55. Ibid.

56. Ibid.

57. Ibid.

58. Ibid.

59. Interview, James Swanson, April 27, 2003.

60. Ibid.

61. Ibid.

62. Interview, Henry Sokolski, March 30, 2003.

63. Interview, administration official, April 3, 2003.

64. Interview, Henry Sokolski, March 30, 2003.

11 ★ FIXING STATE—TO THE EXTENT IT'S POSSIBLE

1. Interview, former Congressional staffer, April 7, 2003.

2. Ibid.

3. Steven Emerson, "Visa for terrorism supporter; State Department bows to political pressure," *Washington Times*, May 19, 2000.

4. Ibid.

5. Ibid.

6. Glenn Kessler, "U.S. Eyes Pressing Uprising In Iran; Officials Cite Al Qaeda Links, Nuclear Program," *Washington Post*, May 25, 2003.

7. Interview, Charles Hill, March 16, 2003.

8. Interview, Henry Sokolski, March 30, 2003.

9. Interview, George Shultz, April 2, 2003.

10. Ibid.

11. "The Importance of Ideas," *American Purpose*, (published by the Ethics and Public Policy Center), Volume 11, Number 1, Spring 1999. This can be found at: http://www.eppc.org/publications/xq/ ASP/pubsID.117/qx/pubs_viewdetail.htm

12. Interview, former State Department official, April 13, 2003.

13. Interview, Henry Sokolski, March 30, 2003.

14. Interview, administration official, May 22, 2003.

15. Patrick E. Tyler, "Hussein Loyalists Rise Again, Enraging Iraqis," *New York Times*, May 8, 2003.

16. Daily Press Briefing, U.S. Department of State, May 21, 2003.

17. Interview, Morton Blackwell, March 27, 2003.

18. Interview, former State Department official Charles Hill, March 16, 2003.

19. Interview, State Department official, April 7, 2003.

Acknowledgments

When I sat down to catalog my gratitude, I realized that I have been truly blessed. None of this would have happened without the help many generous individuals. But trying to extend every appropriate thank you—for everyone from your nursery school teacher to God—is a daunting challenge that is, frankly, beyond my modest abilities. So I will try to be brief.

I owe a "thank you" to:

—Regnery Publishing for taking a chance on a first-time author

—David Limbaugh for connecting me with Regnery and providing guidance along the way

—John Miller for planting the seeds and encouraging me to take the plunge (John, incidentally, edited my first-ever "professional" newspaper column, back in 1996.)

—Linda Chavez for giving me my first break in Washington, particularly since she had no need for another intern when she brought me to DC—and even arranging for me to get paid so I could afford it all

—Heather Nauert for teaching me the lay of the land inside the beltway and helping me develop a better sense of strategy

—Sean Hannity for telling me I was crazy to write a book, but encouraging me to write it anyway

—Pat Roush for inspiring me with her seemingly boundless spirit and unflinching faith that she will rescue her daughters from the desert prison of Saudi Arabia

—all the people whose names I cannot mention, but whose help I will not forget

—all my friends who have supported (and tolerated) me as I wrote this book

—my family for believing in me

I need to reserve a special thank you to the research assistant who helped pull the voluminous material together and who helped me make sense of it all: Cynthia Determan. I wasn't looking for a research assistant, but I am extremely grateful that she devoted several months to this project—with an enthusiasm that often helped keep me energized.

Index